UP TRADE

ONE SHOT – ONE KILL TRADING

JOHN NETTO

McGraw-Hill

New York   Chicago   San Francisco   Lisbon   London   Madrid
Mexico City   Milan   New Delhi   San Juan   Seoul
Singapore   Sydney   Toronto

Library of Congress Cataloging-in-Publication Data

Netto, John.
    One shot one kill trading / by John Netto.
        p.   cm.
    Includes index.
    ISBN 0-07-142794-5
    1. Stock price forecasting—Mathematical models.   2. Investment analysis.
    3. Speculation—Mathematical models.   4. Asset Allocation.   I. Title.

    HG4637.N48   2004
    332.63'222—dc21   2003017388

CONTENTS

CHAPTER 3

Profitable Chart Formations   51

CHAPTER 4

Fibonacci Levels: The Basis of Price Targets   83

CHAPTER 5

Profiting with Inflection Points   107

CHAPTER 6

Going Short: Profiting from Those Less Able   127

PHASE II: From Marksman to Expert   159

CHAPTER 7

Trade Preparation: Using the One Shot – One Kill Method   161

CHAPTER 8

Dynamics of a Trading Day: Where to Focus   179

CHAPTER 9

Entry Techniques: Knowing When to Strike   199

CHAPTER 10

How to Exit a Trade, Lock in Profits, and Limit Losses   217

CHAPTER 11

The Importance of Eliminating Mistakes   243

PHASE III: Locked and Loaded   263

CHAPTER 12

Making A Real-Time Trade One Shot – One Kill: From the Chalkboard to the Battlefield   265

ACKNOWLEDGMENTS

I humbly dedicate this book to all of the military veterans of past, present, and future, whose devotion, commitment, and bravery allow us to enjoy the freedoms of this great country.

My family's love and steadfast support has been a vital component and instrumental in helping me overcome numerous challenges in my life. My mother, Marie, and brother, Alexander, have been there for me during my most trying hours. My father, F. J. Netto, left an indelible mark on my character and work ethic. May his soul rest in peace.

This book could not have become a reality without the great help and critical eye of Scott Newiger, whose vision to help educate others was the catalyst and driving force behind it. Thanks to his wife, Doe, daughter, Heidi, and son, Destry, for sacrificing a husband and father for more than two years. Scott also owes his parents, Patricia and Donald Newiger (may his soul rest in peace), and sister, Hilary, a lifetime of gratitude for their love and support.

Thanks to my life strategy coach Nazy Massoud, who continues to help me live outside of my comfort zone. I am also extremely grateful to my trading partner and close friend, Paul Ierna, whose late-night talks about the market, poker and life continue to inspire.

I would like to also mention some others who deserve recognition for their direct and indirect inspiration, as well:

University of Washington; Scott King; Brett Sharbaugh; Steve Dussault; Ted Wood; Tim and Dana Girard and family; Lenny Rogofsky; Roy Glassberg; Troy Green; Akiko Netto; Marybeth Whyte and Geff Wong; Scott Brindley; Dan Ford; Bruce Thomson; Rob Lee; Bruce Armstrong; Steve Hotovec; Jeff Heely; David Martin; Darrell Jones; Jason Urquhart; Jasmine Waldorf; Victoria Liang; Andrew Hoang; US Ambassador Tom Foley; Dale Kreisher; Professor Jeffrey Pontiff; Professor Walter Novaes; Professor Pansy Lin; Professor Walter Hatch; Brice Wightman;

Angelo Ongpin; Jim and Alan Morphy; Sergeant John Chae; my
godparents Manuel Netto and Sally Burns; Vladimir Lozan;
Daniel Wiggins; Sarah Quinn; Hitomi Miyata; Lars, Barbara,
Amanda and Lauren Blake; First Sergeant Victor Martin -
USMC; Nonnie Granelli (may his soul rest in peace); Jean
"Bubba" Newiger; Doris "Mimi" Granelli; Mel Wyrsch Jr.; Ron
and Bonnie Romero; Virginia Romero; Peter Vigil; Sybil Ravallo;
Rhonda, Raul and Logan Muella; Hilary, Darrell, Nicholas, and
Nelson Baggs; Dolores, Jimmy, Mark, Barry and Lee Langston;
Marvin, Barbara, Eugene, Robin, and Lauren Banks; Randy,
Norman, Jay and Russell Newiger; Scott, Julie, Sloane and Jared
Blair; Robert Weiser; Jeff Rhodes; Alan "Spark" Rifkin; Phil,
France, Daniel and Nicole Schrager; Heidi and Richard Ralph;
Phrancine, Ed, Perynn and Erica Diksa; Steve and Michele
Kirsch; Pam, Clif, and Ryan VanDerWolf; Ron, Celena, and
Isabella Polena; Cristina and Vanessa Camozzi; Rick Camozzi;
Matt and Carrol Curtis; Rita and Brett Weinstein; Stephen,
Yvonne and Gina Pingatore; Ron Gonsalves; Elvis Presley, and
Colonel Tom Parker.

INTRODUCTION

On October 11, 2001, I sat in my hedge fund's office calculating where the market was headed. I was preparing for the next trading setup, which I could see on the horizon. My calculations showed me my next price target for the Nasdaq, which, at the time was sitting near 1389, was headed for a move to 1428 to 1442. Preparing for that setup to go short was the best way to put myself in a favorable position to capitalize from a great trade, with an excellent risk-to-reward ratio.

Six days later, the market was continuing its march up the charts from its September lows. Before the opening bell on October 17, the talking heads on CNBC were beginning to express the kind of euphoric attitude that compels most people to call their brokers and buy stocks, while most professional traders were licking their chops about to go short. The market gapped up that morning about 30 points, to approximately 1435. Based on my analysis, the market had arrived at a spot that would likely lead to a reversal. I had a predetermined price target zone to the downside of this market going to 1305 to 1315, thereby creating a risk-to-reward ratio of nearly 12 to 1 for initiating the short position. Now, it was solely a matter of executing the trade. The market made its high in the first 10 minutes and once the bids started to fade, I initiated my first short position by trading the QQQ (the tracking stock for the Nasdaq 100) by getting short. The trade immediately went my way, as I was surprised by the violent reaction down, and saw myself up some nice gains in the first 15 minutes of the trade. As I got to my breakeven point, I took off half the position, so that I could walk away profitable from the trade. The Nasdaq put in a half-hearted bounce and then stayed rangebound for the rest of the morning. I was not disappointed because I was expecting the market to take at least two to three days to get to my profit target. However, after failing to put in a sustainable rally, with an hour to go, the Nasdaq sold off 60 points. I added back into my original position by offering in on a bounce before the market plunged.

I sat there, slightly surprised, but cognizant of the work I had done, as the Nasdaq plummeted down, watching my profit-and-loss statement increase rapidly to the plus side, while the Nasdaq tumbled down 30, then 40 points. I was content with that and had no problem with the bell closing 30 minutes early, considering the spot I had gotten short. However, that was not to be, as the Nasdaq just kept falling.

People started to pat me on the back and say great call; however, like most traders, I am very superstitious about congratulations on trades that haven't been booked yet, as keeping a clear head and following a plan is the key to success. I had to constantly tell myself not to get greedy and to follow my plan to take profits at my downside target. The Nasdaq closed right on top of my downside target at 1315, as it sold hard right into the close. What had started as a 30-point gap up turned into a 60-point down day. While I was looking for the market to pull back to this support zone, doing it in one day came as a real surprise. I booked it in the after hours at my price target as my plan dictated.

In my career, I have had many profitable days of trading, as well as days that were not so good, but the method I used to enter this trade is the same style I use to trade for a living.

Being ready to execute on these types of setups, at major inflection points in the market, days in advance, is what this book will teach you to do. I was there that day with a plan of attack and executed on it, walking away with a sizeable gain by going short at the open, and adding to the winning position, until it hit my price target.

One Shot – One Kill will walk you through all of the necessary components of the method to systematically and tactically make trades like the one described above. This book provides real-life examples of how to apply this method. Regardless of your skill level now, this book will make sure that when you finish reading you will have a solid understanding of what components are necessary to properly execute on these types of setups.

While it may seem sexier to get straight to the trades, building a solid foundation is critical to successful trading, as it is to every successful business endeavor. This book is set up to cover all of the important aspects of trading this method: from screen setups, software, and brokerage accounts in Chapter 1, to walking-through a real-time trade in Chapter 12. I even go as far as to discuss taxation guidelines and information specifically for traders

The use of Netto Numbers is something that is a critical component to the One Shot – One Kill Method, as it is the Netto Number itself which helps you ascertain how strong or weak a prospective trade candidate is. A trade setup based on a Netto Number is made up of a total of 30 points, with the chart formation accounting for 10 of those points, the Fibonacci levels accounting for another 10, and ancillary technical indicators accounting for the last 10. Chapters 2 through 4 will go over the 30 points and provide the basis for tabulating and creating a Netto Number. As mentioned throughout the book, Netto Numbers serve as a redundant means to help you buy weakness in rising markets and sell strength in falling markets while taking profits at predetermined price targets. The best Netto Numbers for long positions will usually be stocks that have made new highs and have a short-term pullback; for shorts, that would be stocks that have made new lows and have put in a modest bounce.

Netto Numbers are to the One Shot – One Kill Method what a foundation is to a fortress. That is to say, Netto Numbers dictate entry and allocation, while the One Shot – One Kill Method deals with everything from adding into winning positions through the Money Management Matrix to understanding your comfort level. With that being said, the more experienced traders out there may be able to skim through some of the early chapters. Nevertheless, it is still incumbent upon you to have a clear understanding of all of the components that go into this method, so that by the time the book progresses to the more advanced material you will have a solid foundation from which to work.

Basic Trading Tactics

CHAPTER 1

Importance of Ease of Operation

There is an old saying that states that "a 10,000-mile journey begins with the first step." The goal of these early chapters is to begin painting a picture of what a One Shot – One Kill setup entails and how to understand the different elements in it. Those of you who are more experienced traders and money managers, already using direct access trading, may choose to skim through this chapter, as most of what is discussed may already be familiar to you. Whether you choose to read in detail or skim through the paragraphs that follow, keep in mind that you need to have the proper tools and resources to allow you to execute the setups you will learn about in the pages of this book.

Before we begin in earnest, please first take a minute to grab a pencil, paper, and a highlighter. I encourage you to write in this book and highlight some of the ideas I express.

There are just as many trading styles out there as there are traders. The final choice of which trading ideology an individual chooses to employ is ultimately at the discretion of that person. The trading style and method suggestions made in this book come about from my extensive research and discovery as well as long experiences of fighting it out on the field of battle and in the trenches of real-time trading war. My technical knowledge of trading, combined with my understanding of how to best utilize new-generation trading software to soundly uncover profitable trades in real time, has provided me the know-how and insight to the most effective ways to trade.

This book is structured in such a way that you will be able to learn the methods and techniques quickly and easily and put them to work for you immediately. More importantly, you will understand why you'll be making the plays you do, to a larger degree than you probably ever thought possible. A good understanding of why you are doing what you are doing is essential for every trader's success. Guessing is not an option in sustaining long-time success.

This chapter contains a number of points, which I have purposely placed in the beginning of the book, so administering things like data feeds, brokerage services, and trading room setups can be accomplished while you are completing the book.

As with many things in the "big picture of trading," little things can sometimes get overshadowed by what are perceived to be things of greater importance. Two of the most often-overlooked factors that I find important in trading are ease of operation and personal comfort. Because I trade and teach traders for a living, I have found it very important for traders to get comfortable, before they begin trading. Don't get me wrong; when traders make mistakes, they do not do so because they are uncomfortable, but because they are unprepared or indecisive. Nevertheless, being uncomfortable, can easily lead you to a state of unpreparedness. Your comfort level will contribute greatly, though immeasurably, to your overall success as a trader.

Every day in which you find yourself at your trading station is another day on your calendar spent doing what you do to make money. For many of you, it is your sole source of income. From the first time you ever sit down in your chair and make your first trade, till the ten thousandth hour of being on the job and actively trading, if you can make it that far, is a great deal of time. So get as comfortable as humanly possible. Do so even if it means you need a coffee pot and cream puffs at an elbow's distance or jelly beans ready at a moment's notice. Whatever your "little necessities" are, have them with you. Some traders find aspirin a necessity. (No tall, cold ones till *after* the closing bell). Have close at hand everything that you anticipate you will need that is not directly trading-related. You'll find out what trading tools you'll be using and what your screens should look like for the work at hand, but make sure you are as comfortable as you can get. And don't forget to have your reading glasses with you, if you wear them. Being able to see the current, correct market prices is helpful.

You should follow this advice for one important reason. Too many times I have known of traders (especially day traders) "sneaking away" for just a few moments to grab something and then getting detained. It ends up costing them more than they could have imagined. A closer examination of each situation usually reveals that, no matter what the trader went to do or get, the errand was a regular occurrence, and one that in many, if not most, instances could have been avoided.

Now, with everything in place, you should be totally mentally focused on trading, while being as comfortable as you can possibly make yourself (without the aid of another person), and keenly prepared to attack the markets.

Since the sole purpose of this book is to teach you how to sustain success as a trader using my One Shot – One Kill Method, I suggest you start by discovering and experimenting with the trading ideas in this book without trading real money. You will have plenty of time to do that later on. It is best you begin by becoming somewhat proficient with my method first. Paper trading, despite being no match for real trading, is an excellent way to familiarize yourself with various trading methods. Fear not, you will not need an eternity to learn what you need to do to trade with real money.

Now, you *must* read this next sentence very carefully:

Once you learn and choose to employ the One Shot – One Kill Method, you must do so with complete confidence and faith in its efficacy, so that you can derive the greatest benefits from its application.

You need to pay attention to this statement for a good reason, because no matter what plan or method you use to trade, you should be committed to it. If you are not committed to your plan, how can you even trust *yourself* as a trader? If you saw another trader who wasn't committed to his or her plan, what would you think?

This idea can best be conveyed with a blackjack example. Whether or not you know anything about blackjack, it is almost always a smart, high-percentage play to "double down" (double the size of your bet and draw only one card) when you, the player, have an 11 and the dealer has a 6 card showing. Statistically, opting to double down will yield you a higher return than any other play. Yet, many better-than-average blackjack players, who may be keenly aware of those statistics, and who regularly take that bet, don't make that play when they have a large bet on the table. Why? Because putting that much extra money at risk "scares" them. So instead, they typically draw only one card, and probably win the hand and effectively settle for less. If they had bet $100, that is what they would have won. However, if they had stuck to their plan and doubled down, and won the hand, they would have taken home 100 percent more money from that particular bet, and over time, further increased their odds for success. When that setup appeared and their chances for success were optimal, they essentially shot themselves in the wallet by failing to take the action they needed to take.

You shouldn't make that same mistake. You must allow yourself to fully benefit from what you believe is a solid trading plan. However, as a safety precaution, you should only paper trade until your knowledge, faith, and confidence in the method grows.

TRADING ROOM SETUP AND COMPUTER REQUIREMENTS

Your trading room setup is comparable to, and should be, as panoramic as the view a general has when he watches his forces do battle in the field. Having a bird's-eye view of all the action allows you to easily see and readily act when a situation calls for observation and action. A functional, well-set-up trading room is an important ingredient for your success and very helpful for your enemy's demise.

In combat, the supplies and equipment that troops are given can have a great impact on the outcome of the battle. If you are serious about wanting to take an active part in managing your money or trading professionally, spending the necessary money for the correct computer setup is an unavoidable necessity. It is an essential expense that will help you in developing your success. When it comes to handling money and doing battle with the markets, a NASA-like computer setup is not necessary. But good equipment and information can pay for itself in just one good trade and oftentimes can make the difference between profits and losses.

An active trader or investor who wants to watch the market online every day needs to have a Windows operating system, preferably Windows 2000 Professional Edition, or Windows XP. Try to avoid using Windows 98 or 95, both of which have reportedly caused many traders great headaches and, in some cases, great losses by locking up and shutting down in the middle of trading. Although these occurrences are infrequent, just one instance during a trade can be costly. Most of the time lockups happen because the computer system is not able to handle the resource-eating computer trading programs

A computer with a minimum 1 GB processor (or, preferably, the fastest one available), 512 megabytes (MB) of RAM, and a 10-gigabyte (GB) hard drive is recommended. You should also have at least two 19-inch or larger monitors (three monitors is ideal), if you plan to watch and trade the market on a regular basis.

The next essential requirement is the connection to your data. Digital subscriber lines, or DSLs, and other broadband connections are becoming more widespread. Having one is an absolute minimum requirement if you actively trade from home. A cable modem connection is perfectly acceptable and will provide the necessary bandwidth required to run the trading applications on your computers. I do most of my trading from an office where I have a T-1 connection, because having a plentitude of bandwidth is an essential asset when making split-second executions.

The mouse is something that most people may not consider to be too important when they trade, but I highly recommend that active traders learn how to use hot keys as well as purchase a Microsoft IntelliMouse Optical or similarly functioning mouse. It is an amazing innovation that will save you a great deal of anguish and frustration in the heat of the trading battle. It does not need to be cleaned or maintained, and you can use Levi's jeans or a naked thigh as a mouse pad. I consider it an indispensable part of my trading arsenal.

A sound card is also needed, so that you can hear alarms when they go off. Many traders never use alarms and, frankly, I find that alarming.

Finally, a successful trader needs is a backup power supply. Should anything happen, having your system backed up and ready to go is akin to having your reserves ready, in case something happens to your first wave.

Exactly how much to decide to spend on a trading room setup is a personal decision all traders eventually have to make. A number of things should be kept in mind when factoring what is important to include in the ideal trading room. The trading room setup I use, and feel to be quite adequate, consists of three monitors, with the middle monitor sitting directly in front of me and the other two monitors cropped in to my left and my right.

Having access to a Standard & Poor's (S&P) 500 futures pit audio via a squawk box is important because it's one of the best sources for breaking news. I also have financial news on in the background so I can hear what commentators are saying, in case someone gets on the air and starts speaking about a sector or a stock that I have a position in. Actually, most of what they report is a watered-down version for most people who don't follow the market in the way that traders do. However, news stations are the most popular medium out there right now for following the markets. Because it is, you should try to stay aware of what they are saying, and whom they are saying it about, because short-term movement of a stock or sector can be affected.

The following is a checklist for a good system:

- Minimum 1 GB processor
- 10GB hard drive
- Windows 2000 Professional / Windows XP
- 512MB RAM or more
- Video card of 32MB of RAM or more
- Microsoft IntelliMouse Optical or similar mouse
- L-shaped desk
- Two to three 19- to 21-inch monitors
- Access to financial news and S&P 500 futures squawk box
- Comfortable chair

- Wireless, hands-free phone
- Cool temperature and well-lit workspace

DATA FEED AND TRADING SOFTWARE

Over the course of this book, the importance of identifying a trend as the primary focus of the One Shot – One Kill Method will become evident. Understanding who is in control of the market, and picking the best spots to get on their side, is its essence. During the heat of the battle, having software that is catered to your trading style is not enough to win the war. It's a mistake often made by struggling traders. They are very good at getting themselves comfortable in their trading setup and style but, because of a mediocre trading plan, which does not stress strong trading habits, they are often not mentally fit or anticipatory enough to trade as effectively as they could and should. An essential feature of being a decisive trader is being ready to pull the trigger at a moment's notice.

Before you can begin trading online, you need to have a data provider that provides delayed, end-of-day, and real-time quotes, so the software can analyze the market and help you make the calculations you need to. As of this writing, I use eSignal Data, from Data Broadcasting Corporation, as I have found it to be extremely reliable in the fastest of markets and compatible with a number of software providers.

While there are several good trading software packages available, the charts in this book and the analysis performed were done with MetaStock Professional Software, which is put out by Equis International. I personally use this software, as it is extremely versatile, well thought out, and fairly easy to use. Price target creation, the basis of the One Shot – One Kill One Kill Method, is made possible by using this software, and it will make your time in combat more prosperous. The eSignal and MetaStock software I use and recommend can be substituted for any software that accomplishes what they do.

Once you begin to incorporate these software applications together, applied with Netto Numbers, you can begin the process of making your trades with confidence. Having said that, I also want to add that I am keenly aware there are litanies of software programs on the market that may fit your personal trading style more comfortably. Choose the software you like best. Traders have their own trading preferences. However, more importantly, traders have different skill levels, of which they should be aware. Since you are reading my book, I can only presume you are trying to improve your trading results. I am not recommending, nor do I want to change, a trading style that is profitable for you. But in order for you to improve your results, you may have to change at least some of your ways.

Whatever software you use and whatever your trading style is, you must be able to correctly arrive at Netto Numbers to incorporate them into the method. It is the trader who has to make the final decision as to what best suits their needs. However, I have extensively tested a number of software programs on the market and have found the aforementioned software programs have met my level of acceptability. You can find a list of software providers at the One Shot – One Kill Trading Web site (www.oneshotonekill-trading.com or www.osoktrading.com), which will give you additional references and information as far as trend software is concerned.

Keep in mind that software only serves a supporting role in your efforts to become a successful, active money manager. The ultimate decision to buy and sell, hold or pass, lies squarely on the shoulders of the individual, not the technology they employ to reach their trading decisions.

My intention is to teach you to learn to know how, what, when, and why to make a trade. The market is an amalgamation of psyches that come to represent our impressions on the future at a particular moment. The One Shot – One Kill Method teaches you to *trade what is* and not *what you think should be*.

TRADING SCREEN SETUPS

Having the proper setup behind your trading is essential to your success. Not having the right view of the market is akin to boxing with an eye patch and dark sunglasses on. Although it would still be possible to win the fight wearing these items, the odds

[handwritten annotation: SEE → CHAPTERS 4 & 5 / FIBONACCI / INFLECTION POINTS / + PREVAILING TREND]

would be greatly against you. In using the One Shot – One Kill Method, it will help you see what is going on clearly at all times. It is very important never to get blindsided.

This section covers two potential trading screen setups. The first will be for the average investor who makes trades. This screen needs to focus on being able to spot prevailing market trends as well as provide you with a feel for what is going on in the market that particular day. The second trading screen setup is designed for the more active trader, one who follows the market every day and is in and out of several positions a week. This setup incorporates two or more monitors, as the need for information more closely related to the market becomes heightened. Although this book focuses primarily on short-term trading, long-term investors can also benefit from the tactics and strategies brought forth.

Success requires the ability to spot key trends and indicators essential to the success of the One Shot – One Kill Method (such as, Fibonacci levels and long- and short-term inflection points; see Chapters 4 and 5, respectively), and the prevailing trend of the security you are trading. By using the One Shot – One Kill Method, and applying the techniques discussed in this book, you will have a very strong foundation to make your success a reality. I recommend that after reading the following chapters in this book, you frequently refer back to this chapter, in order to better understand the reasoning behind setting up your screen this way.

In order to give you a better idea of the screens and their content, all of the screen setups displayed in this book can also be found and downloaded from www.oneshotonekilltrading. com/screensetup.htm or www.osoktrading.com.

During the time you are reading this book, you should make arrangements to investigate and experiment with the software from the data vendors. Many of them have initial 30-day trial offers that leave you with either no commitment or a full refund, if you are not satisfied.

Many traders, over the course of their lifetimes, will have the opportunity to handle hundreds of thousands, if not millions, of dollars. Having reliable information and effective trading techniques is paramount to your success. When you can make thousands of dollars in one day from just one trade, cheap is not something you want to be, nor is it something you would ever feel good about disclosing. You may try and kid yourself and call it "being tight" and maintain that you are "just being prudent," but when you are actively trading to win, cutting corners brings no advantages. It is not the time to be cheap. If you had to spend your hard-earned cash for a weapon to use in battle, why would you be thinking of buying a handgun when you could buy an Uzi? No one is going to admire you for being a cheapskate, especially when the decision involves your business equipment. And, to whom would you brag about it?

The purpose of the one-screen display is to provide a general overview of the stock, market, and sector. A typical one-screen display is shown in Chart 1.1.

The left side of your screen will consist of approximately 15 quotes. Of these 15 quotes, five of them will be the Nasdaq Composite Index ($COMPQ), the Nasdaq 100 Index ($NDX), the Standard & Poor's 500 Index ($SPX), the Dow Jones Industrial Average ($INDU), and the respective sector the stock that you are playing is in.

For example, if you were planning on trading Intel Corporation (INTC), then you would be watching the Semiconductor Index, which is an index made up of several chip-manufacturing stocks. Its symbol is $SOX.

To the right of the 15 quotes will be a daily chart. The daily chart will have the Moving Average Convergence/Divergence (MACD) indicator with the parameters of 5, 35, and a trigger line of 5 periods. This will make more sense as the book continues (for more info, see Chapter 2). You will need to insert three different moving averages: a 5-, 15-, and 39-period simple moving average from the close.

To the right of the daily chart will be a 60-minute chart, This will be the same size as the daily chart but will only have the 15- and 39-period simple moving averages. This chart will be based on the past 30 days.

Below the 60-minute chart will be a 13-minute chart. This chart will also have a 15- and 39-period simple moving averages.

Directly below the quote display on the left-hand side will be a detail window that will give all of the basic information

CHART 1.1

When looking at the market in the screen setup, you need to have a few of the stocks, sectors, and markets within view. On the left side of the screen, you also need to have a view of the prospective trading candidates for that day.

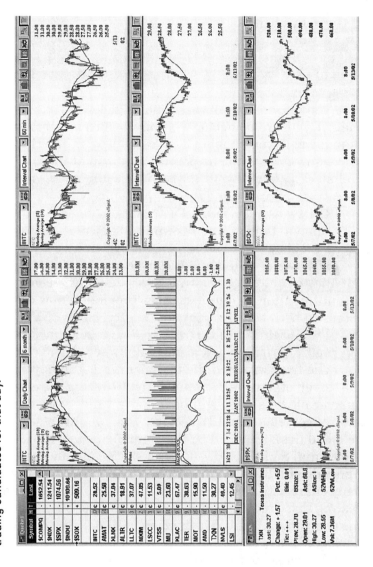

about the stock–for example, the high, the low, the volume traded, and the last price. The first chart to the immediate right of the detail window on the bottom will be a 13-minute chart of the S&P 500, with a 15-period simple moving average. The chart will have a time interval of five days on it. The last chart, to the right of that one, will be a sector chart for the stock that you are going to trade.

The reason none of these charts go lower than 13 minutes is that, if you are someone who buys and holds stock for longer than a week, you shouldn't get caught up in the tiny moves but to keep in tune with the prevailing trend of the market, sector, and stock. I have found that a 13-minute chart enables you to keep track of prevailing trends quite nicely.

The two-screen setup, for traders more active with the market, is understandably more complicated than the one-screen one. Chart 1.2 shows the first screen of a typical two-screen setup.

The two-screen display can be conducted on one monitor, but that is not the best way to go. I highly recommend that a second monitor be purchased to provide you with immediate access to both screens. Having two screens will also help allow you to maintain your focus and be able to instantly reference the information from both screens simultaneously.

The first screen of the two-monitor setup is very similar to the screen of the one-monitor setup. Covering the entire left one-quarter of the screen will be a quote window with 20 stocks, 2 futures contracts, and 10 sectors. The two futures contracts will be listed first; they will be the E-mini Nasdaq 100 (NQ #F), and the E-mini S&P 500 (ES #F). The stocks and indices are listed in Appendix B. To the right of the quote window you will have a daily chart with the same specifications as the other daily chart; that is, three moving averages of 5, 15, and 39 will be placed on the chart and a MACD histogram with parameters of 5, 35, and a trigger line of 5.

The screen to the right of that will be a 60-minute chart, with a 15-and 39-period moving average covering 20 days. Underneath that will be a 13-minute chart, covering 5 days with a 15- and 39-period simple moving average. Moving down and to the left will be a three-minute chart of the stock, also containing a 15- and 39-period moving average. To the right of the three-minute chart will

CHART 1.2

The first screen of a two-screen layout. This screen pertains directly to the stock.

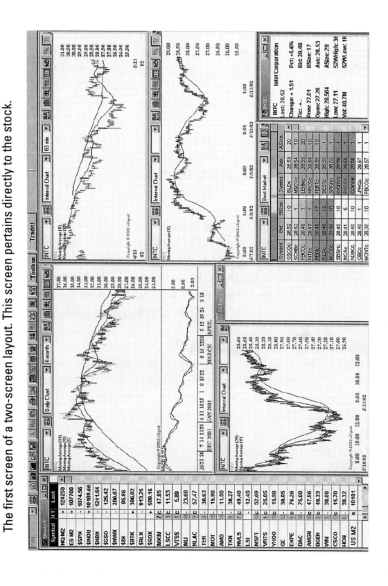

15

be a ticker that will have alerts programmed into it for every stock and index you are watching. It will inform you when the stock is making a high for the day, low for the day, 52-week high, and 52-week low, and when it is hitting a predetermined mark that you will program into the alert. To the right of that and just below the 13-minute chart will be a level-two screen. On the level-two screen, delete the time and the tick of the market maker; also delete the time that the trade went off at in the ticker in order to save space on the screen.

Just to the right of the level-two window you will place a ticker window. This window will have a linking function that will allow you to type in the symbol and it will change all the charts and statistics to match that particular stock. The ticker window is going to have the volume, last price, high, low, open, change from open, and change from close.

Your software provider will be more than happy to personally help you set up all of these functions after you download their platforms. It is in their best interests that you feel comfortable using their software so you remain on as a loyal, happy customer. That wraps up the first screen; now let's look at the second screen. (See Chart 1.3)

The second screen consists of nine charts of the nine different sectors to watch when actively trading throughout the day. The sectors covered will be the Semiconductor Index ($SOX), Networking Index ($NWX), Software Index ($GSO), Retail Index ($RLX), Banking Index ($BKX), Broker Dealer Index ($XBD), ZN #F (U.S. 10-year treasury notes), The Internet Index ($IIX), and the Biotech Index ($BTK). The idea is that you should be able to watch which sectors are performing the strongest throughout the day, which will help you spot and go after the strongest trending sectors, either up or down.

All explanations of chart time intervals should be set for two days, as to give you a visual idea where a sector is compared to yesterday's high, low, and close.

Prudent use of the real estate on your screen is important. The stock or commodity you are really focusing on is in your first screen. The second layout gives you the ability to watch not only the stock or commodity that you own or are about to trade but also the market and sector. As this book progresses, you will

CHART 1.3

The second screen of a two-screen layout. This screen allows you to view a number of different sectors and the overall market action.

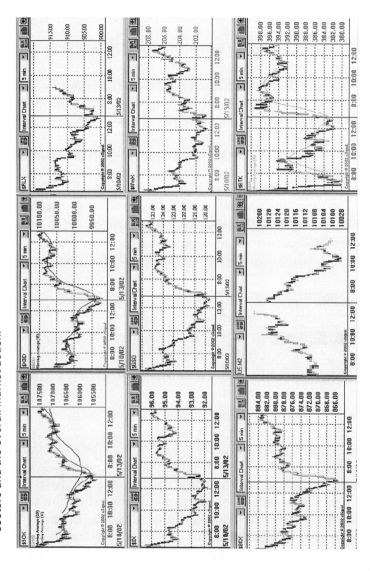

BIFURCATION

come to understand how interconnected the market and sector are. This screen setup was provided through eSignal; however, it can be set up through any number of data service providers. A list of data service providers is included on the One Shot – One Kill Trading Web site (www.oneshotonekilltrading.com or www.osoktrading.com).

For traders using a three-monitor setup, the third screen can be used to have a running version of MetaStock, or other similar software, at your disposal in real time, without having to go through the hassle of changing screens. All the aforementioned screen displays will allow you the ultimate picture of the battlefield, thereby enabling you to make instantaneous decisions based on what is happening in the market at a split-second's notice, without needing to switch screens. If you plan on trading on a full-time basis, a three-monitor setup is highly recommended.

The following list summarizes what needs to be on each screen:

Monitor No. 1. Information that pertains to your stock and to general market conditions

Monitor No. 2. Sector watch allowing you to spot the strongest or weakest trending sectors

Monitor No. 3. Display of real-time market events in order to make instantaneous decisions imperative for day traders

TRADING ACCOUNT SETUP

The structure of trading accounts has drastically changed over the past five years. The recent popularity of online trading, coupled with a demand by investors for faster fills at better prices has created a bifurcation of people who actively manage their money into two groups: those who carry overnight positions and those who day trade (and the majority of the time go flat into the evening).

The type of brokerage services you use is going to play an important role in determining the success of the fills you get, as well as how much you have to factor in for the cost of commissions. The brokerage policies regarding overnight positions, and how they affect buying power, is another key factor in determining which brokerages you should go with.

The best way to handle the brokerage issue is to set up at least two separate accounts. If you have a broker you are comfortable with and feel they are trustworthy, then retaining their services may be in your best interest. However, if you are planning on using the tactics in this book, at least one separate account should be set up with a nontraditional, Internet-based broker. And, on top of that, if you plan on day trading from this account, then a second Internet account should be set up, exclusively for day trading. Day trading needs to be done through a direct-access online brokerage firm. Becoming familiar with your broker's rules is imperative. If you do not have a broker you are comfortable with, please visit www.oneshotonekilltrading.com or www.osoktrading.com and check out through whom we are currently placing our trades.

To summarize, the following are requisite for trading account setup:

- Have at least two separate trading accounts (one for investing and one for trading)
- Understand your broker's rules, fees, margin requirements, inventory of stock and execution system (most of which are negotiable)
- Become intimate with the broker's software before you trade with real money

CHARTING METHODS

Throughout this book I employ the use of two different types of charting methods, which are the same ones I employ in my teaching and personal trading. Although there are several different ways to chart a security, the methods I use on a day-to-day basis *are Open-Close, High-Low bar charts* and Japanese candlesticks.

Open-Close, High-Low bar charts are the most popular type of security charts traders use. A bar chart displays a security's open (if available), high, low, and closing price.

CHART 1.4

The dynamics behind how to read an open,
close, high, low bar.

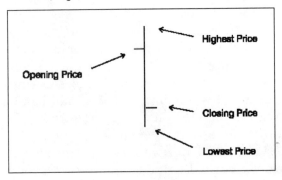

As illustrated in Chart 1.4 the top of each vertical bar represents the highest price a security traded for during a specific period, and the bottom of the bar represents the lowest price it traded for. If opening prices are available, they are signified by a *tick mark* on the left side of the bar. A closing tick mark is displayed on the right side of the bar to designate the security's last traded price of the trading period.

Not as popular, but certainly prettier and more telling, are *Japanese candlesticks*. The Japanese developed this method of technical analysis to analyze the price of rice contracts several centuries ago.

Candlestick charts illustrate the open, high, low, and closing prices, in a display format, which is similar to a modern-day bar chart but in a manner that depicts the relationship between opening and closing prices. Each candlestick represents one period of data. Chart 1.5 displays the different elements of a Japanese candlestick.

Many traders are attracted to Japanese candlestick charts by their mystique. They may think them to be some secret ancient method with special powers behind them.

I wouldn't get that caught up with them; after all, they are only charting methods, not the keys to the Holy Grail. However, I strongly encourage you to explore their use. Japanese candle-

CHART 1.5

Elements of a Japanese candlestick. I prefer using candlesticks, as the body of the candle helps provide insight and clarity in the movement of the underlying vehicle.

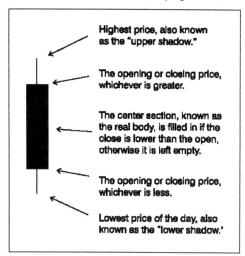

Highest price, also known as the "upper shadow."

The opening or closing price, whichever is greater.

The center section, known as the real body, is filled in if the close is lower than the open, otherwise it is left empty.

The opening or closing price, whichever is less.

Lowest price of the day, also known as the "lower shadow."

stick charts dramatically illustrate the changes in underlying supply-demand lines.

The main reason I use Japanese candlesticks in charting is because of their visual display qualities. They are very easy to understand and descriptive in portraying price action. To learn more about using Japanese candlesticks, I highly recommend reading a book by Steve Nison, internationally recognized as the "Father of Candlesticks," called *Japanese Candlestick Charting Techniques: A Contemporary Guide to the Ancient Investment Techniques of the Far East*. It has just about everything you could ever want to know about candlesticks, explained in an easy-to-understand manner.

SUMMARY

Chapter one provides the you with the necessary components and structure to begin implementing the One Shot – One Kill-Method in your everyday trading. It is critical to attend to these matters and ensure that when you have real money at stake there are no ancillary concerns which may arise beyond the natural ebb and flow of the market. This chapter has gone over how to set up a data feed, multiple trading layouts, the creation of your trading account, as well as a cursory explanation of some basic charting methods.

CHAPTER 2

Technical Analysis Indicators—Weapons of War

The One Shot – One Kill philosophy is adapted from the Marine Corps' rifleman's mantra, which was established during the Vietnam War. When expending large quantities of rounds against the enemy was proving of little use, the Marines implemented this stratagem and slogan to stress the importance of total focus and quality with each shot a rifleman would take. Being that I have felt a heavy influence in both my personal life, as well as my trading life, from the Marine Corps, it is quite appropriate to use a wise slogan symbolizing patience, discipline, and execution to be the basis for developing a strong trading ideology with a decisive battle plan.

ONE SHOT – ONE KILL PHILOSOPHY

The One Shot – One Kill Method can be explained simply as a trading style that buys weakness in up-trending markets, sells strength in down-trending markets, and proactively takes profits at predetermined points, only entering trades with a favorable risk-to-reward ratio. A critical component in this endeavor

INDICATORS = 10 of 30 POINTS

is to be able to use indicators, which allow you to sell into weakness and buy into strength, confirming what the price action of the chart is telling you. In line with building a solid base in spotting potential One Shot – One Kill (OSOK) setups, this chapter will provide another component in calculating a Netto Number (covered in Chapters 7 and 12), and being aware of how to execute on certain setups through the use of technical indicators. Some of the indicators have been around for some time, while others are proprietary to OSOK. New and experienced traders need to understand how these indicators are used to support what this trading method is about.

When a Netto Number is computed, you can tabulate a total score of 30 points. The indicators in this chapter comprise 10 of those 30 points. In Chapters 7 and 12 you will learn what point totals to assign to each indicator. Use this chapter to establish a familiarity for how these indicators are used to support the price target creation.

Many traders believe that to make any real money, they have to make 100 or more trades a day. The focus of this book and purpose of my method is to teach you to make fewer trades but to make them of higher quality. You can do so by using Netto Numbers and accompanying them with precise timing and careful money management. The One Shot – One Kill Method is powerful enough to allow a trader to either build a successful career as a trader or have a more profitable portfolio at year's end. This trading approach is similar to that of a guerrilla sniper, lying in wait in the woods. At certain times every day you will be required to use a great deal of mental discipline not to trade than to haphazardly pull the trigger prematurely and enter or exit a trade. Pulling the trigger prematurely is a common occurrence among traders who don't follow a method. As soon as they get up just a little bit in a trade, they are anxiously ready to cash it all in and trade something else. This fatalistic trading style is caused by too many things to delve into in sufficient detail here. But know that it exists.

On the other side of the spectrum from the trader who trades prematurely are the traders who get a "feeling" that there is not a better trading opportunity out there anywhere. They don't even want to stop and look at anything outside of their frenzy. Somehow this "feeling" paralyzes their fingers while their mind is racing in circles. This costly feeling is usually a result of a lack of discipline. This tendency to jump the gun is a major fault with many traders and it costs them much more often than not. Another reason (and not a very bright one) that leads traders to trade at the wrong time is that they feel that if they don't trade, then they can't make any money for the day. They will see that there are only 45 minutes left in the trading day, and since they haven't made any money that day, they feel they must trade. So, many times they wind up forcing questionable trades, which in my mind is akin to gambling.

As mentioned previously, if you are already familiar with a number of technical indicators and have been trading for some time, you may want to briefly read through this and the next chapter to see if you can gain a new insight or two. After that, move on to Chapter 4. The majority of indicators in this chapter serve a more redundant function in the overall method, rather than the sole basis for making trading decisions. The foundation of the One Shot – One Kill Trading Method is based on the creation of price targets, thereby allowing you to sell strength in falling markets and buy weakness in rising markets. Indicators like the MACD, Vertical Horizontal Filter, and Detrended Oscillator, defined below, are helpful in that they can keep you out of trouble by not allowing you to enter positions that are extended, losing trend strength, or poised to start pulling back. However, after learning and using these indicators for some time, you will get a good intuition for these features, and the need for these indicators takes on a less significant role.

The One Shot – One Kill Method is all about having self-discipline to control and eliminate your trade execution emotions. This ability alone will help remove you from a number of potential problems. Trading and life draw a number of similar parallels. There are times in your life when an opportunity to do something wonderful falls right into your their lap. A trader doesn't know when these situations will occur. However, when these events do occur, you need to be able to trade them with confidence.

After reading through the pages of this book and understanding the material, you will understand how to make the

15 MA (SIMPLE) – MATCHES UP c̄ FIBONACCI RETRACEMENTS, PULLS BACK + THEN CONTINUES IN DIRECTION OF TREND.

15 SIMPLE MA = 20 EXPONENTIAL MA

smart plays, without reckless abandon of money. When you do so, you will be in a position to capitalize upon the situation when even greater trading situations arise, with enough rounds in your magazine to fire or financial resources at your disposal. This type of warfare discipline is what is essential for your success, and success will become more evident when you master it.

MOVING AVERAGES

Moving averages, or *MAs*, set at the right parameters, can serve as an excellent means of containing a stock, or market, in a strong trend. The moving averages that do the best job are the 5, 15-, and 39-period simple moving averages (see Chart 2.1)

Various software programs allow you to perform this simple function. Using the three specific moving averages in the One Shot – One Kill Method gives you a strong, viable weapon in trend delineation for making your trades.

The purpose of using three different moving averages is simple. Each of them serves an important role in quantifying short, intermediate, and long-term trend. The five-period MA does a good job of letting you know where the short-term trend is. You can look at it and instantly know whether the market is getting weaker or stronger, in the shortest time frame you allow yourself to trade. This can be applied on a three-minute or a daily chart.

Pay close attention to the 15-period simple MA, calculated from the close of the bar. It has an uncanny ability to match up with Fibonacci retracements, and serves as an excellent spot for a pullback to find support or resistance and resume in the direction of the trend. The 15-period MA frequently allows traders to reenter positions after they have already gotten in the move. This safe yet simple method for getting into the prevailing trend allows users to benefit from low-risk, high-reward trades. The 15-period simple MA is comparable to the 20-period exponential MA, which accomplishes basically the same thing. I encourage you to use either one, as I have found in my experience the difference between the two is nominal.

As Chart 2.2 shows, Taro Pharmaceuticals' new division, TaroPharm (TARO), is breaking out, and some might even consider it to be getting ahead of itself. Using the One Shot – One

CHART 2.1

Assessing whether or not to buy weakness or sell strength is done largely by using the 5-, 15-, and 39-period moving averages. If the vehicle you are trading is above these respective moving averages, the bias is toward buying weakness, whereas if the market is below these moving averages, the bias is to sell strength.

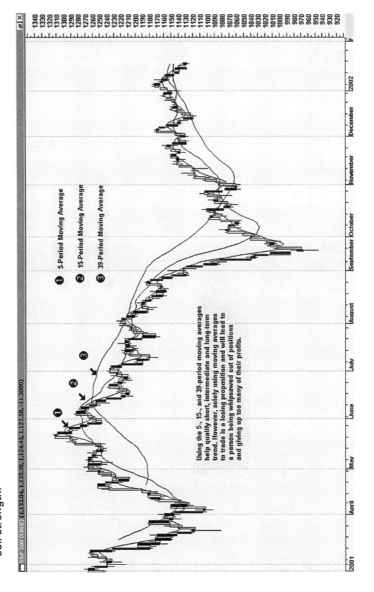

❶ 5-Period Moving Average
❷ 15-Period Moving Average
❸ 39-Period Moving Average

Using the 5-, 15-, and 39-period moving averages help qualify short, intermediate and long-term trend. However, solely using moving averages to trade is a losing proposition and will lead to a person being whipsawed out of positions and giving up too many of their profits.

Kill Method, you will not need to chase stocks or any other prices. One of the reasons is because you can use the 15-period MA to get a very good feel for when a pullback is in order and what numbers will act as support for the stock's next run. Many stocks prices come near their 15-period MAs, as well as having Fibonacci areas of support underneath them (covered in Chapter 4), both of which can act as a good spot for a bounce. These are some of the things that are important for you to decipher.

One problem with moving averages, which you need to watch out for, is the propensity to get *whipsawed* out of trades, meaning the stock moves above the moving average and then below it, causing sell or buy signals too early. It is because of this tendency that no one indicator of the One Shot – One Kill Method should be solely relied upon in making a trading decision. I have been whipsawed out of trades like everyone else, but I have also found that having a confluence of moving averages and using the other indicators I use will greatly increase the ability to make more successful trades.

The 39-period MA shows an example of the moving average containing trend the entire way down on a short position, from September 2000 to January 2001. The One Shot – One Kill Method uses a 39-period MA to quantify the trend in the time period you are trading. If you are swing trading a stock–that is, holding a position and owning it for three to seven days—then, you will want to see where the daily 39-period MA sits. If you are day trading, always be aware of where the 39-period MA sits for the sector and market, on an hourly basis. In order to recognize a trend change, the investment vehicle must have two successive higher closes than the moving average. If it cannot do this, then you will consider the trend to still be in play until you reach your profit target. By using this objective means of adding to positions, you will eliminate emotion from the equation and allow yourself to increase your profits in a very logical, systematic method.

The One Shot – One Kill Method uses the 15-period MA to set stops, which also serves as an excellent short-term gauge to tell you which way the trend is going. However, like most moving averages, when you use them in nontrending markets, there may be a propensity to get whipsawed out of trades.

CHART 2.2

The 15-period simple moving average usually provides low-risk entries on strongly trending stocks. It is at these areas that I look to enter a trade long on a pullback to a rising 15-period MA or short to a declining 15-period MA.

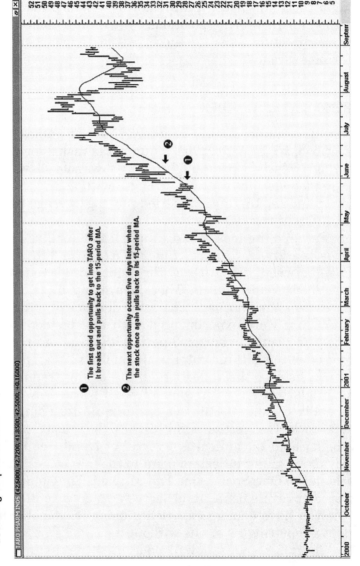

TARO PHARM INDS (42.6000, 42.7200, 41.8500, 42.5000, +0.16000)

❶ The first good opportunity to get into TARO after it breaks out and pulls back to the 15-period MA.

❷ The next opportunity occurs five days later when the stock once again pulls back to its 15-period MA.

29

The application of the three different moving averages provides an objective way to qualify short-term, intermediate, and long-term trends in any time frame as well as provide you a solid method for reentering positions, which are running powerfully in one direction. It is for these reasons I use these particular moving averages.

TREND REVERSAL INDEX

Over the course of this chapter, different indicators will be described, which accomplish a number of tasks, including determining relative overbought and oversold levels with a Detrended Oscillator; trend strength with a Vertical/Horizontal Filter; and 5-, 15-, and 39-period moving average to determine the different trends.

Perhaps the most powerful of all the ancillary indicators I use is the *Trend Reversal Index (TRI)*. The TRI shows divergence between the price of the underlying security and the investment vehicle itself. There are many divergence players out there; however the TRI was developed after numerous parameters were experimented with and tested; finally a 13-period RSI with a shorter 3-period RSI was incorporated. The creation of the TRI indicator would not have been possible without the help of the collective efforts of my trading team and numerous traders with whom I have worked over the years. Appendix C contains the custom formula for using the TRI in MetaStock. This section will illustrate the importance of the TRI in being able to confirm a reversal of trend, coupled with the arrival at a major inflection point in the market, as well as other tools in the One Shot – One Kill Method. The ability of the TRI to predict reversals in trend serves as a good confirmation tool. Once you have enough experience using it, you should become adept at spotting reversals without it.

Chart 2.3 shows how Broadcom is making a higher high while the TRI is making a lower high. This divergence between the price and the index is a very powerful indication that the recent runup in price does not carry with it the same degree of thrust as the first runup. If this second runup meets with resist-

CHART 2.3

The Trend Reversal Index (TRI) is a tool that can tip off reversals at key price levels. Broadcom attempts to retest its former highs, and the TRI shows us a significantly weaker level behind the respective move. This bearish divergence, when coupled with other indicators, is a good indication of a potential reversal.

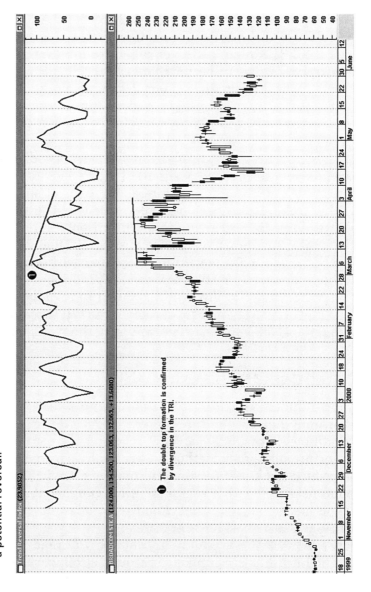

❶ The double top formation is confirmed by divergence in the TRI.

ance at a key level (what's known as a *Fibonacci level of resistance*; see Chapter 4), and creates a divergence, there stands a very good possibility the trend will reverse. As you will see in Chapter 4, many different resistance points exist. However, having the TRI can act as the equalizer in attempting to ascertain which areas stand a better chance of serving as resistance.

The next example in Chart 2.4 shows a huge TRI buy signal generated when the market pulled back to an area of proven support. The Nasdaq 100 made a lower low, but the TRI made a higher low, causing the bullish divergence, which was quickly followed by a powerful rally. Many traders use divergences as a means of entering into positions. Traders look for divergence in stochastic, RSI, and oscillators as a means of spotting a weakening trend. It has been my experience that the TRI serves as a better filter than most of those conventional indicators.

Like any indicator in the One Shot – One Kill Method, the TRI is much more powerful when used with a combination of other indicators. For this reason, don't fall in love with one indicator, as using the TRI will tip you off to reversals in trend but the 15-period MA and Fibonacci Friends (I'll explain this term in Chapter 4) offer the means of entering the position.

TREND LINES AND TREND CHANNELS

Trend lines and *trend channels* are simple yet effective ways to not only gauge potential support or resistance but also to set profit objectives and even spot reversals. Being that the underlying premise of my method is to sell rallies in declining markets and buy weakness in climbing markets, trend lines and trend channels are another complimentary component in this effort. It is for these reasons that trend channels and trend lines are included as one of the indicators.

Much of the explanation that you will read in this book on trend lines was accomplished through a collaborative effort with one of my good friends and colleagues, Paul Ierna, a professional trader and hedge fund manager. It is important to keep in mind when looking at trend lines that it is the buyers who are in control of where the trend line is drawn in most cases. This doesn't

CHART 2.4

A huge TRI buy signal is generated when the market pulled back to an area of proven support.

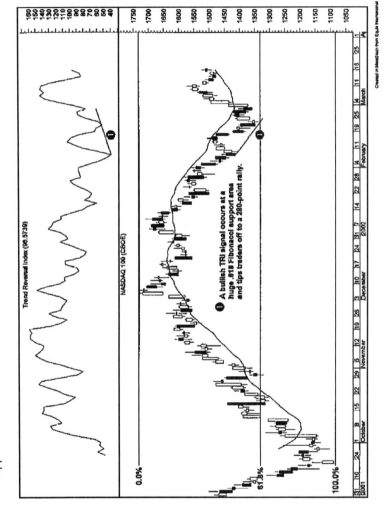

33

mean we can't draw it from its highs, however I have found that they are usually more effective when it is drawn from it's lows, regardless of whether the market is trending up or trending down. Drawing a trend line is a fairly simple endeavor, achieved by connecting a straight line from the lows of the stock all the way to the lows of the stock following its ascension up. As with many other facets of technical analysis, trend lines and trend channels have more validity on a longer-term chart.

There are actually *three* trend lines in effect. The first trend line is the *initial trend line* that is formed following the initial rise or fall of the stock. In Chart 2.4, the initial trend line has little chance of sustaining itself, due to its sharp decline or ascent.

The next and most important trend line is the *primary trend line*. The primary trend line has at least three areas that connect the stock. It is the stock's primary trend line that carries with it the greatest significance and will play a large role in determining whether the stock is in an up trend or a down trend over the time frame you are looking at. Looking at Chart 2.5, you can see the primary trend line provides the most lucid example of when the trend reversed. Whatever the reason with stock prices hitting trend lines, the third time is usually the charm. Expect resistance or support to form the third time that a stock rises or falls to a trend line. If support or resistance does not manifest itself at this level, then it is an indicator that the trend is possibly reversing, and traders should look to shift their trading bias.

Finally, the *third trend line* is much flatter and takes on a much longer time frame than do the initial and primary trend lines. It does so because the first and second pivots that create this flatter trend line are separated by an extended period of time, i.e several months whereas the initial is made up of a few days and the primary a few weeks. Because of this extended period of time, I give the most importance to the primary trend line as opposed to the initial and third trend lines when looking to get into a swing trade.

In line with the rationale of using trend lines to spot overall trends, trend channels can be used to help ascertain direction in the market as well. Both upward and downward trend channels can prove to be highly effective in determining overbought

CHART 2.5

The initial line has very little chance of sustaining itself, while the primary trend line gives a good example of how to assess the present move.

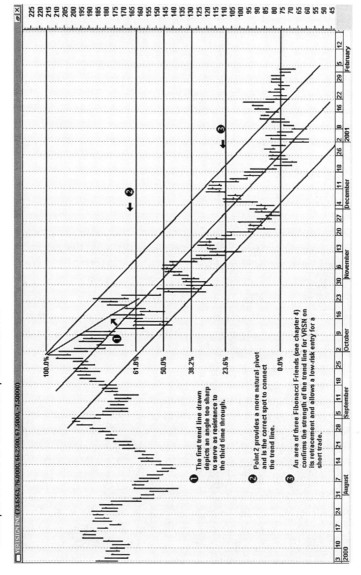

1. The first trend line drawn depicts an angle too sharp to serve as resistance to the third time through.

2. Point 2 provides a more natural pivot and is the correct spot to connect the trend line.

3. An area of three Fibonacci Friends (see chapter 4) confirms the strength of the trend line for VRSN on its retracement and allows a low-risk entry for a short trade.

and oversold levels within the current trending market. Watching a 60-minute chart of trend channels is very helpful when trying to determine the direction of the market over the previous six weeks. I am looking to use the low to establish the slope of the channel. A break in these trend channels can help forecast the next big move to come (see Chart 2.6).

A look at the Nasdaq 100 futures in December 2000 shows a market that is oversold, indicated by the Detrended Oscillator, (see Chart 2.7) with a weakening, indicated by the Vertical Horizontal Filter (defined later). The Nasdaq 100 was trading at the lowest range of the downward-trending channel and had touched the bottom part. While it takes experience to go against an underlying down trend and take a long position, at this point there is a great opportunity to cover a short position, as what followed was an oversold rally. As such, it is important to respect trend lines and trend channels.

In this example, the index rallied for a few days before coming back down again. Once again, good timing means everything. It's the difference between masterfully taking the lion's share of the profits to be had and being "buttonholed" into a position that emotionally and financially drains you. You may not lose big on such a trade, but it will make you feel like your hands are tied all the time you're in it.

Using Trend Lines to Play Reversals

The technical analysis community commonly says that when a major trend line is broken it is time to go the other way. However, while breaking a major down-trending or up-trending line is an important act, to initiate a position solely based upon the line's being broken is, in most cases, foolhardy. Instead, a more powerful, and usually more successful, way to enter on the breaking of a trend line is to let the market pull back to the trend line it broke. The 15-period MA, which is catching up to the move, and hopefully a shallow support area of Fibonacci Friends, increases your chances of making a profitable trade. If it taps that trend line, and then rallies, then by all means enter a position to the long side. However, if the pullback doesn't bounce at these areas and continues to move down, then the

CHART 2.6

The Nasdaq 100 went into a multimonth decline and traded within a solid trend channel during this time. When a channel like this is broken, take note, as a possible trend reversal is underway.

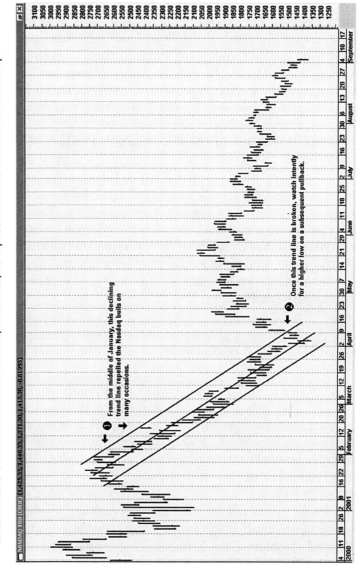

NASDAQ 100 (CBOE) (1,425.53; 1,440.33; 1,371.30; 1,415.30; -8.0 1.995)

1. From the middle of January, this declining trend line repelled the Nasdaq bulls on many occasions.

2. Once this trend line is broken, watch intently for a higher low on a subsequent pullback.

37

break of the trend line is likely to be only a shakeout and not capable of mustering a worthy rally from there.

A look at the Nasdaq 100 Index of January 2001 shows a classic example of a market that breaks through a major trend line only to pull back after breaking out (see Chart 2.8). The subsequent pullback went back to the trend line and then fell to new lows. It was the subsequent pullback that really provided the more profitable move from which to capitalize. It also created a much better entry point than just a buy on the market on the initial breakout over the trend line.

One of the tenets of the One Shot – One Kill Method is to create favorable risk-to-reward ratios. It is a very simple concept in theory. In the above situation in Chart 2.8, if you play the pullback to the trend line, you can put the stop for the long position below the previous days low. However, if you had played the initial breakout, you would have had to put your stop considerably further away. Your ability to muster the discipline *not* to chase the move and to execute your plan as planned normally gives you a decisive advantage. Learn to remember this fact **while** you are trading.

THE DETRENDED OSCILLATOR

The *Detrended Oscillator* is an indicator that I came across during my studies in college, and I was immediately won over by its usefulness. The indicator was created by Joe Dinapoli. It is simple in its constructs yet very effective in its predictive abilities to help determine relative levels of overbought and oversold conditions. For a detailed explanation of its use, see Dinapoli's book, *Trading with Dinapoli Levels* (Coast Investment Software, 1997).

The Detrended Oscillator gives truer readings of overbought and oversold conditions than *most* stochastics, all of which are intended to accomplish the same thing but don't do as well. On a traditional stochastic, a reading above 70 would give you an indication of overbought, while an indication below 30 would give you an indication of oversold. One of the biggest problems with a number of stochastics and other oscillator types of indicators is there propensity to stay overbought or oversold for too long. However,

CHART 2.7

The chart shows the Nasdaq 100 setting up for a possible long entry. These occur on a shorter time period when the daily chart shows a number of extremes on the sell side. Therefore, a possibility exists to take profits from your short position and look for a bullish entry on a shorter time frame to play this move back to the upside.

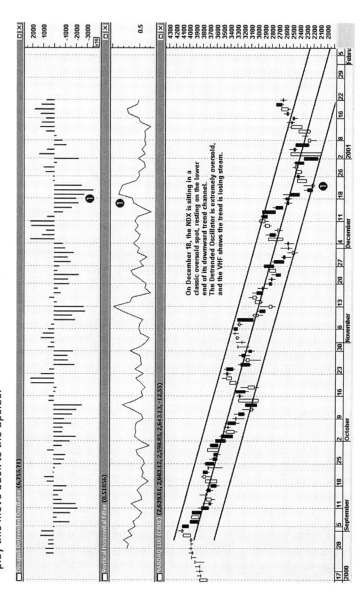

On December 18, the NDX is sitting in a classic oversold spot, resting on the lower end of its downward trend channel. The Detrended Oscillator is extremely oversold, and the VHF shows the trend is losing steam.

39

the Detrended Oscillator, coupled with the Vertical Horizontal Filter, has the ability to react quickly when the market works off its extreme condition. Traditional indicators, on the other hand, have a much more difficult time adjusting as dynamically. Both the Detrended Oscillator, as well as the Vertical Horizontal Filter are very useful indicators when the market begins to go into a strong period of trend, as they will give a clear picture of when the move is losing steam.

Using the Detrended Oscillator is a great way to look over the past to gauge the extreme of markets to both the upside and the downside. Look at Chart 2.8 and you will see how the Detrended Oscillator shows there was a tremendous amount of room left before the market was overbought, while the stochastic alone would have left the trader with the impression the market was already overbought.

This powerful weapon is one of a few specific ones that helps determine entry and exit points in the market. When it is combined with other key aspects of the One Shot – One Kill Method mentioned in the chapters that follow, it provides a powerful collaboration in creating price targets.

Look at Chart 2.9 and you will get a sense of where the stock would consistently hit overbought and oversold levels. This information tells you it is time to take profits in the stock and move on to more profitable scenarios. One of your options would be going the other way on the same stock, which is a ploy very much underused by the common trader. However, do not enter a trade based solely on the Detrended Oscillator readings. It is an effective gauge for booking profits, but you will need to use all of the other aspects of the One Shot – One Kill Method in order to give yourself the best chance for success.

The Nasdaq 100 was looking overbought on the Detrended Oscillator and had a double-top chart formation (discussed in Chapter 3); it also had a negative divergence on the TRI, which followed a huge parabolic run. And right there and then, right in front of everyone's eyes, the Nasdaq was blaring a weather report loud and clear and all you had to do was listen. The market quickly moved down and became nothing short of a panic situation, as people were throwing shares out with the bathwater. The situation

CHART 2.8

The Detrended Oscillator helps provide you with a good spot to take profits at some historical over-bought and oversold levels.

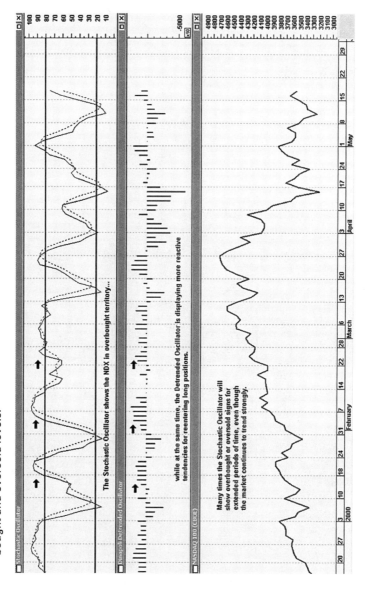

□ Stochastic Oscillator

↑   ↑   ↑   ↑   ↑

The Stochastic Oscillator shows the NDX in overbought territory...

□ Dinapoli Detrended Oscillator

↑   ↑

while at the same time, the Detrended Oscillator is displaying more reactive tendencies for reentering long positions.

□ NASDAQ 100 (CBOE)

Many times the Stochastic Oscillator will show overbought or oversold signs for extended periods of time, even though the market continues to trend strongly.

CHART 2.9

The Moving Average Convergence/Divergence (MACD) indicator coupled with the 15-period MA can help provide some low-risk entry points to get into long and short trades. When both indicators suggest that a market is still trending up or down despite the present pullback, it is a good time to start working positions.

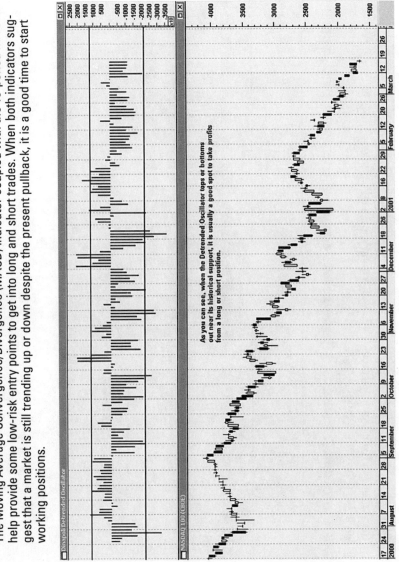

As you can see, when the Detrended Oscillator tops or bottoms out near its historical support, it is usually a good spot to take profits from a long or short position.

42

was unbelievable to watch unfold. I took my profit objective out much sooner than expected, as it kept heading down.

To make a living from trading, on a day-to-day basis, you need to *not* hold out for the dreams of one frenetic week or a day where you are going to make tons of money. Your goal should be to consistently hit singles and doubles. More than likely, big days will come when you may not even seem to do much at all. Preparation is what makes that happen, so be ready!

MOVING AVERAGE CONVERGENCE/DIVERGENCE (MACD)

As articulated earlier in this book, the basis of the One Shot – One Kill Method is to buy weakness in rising markets, sell strength in falling markets, and take profits at predetermined price targets. The *Moving Average Convergence/Divergence*, or *MACD*, helps facilitate this and provides a benchmark to help work all three of those components of the trading method. This indicator is considered to be redundant, in the sense that what a trader should pay particular attention to is not the crossovers but the pullbacks, after the crossover occurs. In other words, traders should learn to use the MACD as a means of buying the dips rather than buying the crossover itself. I like to do so, as I have found there to be considerable lag when waiting for the confirmation of the crossover itself. However, like the 15-period simple moving average, the MACD, with One Shot – One Kill parameters, allows you to reenter pullbacks of the moves and keep your risk-to-reward ratios in check, instead of taking the trade on the retail side by playing crossovers and getting retail results.

For those of you familiar with the MACD and its functionality, you may want to read this section anyway, as I like to use some modifications to the traditional settings. The parameters for the MACD I use are set at 5 and 35, with a five-period trigger line.

The MACD is calculated by taking a shorter-term moving average and subtracting it by a longer-term moving average. The result is plotted on a graph in the form of a line (see Chart 2.10).

The next step to interpreting this indicator is setting up a *trigger line*. This trigger line is simply the moving average of the stock, over a given period. It is beyond the scope of this book to

CHART 2.10

The Moving Average Convergence/Divergence (MACD) indicator coupled with the 15 MA-period MA can help provide some low-risk entry points to get into long and short trades. When both indicators suggest that market is still trending up or down despite the present pullback, it is a good time to start working into positions.

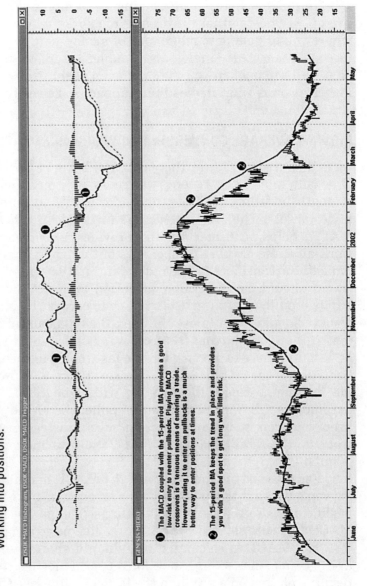

1 The MACD coupled with the 15-period MA provides a good low-risk entry to reenter pullbacks. Playing MACD crossovers is a tenuous means of entering a trade. However, using it to enter on pullbacks is a much better way to enter positions at times.

2 The 15-period MA keeps the trend in place and provides you with a good spot to get long with little risk.

explain all of the dynamics behind the making of this moving average; it is more important to understand how to use it to reenter positions.

Gerald Appel first came up with the MACD nearly 40 years ago and has received much praise for his work. His original parameters were set for the two exponential moving averages at 12 and 26 periods. He used a nine-day exponential moving average in order to establish a line that would help determine a change in trend.

Through my experiences in trading highly fast and volatile markets, I have researched which parameters on the MACD would make it more responsive to potential trend changes without getting me prematurely taken out of a trade. Having said this, I replaced the 12 and 26 periods with 5 and 35 time frames and I replaced the nine-period exponential with a five-period exponential.

The MACD measures the difference between two moving averages. A positive MACD indicates that the 5-day exponential moving average (EMA) is trading above the 35-day EMA. A negative MACD indicates that the 5-day EMA is trading below the 35-day EMA. If MACD is positive and rising, then the gap between the 5-day EMA and the 35-day EMA is widening. This development indicates that the rate of change of the faster-moving average is higher than the rate of change for the slower-moving average. Positive momentum is increasing, and this development would be considered bullish. If MACD is negative and declining further, then the negative gap between the faster-moving average (the solid line in Chart 2.9) and the slower-moving average (the dashed line) is expanding. Downward momentum is accelerating, and this development would be considered bearish. MACD center-line crossovers occur when the faster-moving average crosses the slower-moving average.

One of the primary benefits of MACD is that it incorporates aspects of both momentum and trend in one indicator. As a trend-following indicator, it is very effective and will never be wrong for very long. The use of moving averages ensures that the indicator will eventually follow the movements of the underlying security. If you use exponential moving averages, as opposed to simple moving averages, some of the lag will have been taken out.

Take a look at Chart 2.9 and use the pullbacks in the MACD as a means of providing a low-risk entry in a strong prevailing trend.

As a momentum indicator, MACD has the ability to foreshadow moves in the underlying security. MACD divergences can be key factors in predicting a trend change. However, the TRI is the primary means of spotting bullish and bearish divergences in the market. A negative divergence can signal that bullish momentum is waning and the trend could potentially change from bullish to bearish. This signal can serve as an alert for you to take some profits from long positions. Or, if you are more of an aggressive trader, you may begin initiating short positions, if they match up with price target reversal zones and other One Shot – One Kill indicators.

VERTICAL HORIZONTAL FILTER (VHF)

Traders who work with price targets must fully understand the strength of the underlying trend, corresponding to a major price target zone.

The *Vertical Horizontal Filter*, or *VHF*, acts as a very strong indicator when a trend has run its course. It also serves as a great indicator for detecting when a trend is about to begin from a daily time frame. I use this indicator in conjunction with the Detrended Oscillator to call short-term tops and bottoms, as we are simultaneously hitting areas of Fibonacci Friends, explained in later chapters. It also serves as an excellent measuring stick, when sizing a breakout from consolidation.

Unlike most oscillators and other default technical tools, which should be thrown in the basement and locked away, the Detrended Oscillator and Vertical Horizontal Filter are very responsive to a market that quickly corrects itself and will not remain at extreme levels for long. In other words, a stochastic can stay oversold for days, while the Vertical Horizontal Filter and Detrended Oscillators will back off of their extreme levels very quickly if the market puts in a one- or two-day pullback. This phenomenon is very useful when you are trying to reenter positions. If you can recognize these backoffs, you don't have to be concerned about getting into a move while it is extended or unnecessarily exposing yourself to a violent contramove.

After you use these indicators for some time, your application of them will be more active during times of market extremes. A one- or two-day rally will not put them at levels that render a useful "heads up" as to what is about to come, which is why having a solid understanding of the underlying price action and price targets is so critical.

When analyzing the Vertical Horizontal Filter, you should not focus on the chart while you are analyzing the indicator. If the line on the chart is going up, it means the trend is strengthening. It doesn't necessarily mean that the stock is heading up, only that the direction in which the stock is moving is picking up strength. This indication can be particularly useful from a contrarian standpoint, to gauge when the trend in the market is weakening (and likely to reverse or consolidate). It will be depicted by a topping action in the market when the market appears to be coming out of consolidation. This phenomenon will be exhibited by an extended period of time near the bottom of the chart. It is this ability to accurately measure the strength, or lack thereof, in the trend that will give you another edge over less savvy traders.

After extensive research, I discovered that, to better serve its purpose, the Vertical Horizontal Filer should be set on an interval of seven days. You can do so with MetaStock and most other software packages. This interval is the setting that I have used to eliminate lag while still allowing me to match up the real strength of the move at a major price target.

A look at Chart 2.11 shows that the Vertical Horizontal Filter is topping out and the trend is beginning to weaken. The line starting to come back down depicts this weakness. This trend is in conjunction with the Detrended Oscillator, which is moving back down as well. These two signs together give a strong indication that it is now time to close out your profit and begin waiting for a pullback before rescaling your risk-to-reward ratios.

Chart 2.12 shows a picture of a stock sitting in consolidation with the Vertical Horizontal Filter beginning to break out to the upside.

CHART 2.11

The Vertical Horizontal Filter is topping out and the trend is beginning to weaken. The line starting to come back down depicts this weakness.

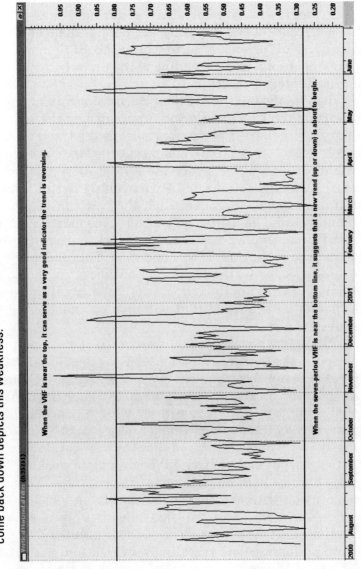

Vertical Horizontal Filter (0.35111)

When the VHF is near the top, it can serve as a very good indicator the trend is reversing.

When the seven-period VHF is near the bottom line, it suggests that a new trend (up or down) is about to begin.

CHART 2.12

Looking at the VHF on THQ, a trader can get a good feel of when a trend is losing strength as well as identifying a good spot to take profits.

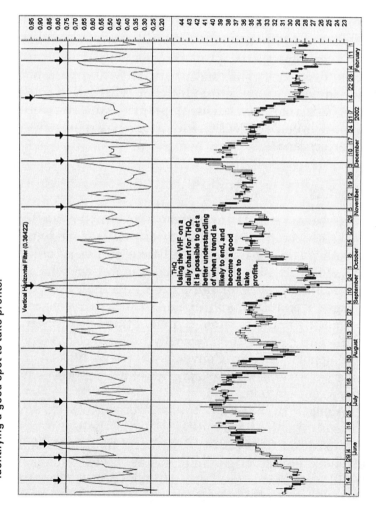

THQ
Using the VHF on a daily chart for THQ, it is possible to get a better understanding of when a trend is likely to end, and become a good place to take profits.

Vertical Horizontal Filter (0.36422)

49

The stock then broke out and set up a play, which was confirmed by the Vertical Horizontal Filter, that in fact, a strong trend was beginning to develop.

Keep in mind one important thing when you use technical indicators to trade: While use of an indicator to gauge the strength of an underlying trend is a necessary part of a good trader's strategy, you are strongly advised not to place trades on this or any one indicator alone. In my second book, which I am currently working on, I explain how to use these indicators to put on certain types of options trades. Once again, this indicator is only used in a confirmation capacity and does not carry as much importance as the underlying price action and price targets. With that said though, proper interpretation, through practical application of this indicator, should improve your trading performance.

SUMMARY

As has been stressed throughout this chapter, the One Shot – One Kill Method looks to buy weakness in rising markets, sell strength in falling markets and take profits at predetermined price points. The indicators in this chapter are what help gauge if we are in a rising or falling market. Indicators like moving averages, trend lines, and the MACD help serve as confirmation for what the market is doing. If all of them determine a strongly trending up market, then typically you will look to buy weakness at the opportune time. Conversely, if they point down, then targeting trades on the short side by selling bounces is usually the desired route to take.

Along with indicators that tip you off to what direction the market is trending are indicators which help you pick spots to exit a position. The vertical/horizontal filter and Joe Dinapoli's Detrended Oscillator can help you assess extreme points in the market and provide good spots to take profits. These indicators help serve as a solid backdrop to the creation of One Shot – One Kill price targets.

CHAPTER 3

Profitable Chart Formations

As you work your way into the third chapter of this book, the steps necessary for understanding Netto Numbers and building the foundation for the One Shot – One Kill Method are evolving. With a maximum of 30 possible points, which can be calculated into making a Netto Number (to be discussed in Chapters 7 and 12), 10 of those points are derived from the chart formation itself, thereby making it essential to understand the concepts of this chapter. Of the remaining 20 points, 10 of those are derived from Fibonacci price levels discussed in Chapter 4, and the remaining 10 points are taken from the technical indicators covered in Chapter 2. With respect to chart formations, the cleaner the formation, the greater the likelihood is that I will get into the position. This chapter will show you the kind of setups that you are looking to get into. However, as you will discover, even the cleanest formations require patience and discipline when it comes to the entry. Again, the underlying premise of our method is that we are looking for entries at inflection points in the market where we can buy weakness when the trend is up, sell strength when the trend is down, and take profits at predetermined price targets.

CHART FORMATIONS

Espousing the ability to accurately prognosticate the future movement of a stock based on what is seemingly an incoherent set of lines on a piece of paper would prompt some reasonably sane people to call you a charlatan or witch doctor. My time at the University of Washington rendered a number of such experiences from my professors and colleagues, who thought that using anything less than the fundamental strengths of the underlying company was merely gambling and could not possibly be means for making an informed investment decision. I am aware of no empirical evidence that conclusively proves the efficacy of technical analysis. Even so, having academics who have never traded say that technical analysis doesn't work is akin to having me test drive a set of economy cars and concluding that it isn't possible for automobiles to go past 90 miles an hour. The One Shot – One Kill Method is BMW's M3 of trading, and can do 90 mph while we are still in third gear.

I humorously, though vehemently, disagreed with those around me who shunned my "nonsensical" approach to buying and, heaven forbid, my shorting stocks. To support my case, I recalled numerous anecdotes and, more importantly, my account statements over a long period of time.

I explained the nuances of reading chart patterns and using certain price targets (known as Fibonacci price targets, defined in Chapter 4) to represent the amount of buyers and sellers at particular price levels. Also, I expostulated on how the chart formations did an excellent job of depicting greed and fear as well as showing the underlying trend in the market. Some took what I said as enlightenment. They were interested in learning something new, and they were very appreciative. Others completely disregarded what I said as hocus-pocus.

Realize that when making a trade you have to be intimately familiar with the recent price movement of the stock. You also need to have a good idea of where the stock is likely to go. There is no better way to do this than by looking at a chart and studying its formation. As we move ahead, I'll explain many of the key chart formations you should always be on the lookout for and what actions to take when they arise.

The chart formations shown in this chapter are not anything new; the knowledge they impart has been around for many, many years. However, unlike the methods espoused in Technical Analysis 101, I like to use these formations in the context of a pullback. That is, normally the first move in a number of the formations you are about to see is not the most profitable one. You need to have patience to reenter on the pullbacks and use well-devised profit targets (discussed in Chapter 4) and the proper application of the One Shot – One Kill Money Management Matrix (see Chapter 10). That is what makes the difference between being the person who almost made some nice profits on the last move and the trader who was right about the move but only walked away with nominal profits or a small loss.

Clearly, more formations exist than the ones in this chapter. As a function of experience and time, you will be able to spot and capitalize on these formations, as the price action behind them takes on an intuitive nature and the need to assign a Netto Number will happen less frequently.

DOUBLE TOP

The point articulated throughout this book is to try to buy weakness in up-trending markets and sell strength in down-trending ones. *Double tops*, if confirmed by our One Shot – One Kill indicators, show a transformation underway from a market that is buying the dips to one that is beginning to sell the rallies.

For example, imagine that you want to buy a stock that has gone on a tremendous run. You tell yourself that if it ever gets cheap again, you will jump in and buy. This yearning to jump in and buy is what forms the first leg of the double top. After the stock falls, it soon begins to rise again, because of all of the traders who bid into the pullback. The shorts have also used the weakness to cover their position, which is only adding gasoline to the fire for another move up.

As the stock approaches its previous high, those who bought near the top are now just looking to get out even, and they begin offering out shares. This initial selling action can gather momentum very quickly and lead to a nice pullback from highs.

Chart 3.1 for the Network Appliance Corporation (NTAP) puts forth a telling story of a nearly perfect double top in October 2000.

The rise was preceded by a tremendous amount of exertion from the previous six months. Those who were not able to be part of the first run got in when the stock traced back to a Fibonacci support level (which will be explained in Chapter 4 in more detail). The market then got its second life and the stock rallied back up to 154 three weeks later.

Unfortunately for investors at that time, the stock turned and took a precipitous drop down, allowing traders who correctly used chart patterns in their trading style to profit handsomely from others' misfortunes as a result of their lack of trading skills. While shorting near the highs may be tempting, what separates a double top from an ascending triangle, explained below, is the how the stock handles the pullback from that second high.

A pullback from that second high that only generates a modest bounce before falling again should offer a much cleaner entry to the short side. Once you begin to actualize some of the profits that exist in detecting and attacking double tops, you will see very good evidence as to why I am so excited about trading.

In order to not get stampeded by a freight train when attempting to enter a double top, you need to understand the five components to every double top that determine whether or not it is worth shorting.

The first thing to measure is the exertion behind the stock's movement before it makes its first high. The longer the time period the stock runs, the more greed that is accompanying its rise, and hence, the greater potential for fear to emerge on a short position. Look at Chart 3.2, concerning the Vitesse Semiconductor Corporation (VTSS), to get an understanding of the exertion that preceded the rise up in February 2000.

The initial rise was accompanied by three straight weeks of upward movement before the stock made its first top.

The second component to a powerful double-top formation is its compression, or the space that exists between the first and second top. Using a time frame of 10 time periods or fewer is ideal. Chart 3.2 shows there is excellent compression being

CHART 3.1

Opportunities like the one seen here occur following a huge runup. A double top forms and the market shifts from buying dips to selling rallies. The first solid entry to the short side occurs near point 2, when the market bounces back up to what is now a declining 15-period MA.

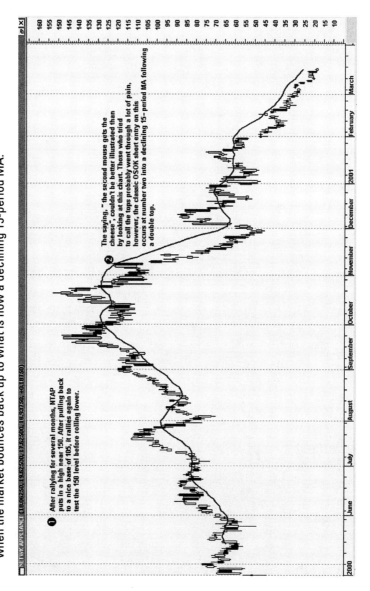

NETWK APPLIANCE (118.05250; 119.82500; 117.82500; 118.93750; +0.18750)

① After rallying for several months, NTAP puts in a high near 150. After pulling back to a nice base of 105, it rallies again to test the 150 level before rolling lower.

② The saying, "the second mouse gets the cheese", couldn't be better illustrated than by looking at this chart. Those who tried to call the tops probably went through a lot of pain, however, the classic OSOK short entry on this occurs at number two into a declining 15- period MA following a double top.

CHART 3.2

The Vitesse Semiconductor Corporation (VTSS) rallied strongly, pulled back nicely, then broke up again to retest highs before finally changing course and retracing all of the gains from the strong rally.

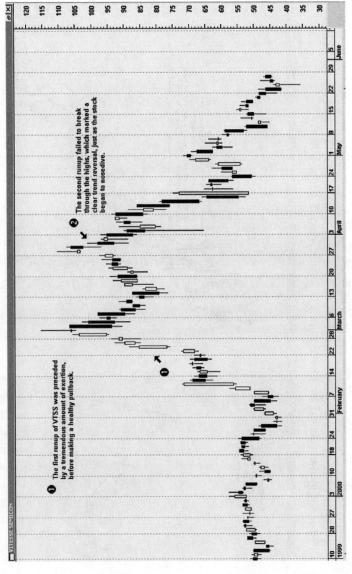

① The first runup of VTSS was preceded by a tremendous amount of exertion, before making a healthy pullback.

② The second runup failed to break through the highs, which marked a clear trend reversal, just as the stock began to nosedive.

formed. An upside-down W, like the one in VTSS, is the kind of clarity that you should be looking for to judge the potential for the downward movement.

The third part of a double top is the deepness of a retracement before it retests old highs. In other words, if a stock only has a shallow pullback before challenging new highs, then attempting to short it is like a salmon swimming upstream. However, if a stock pulls back at least 50 percent of the move and attacks old highs on weakening volume, nice compression, a negative TRI, and breaking down below the 15-point MA, then the probability of a trend reversal increases significantly.

The fourth part of a highly probably double top is the subsequent failure following the pullback from highs the stock or market will experience on its second run. If the stock goes to make new highs on the second run higher and pulls back, you should be alert for a possible short entry. However, if this pullback is met by more buyers, then the stock may not be ready to fall yet and could very well have another higher move in it. However, if this pullback from highs fails to mount another charge and instead fails at a declining 15-period MA, you now have a very lower risk entry to the downside in a stock that has gone from being bought on weakness to now being sold on strength.

The fifth part of making a successful double top is having the stock take out the previous day's low following the scenario in the fourth part. That is, once the subsequent rally after the curve has made a double top fails, making a lower high and succumbing to selling pressure at what is now a declining 15-period MA, you need to enter the position when the stock takes out the previous day's low. This is the spot where most professionals are looking to take aggressive short positions, as the risk-to-reward ratio is excellent.

In summary, you are looking for strongly trending stocks, which have made powerful runs, only to see the subsequent retest of those highs fail. The failure of that retest tells you the sentiment behind the stock has likey changed from that of buying the dips to selling the rallies. You can confirm this by having a *TRI negative divergence reading*. If you see volume weaker on the second run than on the first, then this is usually a pretty good bet that the run has lost steam. You don't need to load the boat the first time the stock breaks down through the previous day's low (PDL) from highs, since, usually, the most profitable short entry from a double top will occur after the second lower high is made. Thereby it provides a more tangible means of entering the position on the short side, using pullbacks to a declining 15-period MA to add to positions to the short side. This loss of momentum usually does a good job of shaking out a lot of buyers. This development offers a tremendous opportunity to playing the downside or at least closing out your long position and watching from the sidelines.

Understandably, many traders don't have the stomach to short stocks. But recognizing this scenario and other formations is helpful in protecting yourself if any of the stocks in your portfolio resemble these characteristics. Understanding the dynamics of this formation alone can save or earn you a tremendous amount of money over the course of your trading and investing career.

DOUBLE BOTTOM

The *double bottom* is just like the double top, except for one key point. The double bottom is used to signal reversals to the upside. The chart is the battlefield showing the war between people's greed and fear. Unlike the double top, which watches traders filled with greed drive the price of a stock higher and higher, a double bottom is accompanied with traders filled with fear, scared into selling the stock on the way down. This downward draft is characterized with a prolonged period of exertion, which is then met by a period of bottom fishers and traders covering short positions. These traders move in to buy when there is temporary support and cause a pseudo rally to the upside. The rally to the upside is short lived, because people quickly use this opportunity to get out of their positions. The selling takes the stock back to the previous low where the sellers begin to lose momentum again.

This loss of momentum by the sellers puts the buyers back in control, as they feel more comfortable that the previous level held as support. This support level serves as an excellent springboard for the rally back up (see Chart 3.3).

A look at Broadcom Corporation (BRCM) shows how strongly this stock was trending, as it created both a double top

CHART 3.3

Movement of Broadcom (BRCM) over a 12-month time frame. The concept with the double top is the same as with the double bottom. Typically, the first pullback after the market has bottomed out provides the best shot at playing the move back up. In the case of Broadcom, shown here, the rally after the first pullback following a double bottom provided for some great trading opportunities.

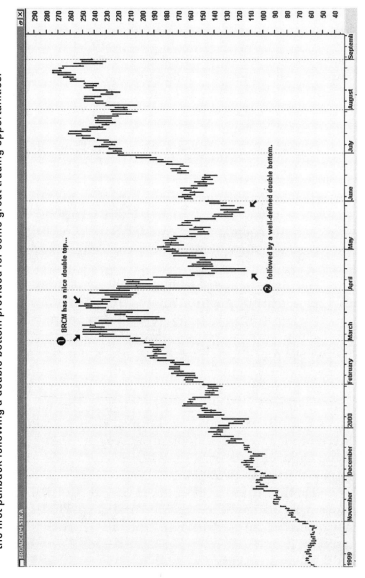

and double bottom within a three-month period. These types of formations provide a great deal of exertion and profitability. The stock ran down for several periods before making a move back up. The move failed, as it ran right into a resistance level (the Fibonacci resistance level, explained in Chapter 4) and headed back down to the previous level of support. However, this time around, the sellers lost momentum and the stock headed back up with a vengeance and tremendous exertion behind it.

Chart 3.4 shows Just Don't Sell Us (JDSU) taking off on a huge parabolic run.

This stock ran into a wall of resistance at 107 and then pulled back to 75, a well-defined level of support (a .618 Fibonacci support level, explained in Chapter 4) from the previous move up. The stock then climbed back up and ran into a top. This set the table perfectly for taking a short position. The stock then went and formed a perfect double bottom and rallied higher

The next stock showing a strong double bottom is BRCM in June 2000 (see Chart 3.5).

The stock fell hard from a classic double top in March 2000 all the way to 105 a share before putting in a low. Following the fall, the stock bounced back up to 180 a share before making a final move lower to retest the stocks low in the 115 area. After falling around 110 a share, the stock rallied powerfully to make a new 52-week high following the bullish formation.

As I do with the double-top formation, I like to look at five things with the double bottom to play the move back to the upside. In order to not get stampeded by a freight train when attempting to enter a double top, you need to understand the five components to every double bottom that determine whether or not it is worth going long.

The first thing to measure is the exertion behind the stock's movement before it makes its first low. The longer the time period in which the stock falls, the more fear that is accompanying its rise, and hence, the greater potential for greed to emerge on the long position.

The second component to a powerful double-bottom formation is its compression, or the space that exists between the first and second lows. Using a time frame of 10 time periods or less is ideal. A "W" formation is the kind of clarity that you should be looking for to judge the potential for the upside movement.

CHART 3.4

Stocks that move strongly off of double tops and double bottoms typically respond well to Fibonacci levels following a retest of highs and lows.

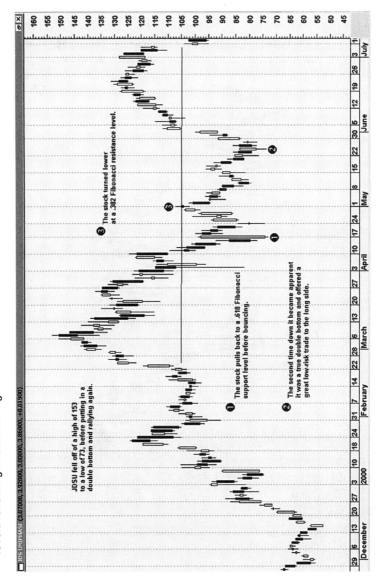

JDS UNIPHASE (3.870000, 3.920000, 3.800000, 3.860000, +0.019000)

JDSU fell off of a high of 153 to a low of 73, before putting in a double bottom and rallying again.

❸ The stock turned lower at a .382 Fibonacci resistance level.

❶ The stock pulls back to a .618 Fibonacci support level before bouncing.

❷ The second time down it became apparent it was a true double bottom and offered a great low-risk trade to the long side.

CHART 3.5

Broadcom shows some nice movement as it reacts well off of both a double top and a double bottom.

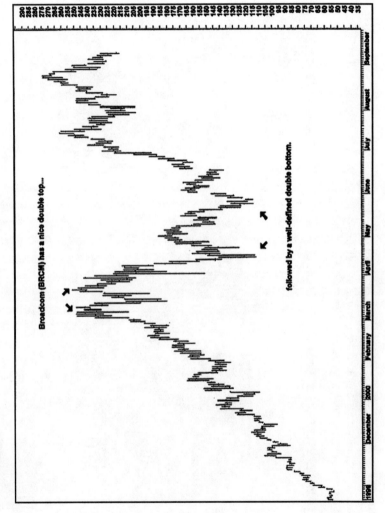

The third part of a double bottom is the deepness of a retracement before it retests old lows. In other words, if a stock only has a shallow pullback before falling back to the lows, then attempting to go long is putting yourself in a precarious position. However, if a stock pulls back at least 50 percent of the move, and falls to old lows on weakening volume, nice compression, bullish TRI divergence, and breaking out above the 15-period MA, then the likelihood of it holding its support is much better.

The fourth part of a highly probable double bottom is the subsequent rally following the pullback from lows the stock or market will experience on its second selloff. If the stock goes to make new lows on the second run and pulls back, you should be alert for a possible long entry. However, if this pullback is met by more sellers, then the stock may not be ready to rally yet and could very well have another move lower in it. But what if this pullback from lows fails to mount another charge and instead finds support at a rising 15-period MA? You now have a very low risk entry to the upside in a stock that has gone from being sold on strength to now being bought on weakness.

The fifth part of making a successful double bottom is having the stock break above the previous day's high following the scenario in part four. That is, once the subsequent pullback after it makes a double bottom holds, making a higher low and finding more aggressive buyers to what is now a rising 15-period MA, enter the position when the stock takes out the previous day's high. This is the spot most professionals are looking to take aggressive long positions, as the risk-to-reward ratio is excellent.

ASCENDING TRIANGLE

Throughout my career, a continually profitable chart formation has been playing the moves from ascending triangle patterns. An *ascending triangle* pattern is part of a continuation pattern. It manifests itself due to the supply of sellers dwindling, as the stock continually battles a consistent line of overhead resistance. At first, the stock will battle the resistance before it retreats south. The next time it battles the resistance level, it also fails to break through, but on the subsequent fall down, it manages to make a higher low. The next time it rises up, it might fail as well, with the subsequent drop leaving the stock in an even narrower trading range.

When a stock finally breaks through its overhead resistance, it is like letting a beach ball out of the water after you have been holding it underneath the surface. It just explodes, with tons of momentum to the upside (see Chart 3.6).

Note that all of these formations can be applied on an intraday chart as well as a daily chart.

The first important factor in gauging the probability of success is having a strong volume on the move. If the breakout is not accompanied with substantial buying interest, then it is not as likely to follow through to the upside. If the break over the base is done on surging volume, this would be a positive sign that the dam of resistance has finally been cracked.

The move over this resistance point is usually fast and furious, leaving many traders to think that they missed the move. However, most breaks, from either an ascending triangle pattern or a descending triangle pattern, come back to retest their breakout point at least once before the real move can begin in earnest. It is this subsequent pullback that really offers the best risk-to-reward opportunity and is the most ideal One Shot – One Kill setup. Again, we are trying to find a spot to buy weakness in what is an up-trending stock. The pullback following a breakout is what offers the best opportunity.

As Chapter 4 (on Fibonacci analysis) will point out, many times, the area of resistance to an ascending triangle will be a solid area of resistance—the Fibonacci resistance. The breaking through of this significant Fibonacci resistance is a very bullish sign for the continuation of the trend. If there is no significant Fibonacci resistance near the line of resistance, ascertain the next area of Fibonacci resistance, as experience has dictated that this is the area where the rally could potentially stall and pull back to the breakout point.

The breakout of an ascending triangle can carry with it great momentum, but as I said before, in most cases, there will be a major pullback to retest the area of the breakout point before the run really takes off. If you missed the first launch, or if you are looking to add on to a winning position, this usually

CHART 3.6

A classic ascending triangle pattern. As with other chart formations in this chapter, the ascending triangle can provide some powerful moves. However, if the move is for real, it will usually provide multiple reentries and give some great opportunities to buy weakness after it breaks out.

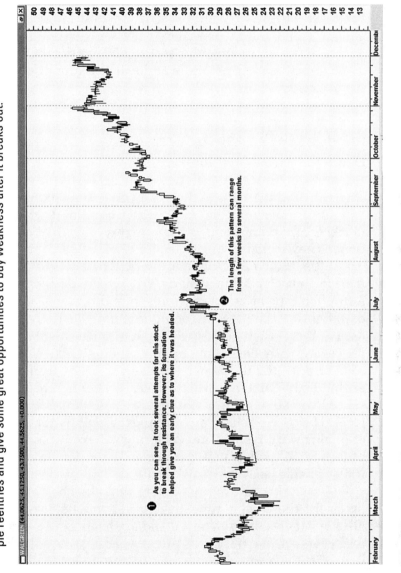

proves to be a good time to get on board. It is for this reason that I particularly like scaling into ascending triangle patterns and patiently increase my position size, after gauging the strength of the trend on the first pullback. If the first pullback holds as I expect, then I will become more aggressive on the second entry.

As always, having the sector and market moving in the same direction as the stock is an ideal situation that you should try to exploit.

DESCENDING TRIANGLE

One of the purposes of this book is to provide you with clear, useful, and important information as it relates to the One Shot – One Kill trading method. I want to couple this knowledge with insight as to how to adequately spot potential downturns in the market. Understanding certain high-probability chart formations is key to doing so.

After the double top, another extremely bearish chart formation that should put you on alert is the *descending triangle* formation. The price action going on in this situation is akin to a dam fighting the pressure of an oncoming rush. As long as that dam is there, then all of the people who are long feel confident. However, with each subsequent rush attack, the dam gets weaker until the floodgates break open. What tends to follow is an incredible amount of downward exertion behind the stock, caused by the panic brought about by the break in the support level. The precipitous drop in a stock is usually the continuation of a downward trend. The stock might have moved lower, then consolidated, and is now gathering steam for its next move to the downside (see Charts 3.7 and 3.8).

A mistake that many traders make is shorting a stock at precisely the wrong time by chasing breakdowns that have already made a sizeable move and are beginning to put in a natural countertrend pullback. Understanding this natural ebb and flow of the markets is why we put the majority of our size on descending triangle patterns after the breakdown and come back up for a breath of fresh air. Unfortunately for the stock, this is the ideal opportunity for One Shot – One Kill traders to

CHART 3.7

A classic descending triangle pattern. As with the ascending triangle, the descending triangle usually sees the stock rally back to retest its breakdown point, which provides a low-risk short entry with a tight stop to get in on the trade. In the case of Loews Cineplex Corporation (LCP), this stock broke down and made a succession of lower highs, thereby giving traders multiple chances to reenter.

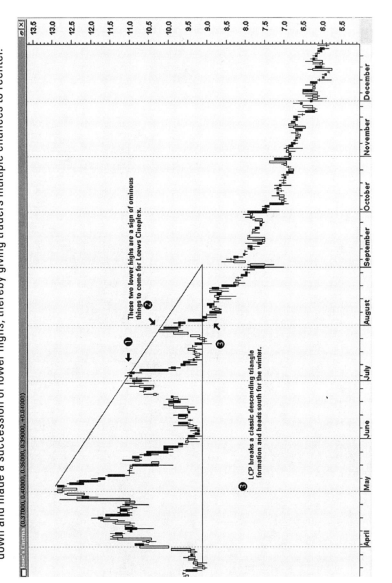

These two lower highs are a sign of ominous things to come for Loews Cineplex.

LCP breaks a classic descending triangle formation and heads south for the winter.

CHART 3.8

LCP continued to trade lower and ultimately went off the trading map.

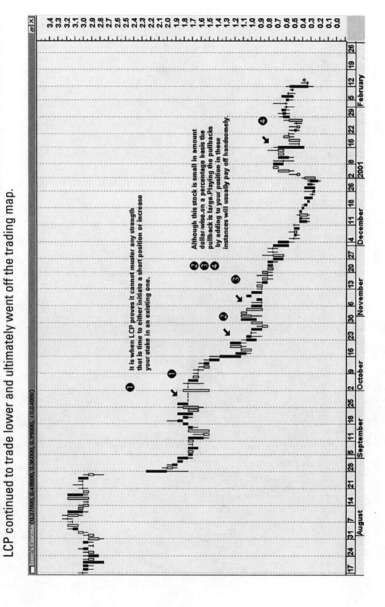

Lowe's Liscena (0.37000, 0.40000, 0.36000, 0.39000, +0.04000)

① It is when LCP proves it cannot muster any strength that is time to either initiate a short position or increase your stake in an existing one.

② ③ ④

② Although this stock is small in amount dollar-wise. on a percentage basis the pullback is large. Playing the pullbacks by adding to your position in these instances will usually pay off handsomely.

offer into the move and capitalize on a move back to the downside with a good risk-to-reward ratio. Sizable profit is what you are after, and shorting a stock at $50, only to watch it rise to $53 or $54 before stopping you out, and then immediately turn back down to $40 (while you are on the sideline), is something I have experienced in the past and hope that you can avoid. This scenario is less likely to happen if you use the pullbacks within the underlying move.

As with every pattern in this book, what time frame you decide upon is up to you, the individual trader/investor. However, a 13- and 60-minute intraday chart is particularly useful for day traders and swing traders, because it does a great job of filtering out a lot of noise. Longer-term investors can look at a daily or weekly chart to get a feel for a potential breakdown in the stock, the market, or both. Again, let me stress, just as with an ascending triangle, you need to have confirmation with a descending triangle before making a trade. Helping you determine the likely chances for profit will be the same indicators used in determining an ascending triangle.

An important factor will be assessing whether or not any major Fibonacci areas could manifest as support. As you will see in Chapter 4, shorting stocks into a heavy area of Fibonacci support can prove to be a costly mistake. It often leaves you with an undesirable risk-to-reward ratio in the trade. It does so because of where you would have to put your stop in order to give yourself a fair chance in the trade, compared to where your likely profit target would be.

The third area, which proves particularly adept, is paying attention to the amount of volume, which occurred when the stock broke through. If, during the downtrend, there is heavy volume relative to the stock's daily average (for example, 25 percent greater than average), then there stands to be a better chance you will see a follow-through on the stock continuing to the downside. In most cases, this formation is a continuation of a down trend, which is merely catching its collective breath before its next thrust down.

A classic example of a descending triangle is shown in Charts 3.7 and 3.8, pertaining to Loews Cineplex Entertainment (LCP). The stock made a high near 13, followed by a lower high at 11 and then, another lower high near 10. The stock had been using a base of support near 9 for some time to rally upward. Following the initial breakdown of support, most of the time stocks will try to make an attempt to retest their breakdown point. It is when that subsequent breakdown point fails that traders using the One Shot – One Kill Method should become more aggressive with their trades and not be afraid to put the boxer to the mat— that is, aggressively adding to a winning position and letting the position work for them. Following the failure of a retest, an increase in your position to the short side would be perfectly acceptable, because if you entered correctly, then you should already be profitable in the trade. You would thereby be allowed to enter a second position, fully knowing that if it goes against you, you should still be able to *at least* break even. However, if the formation follows through, which is what the trend suggests, then you should be rewarded for your proper money management, risk management, and trading ability.

The next example of a classic descending triangle occurred in August 2001, with the Nasdaq 100. The Nasdaq had been using 1600 as a support base and definitively cracked through it in the middle of August (see Chart 3.9).

It is okay to short here. However, it is not prudent to go in with size, until after a retest of that breakdown point fails, thereby giving a much better probability of having a successful trade. More importantly, it gives a better overall risk-to-reward ratio. After the Nasdaq failed its retest, it was time to short with size and watch it roll down. And roll down it did.

These textbook setups should have you take notice, because they are what put the odds in your favor. Once again, all you are trying to do is simply put yourself into trades with positive expected returns, based on logical price calculations. Over time, this kind of trading should allow you to bank bigger profits based on overall better performance.

Remember, however, that at all times you must wear the hat of a well-disciplined risk manager. So it's important to have as many indications in your favor as possible, because each one helps add to the likelihood of a successful trade.

Micromanaging your positions can be one of the worst things you do as a trader. However, it is something, at one time

CHART 3.9

The Nasdaq 100 broke down from a descending triangle base in the middle of August 2001. The retest of the original breakdown point provided a spot for a low-risk short entry to get in the market.

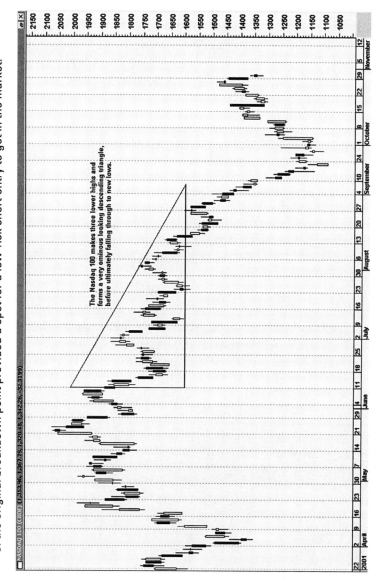

The Nasdaq 100 makes three lower highs and forms a very ominous looking descending triangle, before ultimately falling through to new lows.

or another, we have probably all done. It results from convincing ourselves that somehow, with no real explanation, the trade we entered confidently, just a little while ago, has now changed. It can also result in a lack of confidence in the indicators, method, and/or plan being used. This is not to say the market is not prone to sudden reversals, or that you can't be flexible, but over time, I have found that changing my plan as I go has brought with it more harm than good.

SPOTTING REVERSALS

Market watchers are always asking themselves if the change in direction they are seeing from the movement in a stock price is a natural pullback within the present move or the beginning of a new trend going the other way. While there is no dead-sure way to tell, there are clearly ways to play reversals to determine if your stock is in fact reversing or just retracing before continuing its underlying trend.

The first thing to look at when determining a reversal is the pattern itself. There are a number of profitable reversal patterns, which can provide a quick profit in the near term. The first example of one of those formations is called a *two-bar reversal*. This is a common setup, which accompanies a great deal of pressure to the upside or the downside. When markets trend very strongly without any relief, it is the equivalent of compressing a spring and not letting it unwind. When it finally does unwind, the effect can be a very powerful reversal. This occurs when a market heads up or down very quickly and then makes up its entire gain or loss within the next two bars. This snap back can lead to a huge reversal that will leave many traders wondering if they should buy back in and, if so, will they get suckered?

The second thing you need to look at when attempting to spot reversals are the relevant Fibonacci retracement or expansion levels. Stocks or indices that move into heavy areas of Fibonacci Friends are more likely to reverse than stocks without any support in front of them. With the tools you will learn to use in Chapter 4 on Fibonacci analysis, you can greatly increase your confidence in taking on a trade that appears to be reversing.

Looking at Chart 3.10 for the Dow Jones Industrial Averages, you can see how the market came under tremendous sell pressure on several occasions, before finally and abruptly performing very nice countertrend rallies. These days are marked by explosive moves off of the lows and are confirmed the following day when the market takes out its previous day's high. This event can serve as a good indication that a strong countertrend rally has begun. The reversal can be played as such, by watching to see how it responds to the action off the 15-period MA, major support or resistance points, as well as possible divergences in the TRI. Watch to see how the movement of the stock respects the Fibonacci support level and is unable to move any lower. Knowledge of these areas in advance will make the technical indicators, which were discussed in Chapter 2, even that much more powerful and profitable.

During an up trend, as a stock reverses, it will show a tent-like pattern on the top, indicating the buying at that level has lost its momentum and the stock will more than likely begin a countertrend move (which is sometimes extreme) to the downside.

Viewing the MACD, you will notice that it becomes widely expanded and begins to start turning back in. Take a look at Chart 3.11 or Linear Technology Corporatoin (LLTC.)

You will find it most profitable, if you want to play a reversal based on the parameters set forth in this book for the MACD, that you assess and find areas of a likely reversal, based on historical points of support and resistance, using the MACD Histogram. Like every indicator, this one is not perfect and should not be the sole basis for entering a trade. Use it in conjunction with price targets, formations, and other indicators in order to raise your chances of success.

The other formation that I like to play is the *rounding bottom* on stocks that have been sold off heavily. This rounding motion forms a J-hook formation that is confirmed by a gap-up, after making a nice rounding formation on the bottom (see Chart 3.12).

As it will be explained in greater detail in Chapter 5 on inflection points, determining weekly or even monthly inflection points of either support or resistance is the way to capitalize on

CHART 3.10

The Dow shows the propensity to rally back hard following extended periods of selling.

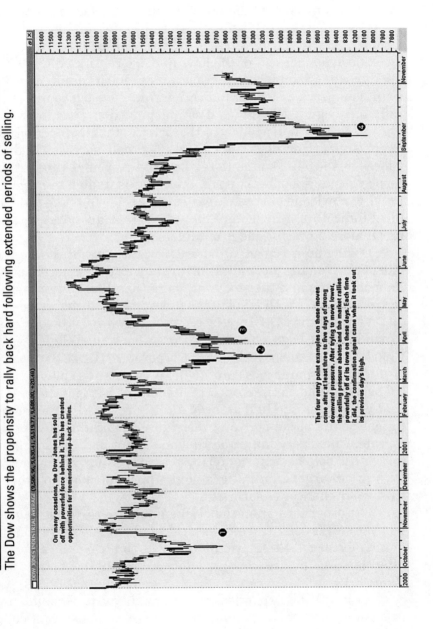

On many occasions, the Dow Jones has sold off with powerful force behind it. This has created opportunities for tremendous snap-back rallies.

The four entry point examples on these moves come after at least three to five days of strong downward pressure. After trying to move lower, the selling pressure abates and the market rallies powerfully off of its lows on these days. Each time it did, the confirmation signal came when it took out its previous day's high.

CHART 3.11

It is important to notice that when the market puts in a solid reversal by closing substan-tially off of its lows and the MACD is showing signs of being significantly oversold, the trend is beginning to change in the short term.

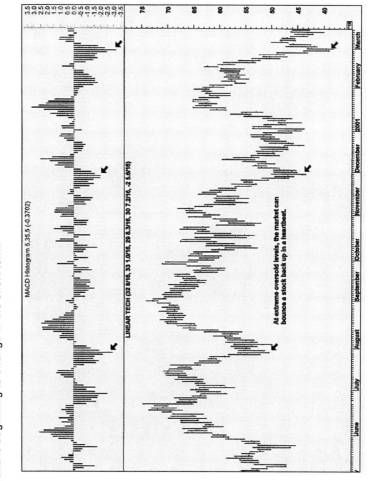

CHART 3.12

A J-hook formation usually occurs after a downturn in the market. It begins when 50 percent of a large daily down bar is retraced (which marks the trade entry point) and is oftentimes followed by either a gap up or a continuation to the upside. This formation offers great profit potential at low risk.

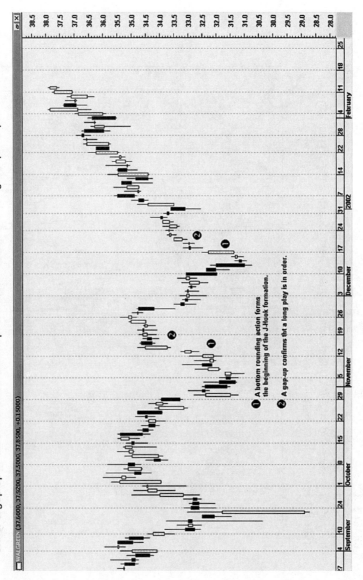

tremendous reversals when most of Wall Street is scratching their heads as to what just happened on the market. Each of the aforementioned methods can serve as signals to a reversal; however, the goal of the One Shot – One Kill Method is to use a confluence of indicators to stack the odds (preferably heavily) in your favor.

The charts shown are all common reversal formations that occur on a daily basis in the market. Identifying them requires some practice and experience. However, knowing and understanding these formations is what is going to keep you alive as a trader and preserve your portfolio if you are an investor.

PLAYING THE BREAKOUT

Playing *breakouts* from consolidations, on both intraday and daily charts, has provided a consistent means of profit for many traders over the years. Patience and discipline is key when these situations arise. By following the One Shot – One Kill Method, you will be attacking these trading formations with a close eye on profitability.

Breakouts and breakdowns occur after a stock hits an area of consolidation, thereby moving sideways, gathering steam before making its next move. Then, once it can break the struggle from either the bulls or the bears, which occurs during consolidation, it moves like hell, with determination in its eyes.

A consolidation breakout occurs after a stock has been trading in consolidation for some time, usually 5 to 15 periods, sometimes a lot longer. While in this consolidation period, the stock is building a base and resting up for its next big run. It is during this next run that you will plan to get into the trade. Charts 3.13 and 3.14, of Maxim Integrated Products (MXIM), shows a stock that was in consolidation for 15 days before breaking big time to the upside.

The longer the stock is in consolidation, the more powerful the breakout tends to be. As expected, the stock retraced somewhat and then traded in another consolidation range between approximately 57 and 64. After 15 days, the stock collapsed to the downside and had "broken down." These breakdowns or breakouts can be very powerful but should not be chased.

CHART 3.13

Movement of Maxim Integrated Products (MXIM), showing how stock was in consolidation for 15 days before moving to the upside.

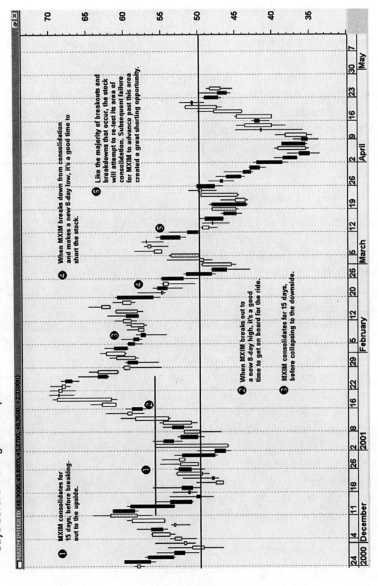

① MXIM consolidates for 15 days, before breaking-out to the upside.

② When MXIM breaks out to a new 8-day high, it's a good time to get on board for the ride.

③ MXIM consolidates for 15 days, before collapsing to the downside.

④ When MXIM breaks down from consolidation and makes a new 8-day low, it's a good time to short the stock.

⑤ Like the majority of breakouts and breakdowns that occur, the stock will attempt to re-test its area of consolidation. Subsequent failure for MXIM to advance past this area created a great shorting opportunity.

CHART 3.14

A classic cup-and-handle formation.

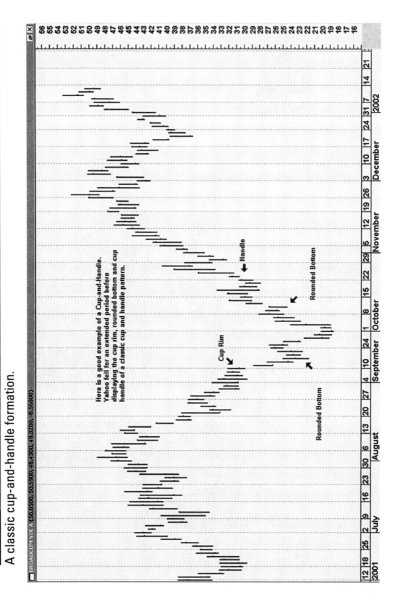

Amateur investors chase breakdowns and breakouts! The pros know that most breakouts or breakdowns will usually pull back and test an area near their initial inflection point. It is this retracement that you should look for, because oftentimes they permit you to get back in the trade, provided the indicators are in agreement. This is usually a good time to scale into the trade with the rest of your position. Determining where the pivot points, 15-period MA, and/or Fibonacci Friends are hanging out serves as an excellent gauge as to where to take profits and move on.

Another kind of breakout is the *cup-and-handle formation*. A cup and handle occurs when a stock runs up. It then retraces and then bases, building up steam for its next run. It comes back up to test that initial level of resistance. This run will usually fail, because those who bought at the previous top will usually use this as an opportunity to sell the stock, just to get even. This first part of the chart formation is called the *cup* (see Chart 3.15).

The *handle* occurs when the stock fails to break through resistance, it moves back slightly, forming what looks to be a handle on the cup. The stock then makes another run at the prize, but this time it breaks through the resistance and moves up with incredible thrust.

Once again, these breakouts will normally retrace and leave you with the opportunity to get back in the trade, if you weren't able to get in at a good spot on the initial move. It is a common occurrence for these breakouts to find resistance at certain points called Fibonacci expansion points (explained in the next chapter), backed up by indicators such as the Detrended Oscillator, TRI, and Vertical/Horizontal Filter showing its time to take profits.

The next example will focus on a stock that broke down from consolidation at a double top and continued moving lower. Chart 3.16 shows how CMGI started its disastrous spiral in a prohibitive downtrend, following its meteoric rise from 50 to 163 and then its subsequent collapse, before finding support with some bargain hunters and short covering at around $35 a share.

While the stock was falling, it continually went into periods of consolidation before it resumed its downward trend.

Eventually, it became sadly apparent to the longs that this stock was not going up again. It kept breaking lower ranges of

CHART 3.15

Disastrous downward spiral of CMGI.

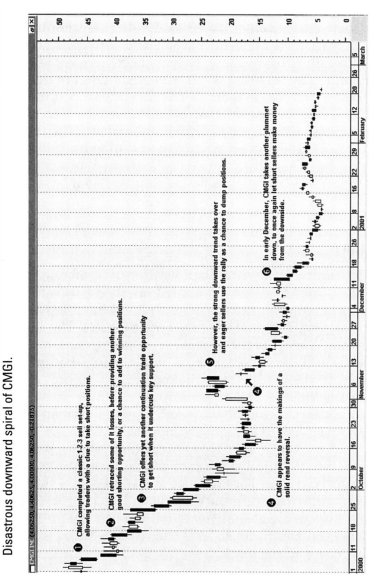

CMGI INC (4.06250, 4.40625, 4.00000, 4.06250, -0.21875)

1. CMGI completed a classic 1-2-3 sell set-up, allowing traders with a clue to take short positions.

2. CMGI retraced some of it losses, before providing another good shorting opportunity, or a chance to add to winning positions.

3. CMGI offers yet another continuation trade opportunity to get short when it undercuts key support.

4. CMGI appears to have the makings of a solid trend reversal.

5. However, the strong downward trend takes over and eager sellers use the rally as a chance to dump positions.

6. In early December, CMGI takes another plummet down, to once again let short sellers make money from the downside.

consolidation and headed lower very sharply. However, like many breakdowns, it also retraced a number of times, to give short sellers another chance to sell strength in a declining stock, continually. As the CMGI chart graphically illustrates, the market will usually give you many chances to get into trade. Having a keen understanding of this offers peace of mind to many professionals, which allows them to look for the best setups.

Like every profitable pattern discussed in this chapter, chart patterns alone do not constitute enough of a reason to "load the boat" and enter a trade. Confirmation from other indicators in the One Shot – One Kill Method is essential to enhancement of your chances for making consistently successful trades.

SUMMARY

As this chapter explained when covering the aforementioned formations, the One Shot – One Kill Method is about buying weakness in rising markets, selling strength in falling markets, and taking profits at predetermined price targets. The chart formation comprises 10 of the 30 points that go into making a Netto Number. Formations like double tops, double bottoms, and ascending triangles are fairly common in the market and provide some great trading opportunities. However, it is not my style to chase the initial move off of these formations, but instead to wait for the subsequent move to emerge as it will usually provide a better risk-to-reward ratio. It is important to understand that within these formations, there are good spots and bad spots to enter both the long and short side of the trades. By using pullbacks within the underlying trend to get in, as well as profit targets to get out, you stand the best chance to profit from these setups and consistently give yourself the best chance to make money in the market.

CHAPTER 4

Fibonacci Levels–The Basis of Price Targets

The progression of the One Shot – One Kill Method has so far touched on how to account for 20 of the 30 possible points needed for creating a Netto Number. Later, I will discuss how to apply them when trying to spot a One Shot – One Kill trading setup. As stated throughout the book, you look for your entries and exits based on major inflection points in the market, allowing you to sell strength in down-trending markets and buy weakness in up-trending markets, determined in large part by Fibonacci retracements and expansions. These Fibonacci numbers are what allow you to stay two to three steps ahead of the market and logically anticipate where the bulls and the bears will do battle.

Creating price targets will put you in position to take on trades that offer exceptional risk-to-reward ratios. It is the application of the indicators in Chapter 2, the proper interpretation of the chart formations in Chapter 3, matched with the Fibonacci levels in this chapter that will give you the foundation to understand the One Shot – One Kill Method. This chapter provides the explanation behind arriving at Fibonacci levels, as we continue our succession into understanding how to properly calculate and apply Netto Numbers.

BRIEF HISTORY OF FIBONACCI

A major contributing factor for the creation of price targets in the One Shot – One Kill Method came from a man named Leonardo Pisano, who was born in Pisa, Italy, around 1170.However, during his childhood, he earned the nickname Fibonacci. The Fibonacci sequence relates to many traders in a big way. Correct interpretation of these levels and how to use them effectively in trading is discussed in substantial detail, as they relate to the One Shot – One Kill Method, in this chapter. I acknowledge Fibonacci, because I like to give credit where credit is due, and teaching you a little something about him may make you appreciate and respect him more.

Some time after 1192, Leonardo's father took him to Bugia. His father intended for Leonardo to become a merchant and so arranged for his instruction in calculational techniques, especially those involving the Hindu-Arabic numerals, which had not yet been introduced into Europe. Fibonacci was a strong supporter of Hindu-Arabic numerals and is one of the first people credited with making them the standard in Europe. Eventually, his father enlisted Leonardo's help and sent him on trips to Egypt, Syria, Greece, Sicily, and Provence. Leonardo took the opportunity offered by his travel abroad to study and learn the mathematical techniques employed in these various regions.

Around 1200, Fibonacci returned to Pisa, where he worked on his own mathematical compositions for at least the next 25 years. The five works he completed during this period are the *Liber Abaci* (1202, 1228); the *Practica Geometriae* (1220–1221); an undated letter to Theodorus, the imperial philosopher to the court of the Hohenstaufen emperor Frederick II; *Flos* (1225), a collection of solutions to problems posed in the presence of Frederick II; and the *Liber Quadratorum* (1225), a number-theoretic book concerned with the simultaneous solution of equations quadratic in two or more variables. So great was Leonardo's reputation as a mathematician that, as a result of these works, Frederick summoned Leonardo for an audience when the mathematician was in Pisa around 1225.

After 1228, virtually nothing is known of Fibonacci's life. Fibonacci died some time after 1240, presumably in Pisa. Traders have been fascinated with Fibonacci numbers for many years.

Those who have a grasp of formulating *Fibonacci retracement and expansion levels*, as described in my trading method, have a decided edge in trading profitably for a living.

Except for his role in spreading the use of the Hindu-Arabic numerals, Fibonacci's contribution to mathematics has been largely overlooked. His name is known to modern mathematicians, mainly because of the Fibonacci sequence derived from a problem in his work: *Liber Abaci*.

A certain man put a pair of rabbits in a place surrounded on all sides by a wall. How many pairs of rabbits can be produced from that pair in a year if it is supposed that every month each pair begets a new pair, which from the second month on becomes productive?

The resulting number sequence, 1, 1, 2, 3, 5, 8, 13, 21, 34, 55 (Fibonacci himself omitted the first term), in which each number is the sum of the two preceding numbers, is the first recursive number sequence (in which the relation between two or more successive terms can be expressed by a formula) known in Europe.

In the nineteenth century the term *Fibonacci sequence* was coined by the French mathematician Edouard Lucas, and scientists began to discover such sequences in nature. For example, they were found in the spirals of sunflower heads, in pinecones, in the regular descent (genealogy) of the male bee, in the related logarithmic (equiangular) spiral in snail shells, in the arrangement of leaf buds on a stem, and in animal horns.

THE IMPORTANCE OF FIBONACCI RATIOS IN THE MARKET

Traders today have many ways to determine profitable entry and exit points. The first place many traders look is to former levels of support and resistance. These levels can give a good idea of where to secure a logical profit or keep a loss to a minimum. The application of Fibonacci numbers is something traders and institutions have been using for years to determine where the markets, or individual stocks, could potentially and most likely turn around. Fibonnaci numbers are a powerful part of many professional traders' trading strategies and now, because of the recent surge of online traders, are becoming popular with newer traders as well.

What are *Fibonnaci numbers*? An example would be the numbers .382 and .618, which can be used to multiply by the previous fall or rise of a stock in order to help determine how far the next move will be. For example, imagine you have a stock that is trending very strongly and has moved up in price from $20 to $45 over the course of a few weeks. It begins to lose momentum, turn back around in price, and start falling. After such a run, many traders might wonder where a good entry point would be to go long, or where a good point to cover a possible short position would be. A good way to get this information is to calculate the Fibonacci ratio of the rise, using the first of the two significant Fibonacci numbers: .382.

1. First, determine the difference between the end and the beginning of the rise:

$$45 - 20 = 25$$

2. Then multiply that figure by .382:

$$25 \times .382 = 9.55$$

3. Now, subtract that figure from the high:

$$45 - 9.5 = 36.5$$

This 36.5 level looks like a significant one of support to develop for the stock. But what if the stock turns around and falls right through 36.5, like a hot knife through butter?

That is why it is important to calculate the next Fibonacci ratio, using the next significant number: .618:

1. Again, calculate the difference between the end and the beginning of the rise:

$$45 - 20 = 25$$

2. Then multiply that figure by .618:

$$25 \times .618 = 15.45$$

3. As you did with the last .382 measurement, subtract that figure from the high:

$$45 - 15.45 = 29.55$$

That 29.55 level serves as a second means for the pullback in the price of the stock to find support. From here, you have two possibilities for spotting a reversal and determining where to close a short position, or where to go long. Fortunately, plenty of software is available that does all of this type of calculation and clearly displays results on charts so you will not have to bother with the chore of constantly determining these numbers. There are many tactics available using Fibonacci analysis to determine price targets, which will be discussed later in this chapter and book.

For an example, let's examine the price action of the Nasdaq market over a one-year period. Near the end of October 1999, the Nasdaq began its record runup, with the index almost doubling by the end of March. However, at the end of March 2000 the Nasdaq seemed doomed. After forming a *compressed double top*, it immediately headed south. Selling pressure was fast and furious. Over the next two weeks, the index fell almost 2000 points, to a low of 3227. From there, the index staged a two-week rally, which, from its March closing high of 5046 to its April closing low of 3227, left a lot of work to be done. The rally failed precisely at the .382 Fibonacci resistance level from that decline (see Chart 4.1).

Following that rally, the market headed south again, continuing its almost steady downtrend from before, and made a lower low at 3042. The Nasdaq then rallied powerfully over the next seven weeks, to a high of 4289, which happened to be another perfect .618 Fibonacci retracement of its decline from 5100, to its low of 3100.

A side note regarding the action shown in Chart 4.1: Looking at the chart, you can see the market managed to break through the .382 Fibonacci level; however, it proved to be only a two-week consolidation, where taking profits from a long position would have been justified. After rallying to 4289, the index came down from the Fibonacci resistance level and headed south again, to ultimately another .618 retracement of its recent run (from 3042 to 4289), to where it fell to 3540 (see Chart 4.2). The market then rallied off that level, for nearly all of August, back to 4260 and then fell back to 3760, which, coincidentally, was yet another .618 Fibonacci retracement level.

CHART 4.1

The Nasdaq Composite Index broke down from a double top in March 2000. The bounce following the selloff gave a nice shorting opportunity right at the .382 retracement before it sold off again and broke down to new lows.

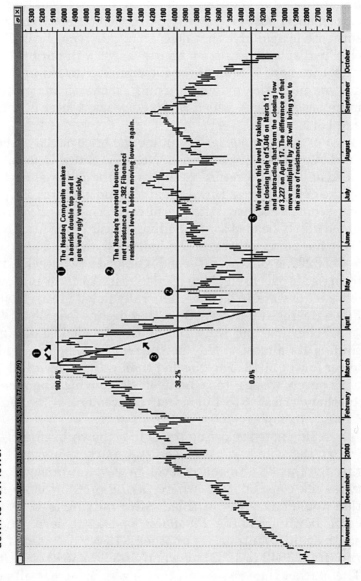

NASDAQ COMPOSITE (5,054.55, 5,316.97, 5,054.55, 3,316.77, +242.09)

① The Nasdaq Composite makes a bearish double top and it gets very very ugly very quickly.

② The Nasdaq's oversold bounce met resistance at a .382 Fibonacci resistance level, before moving lower again.

③ We derive this level by taking the closing high of 5,046 on March 11, and subtracting that from the closing low of 3,227 on April 17. The difference of that move multiplied by .382 will bring you to the area of resistance.

CHART 4.2

Following a powerful move down, the Nasdaq rallied to a .618 retracement of the entire move down.
You need to be aware of these levels before the market arrives at these points, as they create some
very powerful opportunities.

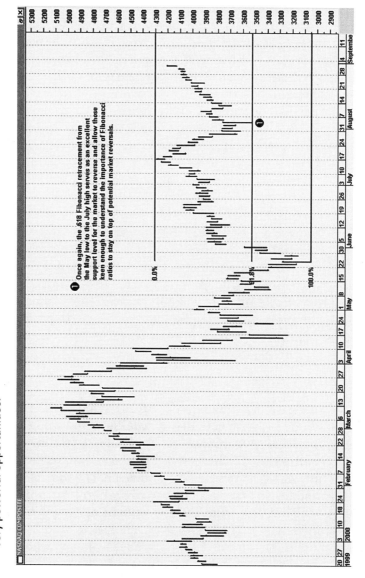

① Once again, the .618 Fibonacci retracement from
the May low to the July high serves as an excellent
support level for the market to reverse and allow those
keen enough to understand the importance of Fibonacci
ratios to stay on top of potential market reversals.

89

You really need to understand the importance of Fibonacci levels on the markets. The Nasdaq often stages very impressive turnarounds off of Fibonacci retracements or expansions. This chapter focuses on familiarizing you with the basics of Fibonacci retracement analysis and applying it to the market. Many beginning and experienced traders who learn about Fibonacci ratios are taken aback when they learn about the uncanny relationships that these ratios have on the market. After fully understanding Fibonacci analysis, they often wonder how they ever traded without incorporating it into their trading.

When watching the market, you must pay close attention to where key Fibonacci retracement levels exist as, many times, a .382 or .618 level provides a logical point for the market to witness either a strong, countertrend rally or begin a trend reversal.

This basic explanation only scratches the surface of how to use technical analysis and Fibonacci levels to determine your best potential trading opportunities. When combined with the other tools in the One Shot – One Kill Method, Fibonacci levels become an invaluable part to a person's trading plan. When trading, you should always keep in mind the Fibonacci levels, so you will have a much clearer picture of how to profit from time-tested areas of support and resistance.

PROFITING FROM FIBONACCI FRIENDS

As has been touched upon many times in this book, creating highly probabilistic price targets to buy weakness in strong markets and sell strength in weak markets is the basis for trading the One Shot – One Kill Method. The use of Fibonacci expansion and retracement analysis is critical in this endeavor. The idea is to create predetermined price targets of not only where the present move is likely to go but also what the subsequent move will be. This calculation gives you a tremendous psychological and tactical advantage akin to that of a champion chess player, who attempts to think out several moves of his opponent before making any move. It is a very proactive way of approaching the markets.

Much as mammals often travel in packs in the wild to enhance their chances of survivability, traders in the market tend to move in clusters. Thus, the majority of your profitable

Fibonacci ratios are going to occur in the same area, as a result of a prolonged down trend or up trend. The stock or market will run for a while as part of a strong trend. The market will usually retrace part of those gains until it can gather more steam and move forward again. The first move naturally creates a set of Fibonacci ratios that are specific to that first move. As the second move begins, it becomes clear that there is a second set of Fibonacci ratios to compute. Remember, when you calculate where potential Fibonacci support or resistance will manifest itself, you must do so by taking the rise or fall of the stock price and multiplying it by .382 and .618. The following example on the Nasdaq will better illustrate how to use these technical tools.

These two computations show that there is relatively close proximity between a .382 retracement of the entire run from the start, which sits next to a .618 retracement. This relative proximity is what the One Shot – One Kill Method calls an area of *Fibonacci Friends*. These are also known throughout the trading industry as *Fibonacci price clusters* or *Fibonacci areas of confluence*. These Fibonacci Friends provide a solid area of support for a further rise up or resistance for a further drop down.

The paragraphs that follow will explain, in a step-by-step fashion, the process that you must go through when attempting to find an area of Fibonacci Friends. In Chart 4.3, we see an example of the Nasdaq 100, on its rise from 1348 to 1981.

The first place the Nasdaq 100 paused for a breather was around 1600 before it continued its ascension up. The move finally stopped at 1981, before beginning a more meaningful retracement (see Chart 4.4).

It is from this point of 1981 that you can come up with two powerful sets of Fibonacci resistance numbers, with the hope of finding two numbers that will fall in the same area. If you are so fortunate, the odds of a major move off of that level is very high.

The first measurement will come from the April low of 1348 to 1981 and give a retracement level of 1742 for a .382 retracement and 1626 for a .618 retracement. The second measurement was taken from the second pivot point of 1743 to the high of 1981. The Fibonacci retracements from this level were a .382 of 1837 and a .618 of 1743. These two measurements produced an area of Fibonacci Friends at 1743, in that a .382 retracement of

CHART 4.3

When finding an area of Fibonacci Friends, you need to locate the two pivot points from which to project the areas. In the case of the chart shown here, the points 1 and 2 are the levels you should look to measure your retracements from point 3.

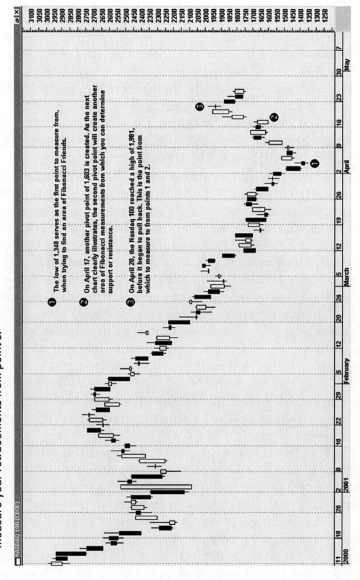

1. The low of 1,348 serves as the first point to measure from, when trying to find an area of Fibonacci Friends.

2. On April 17, another pivot point of 1,603 is created. As the next chart clearly illustrates, the second pivot point will create another area of Fibonacci measurements from which you can determine support or resistance.

3. On April 20, the Nasdaq 100 reached a high of 1,981, before it began to pull back. This is the point from which to measure to from points 1 and 2.

CHART 4.4

After rallying sharply from the lows, an area of Fibonacci Friends is setting up around the area of 1750. The pullback to this level provided a nice low-risk One Shot – One Kill long setup.

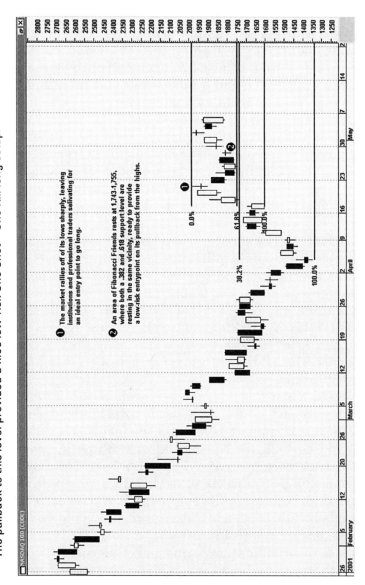

1 The market rallies off of its lows sharply, leaving institutions and professional traders salivating for an ideal entry point to go long.

2 An area of Fibonacci Friends rests at 1,743-1,755, where both a .382 and .618 support level are resting in the same vicinity, ready to provide a low-risk entrypoint on its pullback from the highs.

one measurement and a .618 retracement of another measurement both fell in the same area, as shown in Chart 4.5.

For those more comfortable with Fibonacci expansion analysis, which is covered in the next two sections, also observe that the low of 1348 to the high of 1714 created a 374-point run. If you were to project those 374 points off of 1603, the next pivot low, you would have had a Fibonacci 1 × 1 projection higher to 1977. The Nasdaq made its high at 1981. So, had you gone long and were looking for a predetermined price target to book your profits, or were looking for a place to short the market, using the Fibonacci 1 × 1 expansion, or higher price target shown by the lines AB and CD in Chart 4.6 would have provided such an opportunity. However, until you are comfortable with the One Shot – One Kill Method, you need to gradually work yourself into these kinds of trades.

What many short-term traders do to really harness the power of these numbers is take long-term Fibonacci numbers, like the ones above, and day trade off them. On the aforementioned move, a savvy day trader can use this information to get into a trade and conservatively create a possible 12:1 risk-to-reward ratio by risking 10 to 15 points near the area of Fibonacci Friends, with the idea of playing the move back to its old highs. These kinds of powerful tactics are what One Shot – One Kill trading is about.

Since the use of Fibonacci Friends is very common, many institutions and professional traders have also been aware of this technical support level as a means of entering a market rally. In Chart 4.5, the Nasdaq did what it was "supposed" to and pulled back to the area of Fibonacci Friends, allowing those aware of the price targets to enter into a long position, with a good risk-to-reward profile on the trade. As has been articulated throughout this book, one indicator alone should not be used as the sole basis for entering a trade.

It is the combination of this and other certain, specific indicators that will give you the confidence to enter a trade knowing that your chances of success are very good.

The use of Fibonacci Friends is something essential to understanding the One Shot – One Kill Method and will allow you to create great risk-to-reward ratios for your trades.

CHART 4.5

The market bounced solidly off of the area of Fibonacci Friends to give traders an excellent opportunity for a low-risk setup.

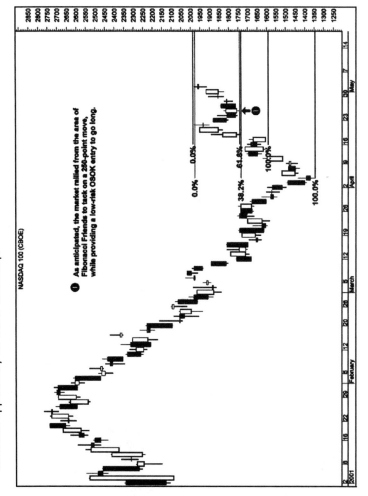

NASDAQ 100 (CBOE)

❶ As anticipated, the market rallied from the area of Fibonacci Friends to tack on a 250-point move, while providing a low-risk OSOK entry to go long.

CHART 4.6

An AB = CD move up, or 1 × 1 expansion, can help provide a great place to take profits and look to reload on a pullback. As with the case of Nvidia (NVDA), the 1 × 1 expansion happens on a daily time frame.

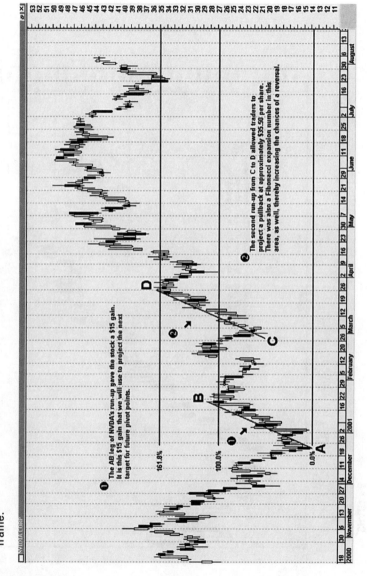

❶ The AB leg of NVDA's run-up gave the stock a $15 gain. It is this $15 gain that we will use to project the next target for future pivot points.

❷ The second run-up from C to D allowed traders to project a pullback at approximately $35.50 per share. There was also a Fibonacci expansion number in this area, as well, thereby increasing the chances of a reversal.

FIBONACCI EXPANSION ANALYSIS

One of the most important tools in the arena of price targeting is the use of *Fibonacci expansion analysis*. You do not have to be overly intelligent to understand how to use it, but its proper use should enhance your intuition of the market.

As with natural Fibonacci retracements, Fibonacci expansions play a very vital role in building price targets and creating sequence setups that can allow traders to stay two to three steps ahead of the market. This analysis is fairly simple to do with a number of software packages or just a common Excel spreadsheet. Each one of the many Fibonacci expert software packages available seems to have a slightly different way of using Fibonacci numbers to project price targets to the upside or downside. If you follow the One Shot – One Kill methodology to Fibonacci expansion analysis, you will soon realize that the method is not very time consuming and can prove to be richly rewarding.

Three projection points are used to derive a price target, conceived by using the two inflection points of the previous run. For example, if the Dow ran from 9400 to 9800, the first point from which you would measure would be 9400, or point A. The second inflection point would be at 9800, or point B. Taking the run from point A to point B will construct the expansion points. The three ratios that will be projected off point B will be 1.382, 1.618, and 2.618. However, of these three expansions, the 1.618 area is the one to pay the most attention to. So in the case of the Dow, the first of the three expansion points would be calculated as follows:

1. Determine the difference in the run from 9400 to 9800:

$$9800 - 9400 = 400$$

2. Multiply the ratio at point A by 400:

$$1.382 \times 400 = 552.8$$

3. Project that figure off the low in the run:

$$9400 + 552 = 9952$$

Thus, 9952 would become the first Fibonacci expansion point.

So with the first expansion point complete, we would then perform the same function with the other two expansion ratios with the 1.618 ratio projecting a move on the Dow to 10,048:

$$1.618 \times 400 = 648$$

$$9400 + 648 = 10{,}048$$

The 2.618 expansion ratio would take this move to 10,447:

$$2.618 \times 400 = 1047$$

$$9400 + 1047 = 10{,}447$$

These points are projected so that you will be able to generate an area of Fibonacci Friends, akin to those found in natural Fibonacci retracements. Suppose you see a .618 retracement from one price run in the same area as a 1.618 expansion match-up from another price run. Then there stands a better-than-average chance that there will be a price reversal at that point—or at least the price of the stock will consolidate. With timing being such an important part of when to get in and out of a trade, understanding where Fibonacci retracement and expansion points are located will do a great deal to help you get into positions with confidence.

As Chart 4.7 shows, the Nasdaq was headed in a downward spiral after September 11, 2001. The market underwent severe selling pressure and had many people asking where the market would bottom. While no method can assure you of where a bottom will be, using the Fibonacci projection analysis from the One Shot – One Kill Method would have allowed you to find a strong area of Fibonacci Friends, which sat between 1072 and 1090. The market moved to the area before finding support and rallying sharply off it. This movement had many people shocked, but those who used this price projection method stood ready to attack the markets for a very low-risk long position, or an ideal place to book profits from their short positions.

As mentioned above, I have found expansion points to be most powerful when they agree with natural Fibonacci retracements themselves. Expansion points are also powerful when they agree with other expansion points from previous moves.

For example, if a 1.382 expansion from one move is in the same area as a 2.618 expansion from another move, then this is an area worth watching. If multiple expansion points come together with multiple natural Fibonacci retracements, then you have a very likely chance that the market or vehicle you are trading will reverse. If it does not reverse, then you should take notice, as the market is making a powerful statement and a shift from buying the dips on weakness to selling strength on rallies may be underway (or vice versa).

The next twist the One Shot – One Kill Method adds to Fibonacci expansion analysis involves a *1 × 1 Fibonacci expansion*, or an *AB = CD expansion*. This ratio is the most powerful expansion I use, and therefore is worth paying significant attention to when it is being approached in the market. Obtaining this level is very simple, in that you merely measure the run from point A to point B, using that as a base from point C to determine point D. This analysis can be applied to any time frame, either intraday or daily, in determining likely reversal points, and like most Fibonacci work, is more effective and applicable to widely traded stocks and indexes. Chart 4.6 shows that after NVDA ran from about 13.50 to 28.50, it pulled back to 20.5.

Using the run from A to B to get 15 (the difference between 13.50 and 28.50) and projecting that off of 20.50, tells us that if the stock begins to head up again, it could move as high as 35.50, before pulling back. Over the next five weeks in April, NVDA ran to 35.50, before pulling back to 27.

When an AB = CD price expansion coincides with a natural Fibonacci retracement and other Fibonacci expansions, the deck is stacked even more in your favor. A look at Chart 4.8 shows the setup discussed in the introduction, as I was analyzing the market using the Fibonacci levels and trend lines to ascertain its futures direction.

On October 11, the Nasdaq was sitting near 1389. Based on the chart, you can see that a move to the down-trending line and an area of Fibonacci Friends brought the move to the 1428–1452 zone as you had a host of natural retracements from a number of intermediate pivot highs from 1973 all the way down to 1610

CHART 4.7

Following the market extreme move down after the September 11 tragedy, the Nasdaq found support at a number of Fibonacci expansion points that matched up in the same area. The bounce from this level was very powerful.

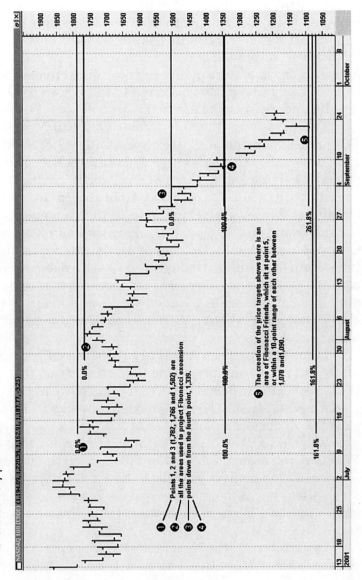

Points 1, 2 and 3 (1,782, 1,766 and 1,502) are all the areas used to project Fibonacci expansion points down from the fourth point, 1,339.

⑤ The creation of the price targets shows there is an area of Fibonacci Friends, which sit at point 5, or within a 10-point range of each other between 1,078 and 1,090.

CHART 4.8

When the market arrived at this area on a massive gap up, the market makers and professionals were waiting to offer into the move. The reaction from this level was nothing short of phenomenal as the Nasdaq fell by more than 100 points the first day it hit this level.

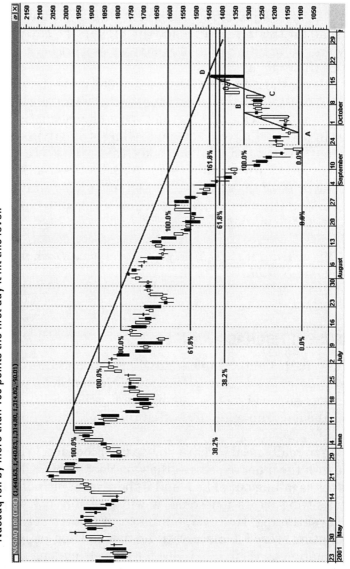

NASDAQ 100 (CBOE) (1,440.53, 1,440.53, 1,314.80, 1,314.80, -90.01)

being, projected off of the low of 1088. This was coupled with a natural 1.618 expansion from the move from 1101 to 1313 which took it to 1450, and an AB = CD higher which also took it to 1,433. As you can see from looking at Charts 4.7 and 4.8 that the Nasdaq hit this zone and made the high in the early part of the day and off to hit an area of Fibonacci support back down to the 1305–1315 range.

Using the collaborative tools to determine the price targets allows you to effectively anticipate where the market is going. The One Shot – One Kill Method is not only about buying weakness in up-trending markets and selling strength in down-trending markets but about having a keen sense of where you and the market are at any given moment through the creation of probabilistic price targets. Every day you must keep yourself in command of being able to go where you want and you do that by following the market.

"We are what we repeatedly do. Excellence, then, is not an act, but a habit."

ARISTOTLE

MISUSE OF FIBONACCI RATIOS

While the benefits of understanding Fibonacci levels will dramatically improve your perception of the markets, poor application and slipshod money management will result in lost money over the long run and, more often than not, the even not-so-long run.

You really need to learn how to use Fibonacci Friends in unison with the other aspects of the One Shot – One Kill Method. If a stock is falling out of bed, and if there is an intraday Fibonacci level sitting by its lonesome, it will probably not stop the fall from continuing. However, a number of traders get wrapped up in locating every Fibonacci ratio on the map and sloppily use that information as their sole indicator for getting long or short in a trade. As mentioned before, the daily, weekly, and monthly Fibonacci levels stand a much better chance of holding up as support or resistance than do short-term levels generated from short-term inflection points. The Fibonacci levels that come from isolating the pivot point of a longer time frame (one that lasts several weeks) will usually hold up better than the Fibonacci points from a shorter time frame (a few days or hours).

Another common misuse of Fibonacci levels is when a major Fibonacci zone has been violated. I have seen many traders not update their Fibonacci grids and erase that support zone from their charts. For example, if you have a major support zone on the Nasdaq at 1330, and the Nasdaq falls down to 1300, this is a clear break of the Fibonacci support zone and should therefore no longer be regarded as a viable place of Fibonacci support. After the Nasdaq broke down through this, over the course of the next couple of days, it rallies back to 1360, before falling again down to 1330. However, this time I do not give the same respect to this level, since it has already been significantly violated to the downside. You should still be aware of it, but just remember to keep your price target grid clean of old Fibonacci Friends and update it on a continuing basis.

Many traders will blindly fight the trend using the Fibonacci levels as a means to keep raising their stops in losing trades instead of just cutting the loss when they are supposed to. I have seen traders attempt to reenter a long-term down trend by placing their short sell order in front of a number of Fibonacci Friends, which serves as resistance. They are filled. There is nothing wrong with this entry, as these are the types of spots you usually want to be in. However, the market continues to move right through the area of Fibonacci Friends and is now moving up. Instead of being stopped out, the trader will look for the next area of Fibonacci Friends, which may be a good distance away, to place his stop. The whole purpose of him taking on the trade initially was to put himself in a trade with a good risk-to-reward ratio and an easy out if the trade went against him. However, by raising the stop the trader has completely undermined his strategy and has lost his tactical advantage. This type of application of Fibonacci analysis is nothing short of suicidal. The setups we are looking at in this book are ones we want to take on hundreds of times; therefore, consistently entering and exiting on the same parameters is paramount in analyzing your success.

By having a knowledge of where these Fibonacci price targets are, you can watch for some kind of support or resistance manifest itself, before entering the trade. This observation can come in the form of watching the intraday TRI show divergence to support your position, the market moving back over the 15-period MA, the Vertical Horizontal Filter on the daily chart showing that the trend is losing steam, and the daily Detrended Oscillator showing extreme overbought or oversold conditions.

In line with the aforementioned mistakes, people will use Fibonacci levels as a means of countertrend trading, which is something that I strongly discourage. If a number of technical indicators—for example, things like rising moving averages, upward-moving trend channels and trend lines, and a positive MACD—should tip you off to be using major areas of Fibonacci resistance to book profits from the long side, you should *not* aggressively short, or vice-versa, for stocks that are falling. This does not mean there are not strong and violent reactions off of these points; however, when you enter trades against the grain with Fibonacci levels being your primary reason, you will usually draw a lower Netto Number. Profitability can be enhanced by using the indicators, chart patterns, and Fibonacci Friends in unison, as the power of a collaboration of indicators is a strong ally in your battle to be a profitable trader.

Patience is the key when employing any aspect of the One Shot – One Kill Method. When trading intraday, a few minutes can mean a swing of hundreds or even thousands of dollars. Timing can be critical in initiating a trade, and, just as patience is a valuable attribute to your trading, so is unwavering and immediate action when the time calls for it. Avoiding the aforementioned misuse of Fibonacci ratios is an important discipline needed to properly execute the One Shot – One Kill game plan.

SUMMARY

This chapter has discussed three types of Fibonacci measurements—retracements, expansions, and projections—all of which give you the tools to anticipate price movement of an underlying security or market in unison with other technical indicators and chart formations. There are 30 points that help compose a Netto Number, with the creation of Fibonacci price targets accounting for 10 of those. Being able to create an area of Fibonacci Friends allows you as a trader to find spots on the charts to buy weakness in rising markets, sell strength in falling markets, and take profits at predetermined price points. Now that you have been exposed to a cursory knowledge of Fibonacci analysis, Chapter 5 will take some of the tools from the early lessons and put them to work to help reinforce these early concepts.

CHAPTER 5

Profiting with Inflection Points

Learning to trade using inflection points is the most critical part of employing the One Shot – One Kill Method. Inflection points are the summation of the previous three chapters when applied and put into one respective price area. This chapter will take the tools taught in the last three chapters and implement them to show how you as a trader can anticipate market moves two to three places in advance. By being able to anticipate this market movement, you can stay a step ahead of the herd while systematically taking money out of the market.

TRADING INFLECTION POINTS

When the market moves from major inflection points it can create phenomenal trading opportunities yielding exceptional risk-to-reward ratios. Inflection points appear at places on the chart where the bulls and the bears go to battle to fight for supremacy. This battle rages on at these points, and as such, you should pay them a great deal of attention as to whether you should be looking to buy the weakness for the day or sell strength.

Inflection points are commonly used by institutional traders, the ones who are primarily responsible for initiating the majority of the buy and sell programs that go on in the market. From understanding where these inflection points are at, you can then deduce where the market will likely head next. This type of *sequence trading*, as it has been called, or *anticipatory trading*, keeps you thinking objectively regardless of which direction the market goes. Inflection points, in the One Shot – One Kill Method, give you the edge as a trader.

Inflection points can be used when you trade bonds, currencies, stocks, and options contracts. However, when comparing them with Fibonacci analysis, the deeper and more liquid the market being traded, the more likely you will see an expected reaction from those numbers. In other words, a thinly traded stock is less likely to react from an inflection point as is the Nasdaq 100 or the S&P 500 Index.

Initially, it may seem that a great deal needs to be learned in order to become a successful trader. Rest assured: The contents and purpose of this book is to provide you with a fundamentally sound basis from which to make informed trading decisions. From there, you can decide for yourself what fits into your style and how much you want to assimilate into your trading.

CREATING INFLECTION POINTS WITH THE NASDAQ 100

The first example of inflection point trading will be done with the Nasdaq 100. The methods I am about to discuss helped me stay in touch with the market; you should give them a great deal of attention.

Chapter 4 included a discussion of three very important types of Fibonacci measurements: Fibonacci retracements, namely the .382 and .618; Fibonacci expansions, namely the 1.382, 1.618, and 2.618; and Fibonacci projections, or what I call a 1×1 move up or down. Using these respective measurements, coupled with other ancillary technical tools such as trend lines, moving averages, the TRI, VHF, MACD, and Detrended Oscillator, traders can anticipate key spots to enter and exit positions in the market.

If you look at the Nasdaq 100 Index from September 2002, you will note that market participants had witnessed a prolonged down move from the previous nine months in what was now the third year of one of the most tumultuous bear markets in history (see Chart 5.1). Recall from Chapter 4 that you are looking to create an area of Fibonacci Friends for every trade you put yourself in. You can use inflection points to create price targets to the downside and upside. In the scenario illustrated in Chart 5.1, the high from December 2001 sits at 1734. There is also a pivot high before the major selloff in May 2002, which sits at 1350. The goal from these two major inflection points is to match them up and create an area of Fibonacci Friends on both the downside and the upside. With that said, you now must ask yourself: What area on the downside will allow those two respective pivot highs to form an area of Fibonacci Friends of a .382 retracement from the 1734 area and a 618 retracement from the 1344 spot?

The answer to that question puts a move down to 795 to 805, which, as of September 2002, was 120 points away, as the Nasdaq 100 (NDX) at that time sat at 920. Many people were trying to buy the lows at this time and bottom fish; however, those who were trading with a viable price target in mind understood the potential for the inflection point that was about to hit them.

After forming an inflection point at the 795–805 area on a long-term chart, you now begin to look for shorter-term Fibonacci ratios that set up and confirm your suspicion as to how viable this area of support is. You know that looking at the 795 to 805 targets would create an area of Fibonacci Friends at 1144 to 1155. This knowledge is important, because this area from 1144 to 1155 is the bottom of the pivot low from the action in May. As has already been mentioned, don't feel the need to chase breakdowns or breakouts, because they normally return to their spot for some kind of a retest. With that said, the fact that the area of Fibonacci Friends lines up with the pivot low in May gives a great deal of credibility for the Nasdaq to bounce from the 795–805 level.

This point is merely the first leg of the inflection point trading scenario or trading sequence in which you will learn how to create and trade off of these respective inflection points.

The Nasdaq continued its trek down to the anticipated price movement and found a bottom at the 795.25 mark (see Chart 5.2), the number that created an area of Fibonacci Friends serving as resistance right at the 1144–1155 mark, if the 795 level held. It did, and the Nasdaq began a furious rally

CHART 5.1

Setting up a nice price target and creating an inflection point is critical to taking profits at good spots. In the chart shown here, the 800 level on the Nasdaq is shown as a key inflection point.

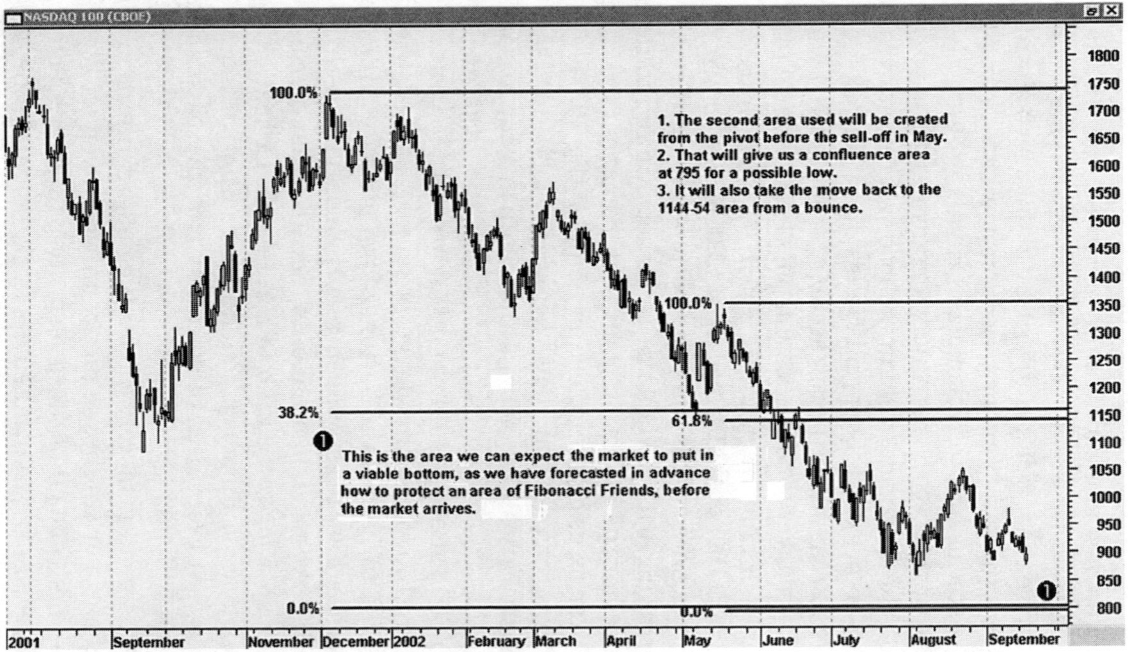
NASDAQ 100 (CBOE)
100.0%
38.2%
0.0%
100.0%
61.8%
0.0%
1. The second area used will be created from the pivot before the sell-off in May.
2. That will give us a confluence area at 795 for a possible low.
3. It will also take the move back to the 1144-54 area from a bounce.
This is the area we can expect the market to put in a viable bottom, as we have forecasted in advance how to protect an area of Fibonacci Friends, before the market arrives.
1800
1750
1700
1650
1600
1550
1500
1450
1400
1350
1300
1250
1200
1150
1100
1050
1000
950
900
850
800
2001
September
November
December
2002
February
March
April
May
June
July
August
September

CHART 5.2

The reaction from the 800 level, a spot you can create weeks in advance, is very strong back to the upside.

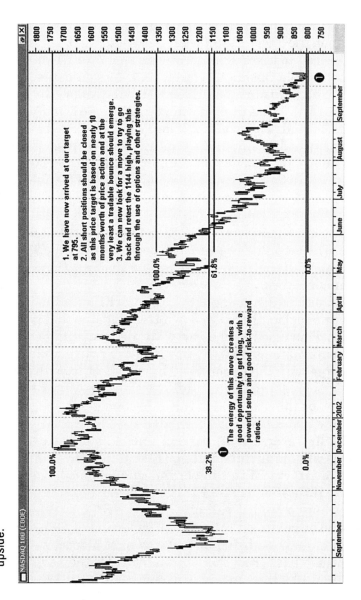

over the course of the next eight weeks, offering numerous chances to go long and challenge the 1144 level (see Chart 5.3).

Up to this point we have used the natural retracements to show that the 1144–1155 target is the one that offered a viable point to look to cover short positions at 795 and look to get long with a possible upside target of 1144. As you can see from the chart on the Nasdaq, the market made a move higher to the 1007 mark in late October, pulled back to 941 and a rising 15-period MA, and headed higher again. As I mentioned in Chapter 4, most major selloffs or rallies on any time frame will typically generate a 1×1 correction counter to the move. This development is important, because the move from 941 would give us a 1×1 at 1155 on the Nasdaq. Again, we would get this by taking the length of the move from 795 to 1007 and projecting it off of 941. The first move up was 212 points and lasted about three weeks. The second move can also be the same length and would match up with the 1155 target within 2 points. Good enough for government work.

More than just an area of Fibonacci Friends that is developing in this region, there is a down-trending line that goes back 18 months. This also matches up with the level and provides even more confirmation as to why this is such a critical inflection point and in line with the major trend line in effect from the May 2001 high. This is very powerful stuff and shows how important it is to be ready for the potential of this inflection point.

Now that a point has been identified where the market will potentially reverse from several weeks before it even arrives, the next step in understanding these inflection points is to create price targets off this major inflection point. If the Nasdaq is going to reverse at 1144–1155, then the next exercise is to determine where would it sell off. From Chart 5.3 we see the two major pivot points on the way up, one being at 795, the original pivot low, and one being at 940, the next pivot low. Should the Nasdaq sell back from this 1144–1155 zone, then a move back to 1020 would be in order. This would be about a 130-point move lower, as there is a .382 retracement from 795 to 1155 and a .618 retracement from 941 to 1155. This is a very powerful method of planning trades out weeks in advance. It also gives you the patience and discipline to execute when the time comes.

CHART 5.3

The subsequent rally over the course of the next few months caught a number of market participants by surprise. But it gave those who were looking for the move a low-risk trading opportunity.

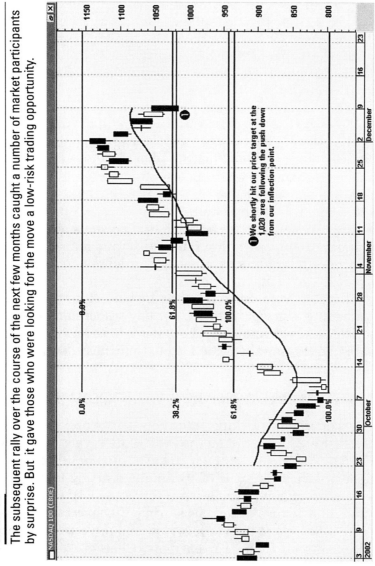

1 We shortly hit our price target at the 1,020 area following the push down from our inflection point.

Fast-forward to December 2, 2002 (see Chart 5.4). The Nasdaq gapped up 25 points into the 1144 target. The Nasdaq ran 11
points higher in the first 30 minutes and then tanked for the
next five days following this climax high at the price target.
Over the following five trading days, the Nasdaq plunged down
nearly 130 points and hit the 1020 target.

The next major inflection point is once the Nasdaq hits the
1020 target (see Chart 5.5). This is the spot you should be looking to use as a means of taking profits from the short side and
playing the move back up again. However, unlike most traders
who may be reacting, you would be proactively mapping out the
prices on your chart and anticipating where inflection points are
and trading off them. Inflection points offer tremendous risk-to-
reward ratios, and working off of them is critical to trading the
One Shot – One Kill Method well.

Trading is about putting yourself in good spots on a consistent basis, repeatedly executing your trades, and managing your
risk. Getting into trading setups like the aforementioned one
can provide a viable means of taking on positions in which you
are actually positive most of the time instead of getting into a
spot and having it go against you. For day traders and smaller
time horizon traders, knowing where these long-term inflection
points are and trading them can lead to some nice gains.

PROFITING FROM INFLECTION POINTS WITH EXPEDIA (EXPE)

The next example of working inflection points and sequences
into the One Shot – One Kill Method will come via a stock, Expedia (EXPE). The stock went on a huge run for about eight
months before showing signs of strain and starting to roll over
from a quasi-double-top formation (see Chart 5.6). One of the
methods I like to use when measuring Fibonacci expansion
points is to take a pivot high or pivot low and project expansions
or retracements off them. For example, Chart 5.7 shows that
EXPE made a pivot low at 36 before attempting to challenge its
high of 42.5. The attempt to retest that high failed and forced
traders to measure what area would make that pivot low a .382
retracement from the high at 42. This is the spot to which you

CHART 5.4

As the Nasdaq continued to rally, it met up nicely with an 18-month trend line and a number of areas of Fibonacci resistance to create a huge inflection point on the daily chart. This is a great spot to look to take profits as well as a spot to possibly shift your bias from buying dips to selling rallies.

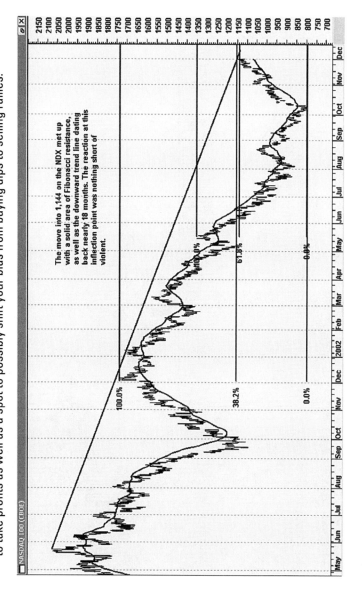

The move into 1,144 on the NDX met up with a solid area of Fibonacci resistance, as well as the downward trend line dating back nearly 18 months. The reaction at this inflection point was nothing short of violent.

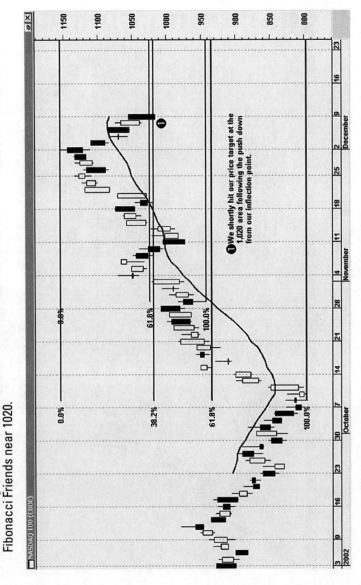

CHART 5.5

After hitting the downward trend line, the Nasdaq sold down 130 points in that time period to some Fibonacci Friends near 1020.

116

CHART 5.6

Expedia (EXPE) is setting up for a healthy pullback after a strong rally and subsequent double top.

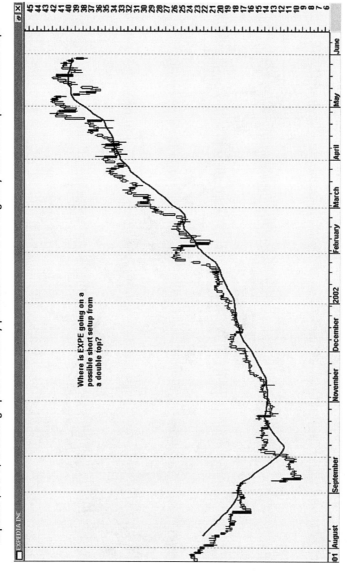

Where is EXPE going on a possible short setup from a double top?

CHART 5.7

When creating inflection points on EXPE, you should take into account all of the recent pivot highs and pivot lows to see where the stock might go. From these pivot points, you can create the necessary collaboration of price levels, which will give you highly probabilistic inflection points.

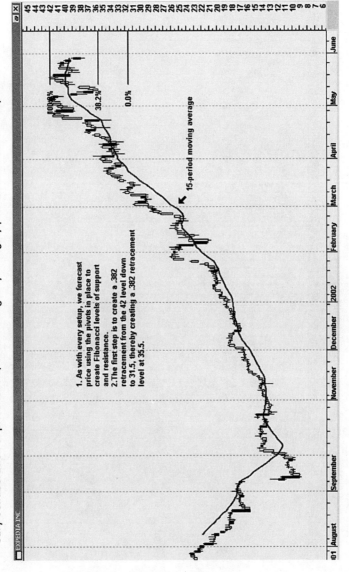

1. As with every setup, we forecast price using the pivots in place to create Fibonacci levels of support and resistance.
2. The first step is to create a .382 retracement from the 42 level down to 31.5, thereby creating a .382 retracement level at 35.5.

100.0%

38.2%

0.0%

15-period moving average

EXPEDIA INC

are looking for the initial selldown to head before it starts to rally, which, in this case, is near 31.5 (see Chart 5.8).

Along with creating a move down to 31.5 via the expansion point, you would also be looking to see if the movement matches up with any natural Fibonacci retracements along the way. In this case, there is a move from the low in December at 16.5 to its high at 42.5. A natural .382 retracement is created near 65, close to the expansion level down to 31.5 and near some historical support on EXPE at 32. So, based on the information, you should be looking for the fall to head to 32, about $7 below the price of 39, where Chart 5.8 is.

Like the example with the Nasdaq, you would also be expecting a bounce to happen when the price hit your area of support at 31.5 to 32.5. As the days come, EXPE takes a nice plunge and heads down to the inflection point near 31.5. From this point, you are looking for a bounce, as the stock and the market like to move in a natural ebb and flow, with you offering into rallies during a declining market, buying weakness in a rising market, and taking profits at predetermined price points (see Chart 5.9).

As expected, EXPE mounts a nice bounce to the inflection point at 35.5 and the Fibonacci resistance from the high at 42, as well as a declining 15-period MA (see Chart 5.10). This is a classic One Shot – One Kill setup—offering into the subsequent bounce following a breakdown and playing this as a measured move for a 1×1 down to the next area of Fibonacci support (see Chart 5.11). If you were able to play the move long, then this is where you would be looking to blow out of your long positions and start offering into the short trades, putting a pasting on it when it broke through previous day's low, which would be around $35. After entering, you would look to measure a 1×1 down to 26.5 by taking the length of the first down move from 41 down to 31.5, or 9.5 points, projecting that off of 36, and lining up around 26.5, which is also a 618 retracement. After entering the position, you can place your stop about 50 cents above the previous day's high, thereby risking about 1.50 to make 10, not including if you add into positions along the way (discussed in Chapter 10).

CHART 5.8

The ideal situation occurs when you can get a collaboration of Fibonacci levels, or Fibonacci Friends, to line up at one respective level. After seeing these levels emerge, you should be able to target your trades at this price area. In the case of EXPE, 31.50 to 32.50 is a great spot to look to cover any short positions as well as look to go long.

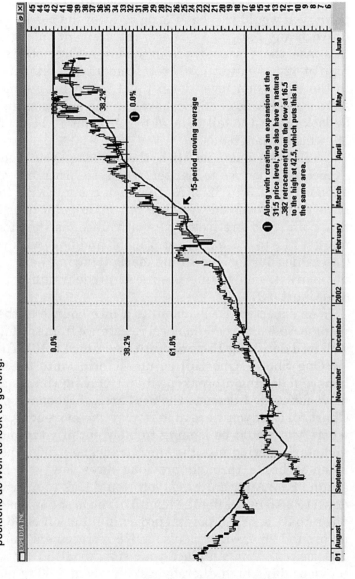

CHART 5.9

Once the target is hit, it is not a time to get greedy and dismiss your plan. Instead, you should execute and wait patiently for a bounce to reload. Either that, or look for a shorter-term long setup to play a potential snap-back rally higher.

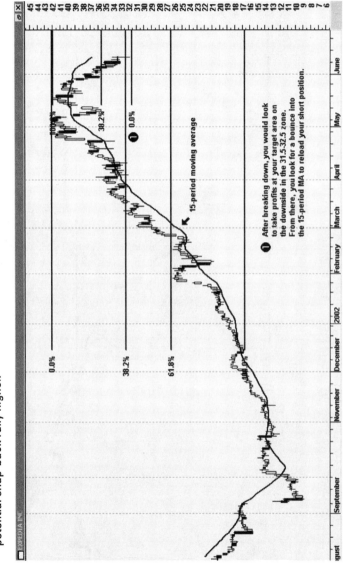

15-period moving average

1 After breaking down, you would look to take profits at your target area on the downside in the 31.5-32.5 zone. From there, you look for a bounce into the 15-period MA to reload your short position.

CHART 5.10

The bounce on EXPE takes us back to our pivot low at 36 and hits a declining 15-period MA. This level then becomes a low-risk entry spot to reenter a short position, and look to play for another leg down.

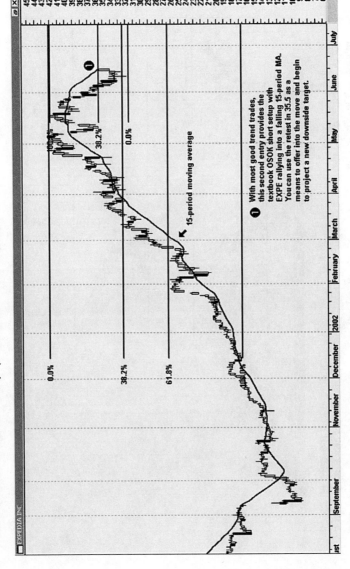

With most good trend trades, this second entry provides the textbook OSOK short setup with EXPE rallying into a falling 15-period MA. You can use the retest in 35.5 as a means to offer into the move and begin to project a new, downside target.

15-period moving average

0.0%
38.2%
61.8%

0.0%
38.2%
0.0%

EXPEDIA INC

CHART 5.11

The next move down looks to set up near point 4, which is a natural Fibonacci retracement near 27. This is also an area where a Fibonacci 1 × 1 projection takes us, thereby giving more validity to the target.

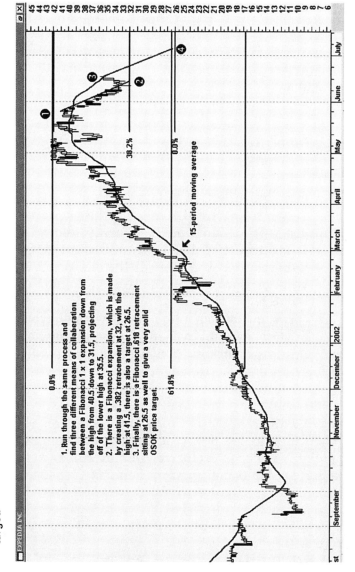

EXPEDIA INC

1. Run through the same process and find three different means of collaberation between a Fibonacci 1 x 1 expansion down from the high from 40.5 down to 31.5, projecting off of the lower high at 35.5.
2. There is a Fibonacci expansion, which is made by creating a .382 retracement at 32, with the high at 41.5, there is also a target at 26.5.
3. Finally, there is a Fibonacci .618 retracement sitting at 26.5 as well to give a very solid OSOK price target.

0.0%

100.0%

38.2%

0.0%

15-period moving average

61.8%

In line with the profit target, EXPE spirals down to 26, a major inflection point for this stock and a spot from which a trader would be looking to take profits, as the premium from the trade is gone. If the market keeps on plunging without you, you wouldn't have to worry, because the next bounce will probably take you back to the same spot you covered. Again, trading is about putting yourself in good spots on a consistent basis. And you would be waiting for the target to match up and could look at covering your shorts there and taking on a long position to play back up to your last downward pivot around 31.5 (see Chart 5.12).

SUMMARY

This chapter on inflection points is intended to teach you, a future One Shot – One Kill Trader, to be proactive and antici-pate future market movements, thereby allowing you to put yourself in good spots again and again. Executing on this type of trading style requires work outside the market. It is not for peo-ple who can't or won't put in the time and effort to create this type of research.

The previous four chapters and this one have provided you with some very powerful tools in understanding how to success-fully trade these markets. You need to continually take notes and review your trades to see if you were getting in at good spots or if you were exiting at your price targets. Learning this method is the easy part; going out and seamlessly executing it is an entirely different matter. Inflection points can be used to play both the up and the down side of the markets, which is why Chapter 6 will focus exclusively on short-side setups and the dynamics behind benefiting from sell offs in the market.

CHART 5.12

On cue, EXPE heads toward the target and puts in a very healthy bounce on an intraday basis. At this spot, many traders are looking to get long as well as cover short positions.

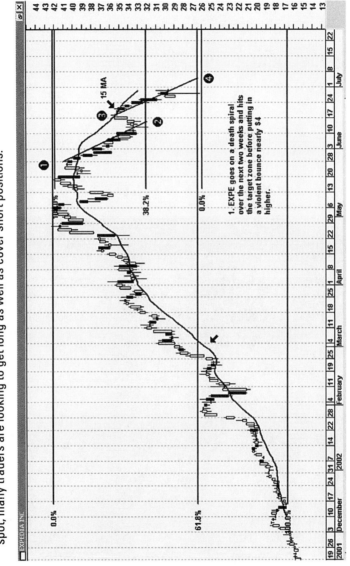

1. EXPE goes on a death spiral over the next two weeks and hits the target zone before putting in a violent bounce nearly $4 higher.

125

CHAPTER 6

Going Short–Profiting from Those Less Able

The One Shot – One Kill Method does not carry a long or short bias and looks to profit from both up and down markets. However, because stocks historically fall significantly faster than they rise, and because people have much less experience with shorting stocks than with buying them, learning the art of short selling is a powerful weapon to have at your disposal. This chapter will cover the ways to short stock and the implications of doing so. This topic should be fully understood before the discussion of Netto Numbers can begin in earnest.

WHY SHORTING CAN BE SO PROFITABLE

There are many misperceptions and a general lack of understanding of shorting. Most people have a hard time with the concept of selling something they don't own with the anticipation of buying it back at a lower price. The general public (when you learn my method, that won't include you) rarely capitalizes on this avenue of revenue. Clearly, the shorting of stocks has a speculative aspect that, along with a lack of knowledge, prevents most people from shorting. A person who is only willing to go long is just like someone who will only date redheads. You

need to be able to go both ways as a trader. The One Shot – One
Kill Method teaches you to optimize the entire spectrum of situations that the market delivers to the table each day. Like anything else in trading, proper risk management is imperative for
success. However, shorting is more than just mere speculation.
It represents a viable means of not only protecting your investments from sudden market downturns but also proactively taking advantage of them. By having the ability to go both ways in
the market, you, as a trader, can make money on both sides of
the market.

As you no doubt are aware from previous market experiences, stocks fall much faster than they rise. In fact, on average,
stocks fall 60 to 75 percent faster than they rise. An unfortunate
and, in most cases, unnecessary sight is to see people who diligently put money away have a significant portion of it wiped out
by a swift and sudden downturn. I consider that sight to be
unnecessary because quite often the writing is on the wall. This
chapter will go over what signs stocks and markets exhibit when
they are setting up as possible short candidates and how to go
about trading these setups. Remember, the majority of people
who short stocks are professionals: market makers, specialists,
hedge fund managers, and institutions. Understanding the
methods and styles these professional traders use will be crucial
to your success as a trader.

ONE-DAY REVERSALS

One-day reversals are one of the most profitable chart formations for shorting, as they provide a clear picture of a stock
whose upward trend is weakening. Two types of one-day reversals are important for our purposes.

The first type of one-day reversal signals that a short-term
rally from an oversold condition is coming to an end. Typically,
stocks that have fallen between five to eight days mount a countertrend rally that normally lasts for two-and-a-half to three-
and-a-half trading days. These types of one-day reversals
usually encounter some type of resistance near a declining 15-
period MA, Fibonacci resistance levels, oversold levels that have
now leveled off, as well as shorter-term time frames like an

hourly or 30 minute chart that have gone short term over-bought. These setups are spots where One Shot – One Kill traders are looking to enter short positions because, of course, we traders are looking to sell strength in a declining market. By offering in at these spots, we are consistently putting ourselves on the side of the trend in fairly low-risk spots. If this situation plays out like we hope, the stock will lose strength and get turned back down, leaving the short-term bounce finished, and resuming its downward ways.

The second type of one-day reversals are preceded by at least 7 to 10 periods of exertion on the run up and experience a *blow-off top*, which results in the stock reversing substantially and closing in the lower 25 percent of its daily range. The second one-day reversal will not render as good a Netto Number because it will still be showing a bullish bias. Nevertheless, you need to under-stand when to close out a long position, or enter the short trade on a shorter time frame, such as an hourly or 13-minute chart that will be exhibiting more bearish characteristics. These types of one-day reversals are commonly associated with the end of a par-abolic run. This pattern can result in a very profitable trade, because the joyous greed that accompanied the rise up is now being replaced with the dreadful fear of being left holding the bag.

For both of these setups the indicators on the stock will sig-nify an overbought condition, as part of a prevailing down trend or the completion of an upward move. These are the types of setups we want to take advantage of. A common setup is for the Vertical Horizontal Filter to be touching near its high, the Detrended Oscillator to be showing an overbought condition, and the TRI to be showing major bearish divergence on a shorter-term chart like an hourly or 13-minute chart.

For those learning to take advantage of such situations, what helps many is doing a Fibonacci expansion analysis. By doing so, you can project the potential price at which a market or stock can reverse, thereby offering confirmation to the one-day reversal. I teach my students to use it as a confirming tool. If these indicators are in agreement, then you have a good case to get short and manage the risk. Look at Chart 6.1, for Rambus Inc. (RMBS) back in March and July 2000, which was on a solid up trend for some time.

CHART 6.1

Movement of Rambus, Inc. (RMBS), showing reversals happening following several periods of exertion in the stock or market. As is typical with such reversals, the short-term top is tipped off by the stock pulling back significantly from its highs and closing in the lower range of the trading day. RMBS shows this action on a few occasions and pulls back significantly from those levels. As with other trades, it is more valuable if the pullback happens from a key inflection point.

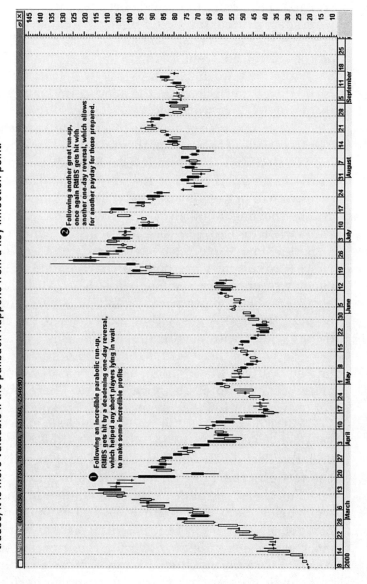

The stock took off on a parabolic run and closed at a presplit price of $480 a share in March 2000, which was in the lower half of the day's trading range. This closing price was a signal that the buying pressure on the stock was starting to lose momentum.

The entry for the short position, or stop-loss if you were long, would be when the stock takes out previous day's low. Some traders would try to get short at the top. One Shot – One Kill traders will occasionally take on countertrend trades per market dynamics, if the risk-to-reward ratios are good, with smaller share size and/or through the use of options. However, we put the big size of our short trades on the first type of one-day reversals for down-trending stocks that are pulling back to resistance.

The two respective setups from this section are also discussed in more detail in the next two sections, with the next section touching more on the parabolic nature of the move and the following section looking at playing dead cat bounces, which resemble the more textbook One Shot – One Kill trade setups.

PARABOLIC RUNS

Parabolic runs occur in stocks that exhibit extreme behavior to the upside, which is unsustainable. These stocks take off for a number of reasons, but they often leave their investors holding the bag after they retrace a large portion of their gains. Parabolic runs occur on every time frame, from a five-minute chart to a monthly chart. A parabolic run depicts greed at its finest, with buyers tripping over one another, trying to get long.

Parabolic runs, on an intraday chart pattern, commonly occur within the first 20 to 30 minutes of the trading day. Take a look at Chart 6.2. It shows that on the start of this particular day the Nasdaq 100 took off on a parabolic run.

Such situations are incredibly tempting for investors, who want to chase what they are trading and buy in as the trading seemingly runs out of control while leaving behind those who are not on board. Knowing what to do during these instances can create substantial wealth. Remember, the situations happen on a recurring basis. Knowing this fact should enable you to also

CHART 6.2

The market takes off on a huge rally and continues to make higher lows and higher highs. These types of moves typically look to pull back at some point in time.

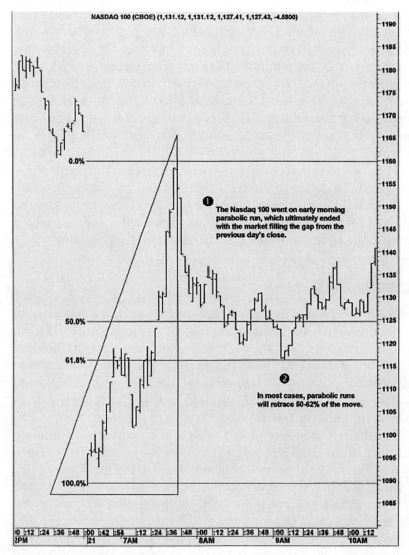

NASDAQ 100 (CBOE) (1,131.12, 1,131.12, 1,127.41, 1,127.43, -4.5800)

❶ The Nasdaq 100 went on early morning parabolic run, which ultimately ended with the market filling the gap from the previous day's close.

❷ In most cases, parabolic runs will retrace 50-62% of the move.

understand the importance of cutting losses quickly. Because of the preponderance of trading opportunities that exist, there is no reason to sit in one that isn't working as you would like. These runs can normally provide very profitable opportunities to trade from the short side or help determine when best to close out a long position.

Parabolic runs usually last from three to five time periods. After five time periods, most stocks will consolidate or pare their gains. Understanding the natural cycles behind parabolic runs will help you profit from them on a more consistent basis. Chart 6.3 demonstrates a massive parabolic run and the nasty retracement that the stock took when it fell back down again.

The parabolic run that many investors will remember for a long time to come came via the Sonus (SONS) IPO, which is illustrated in Chart 6.3. Never wanting to be an underachiever, SONS tacked on a modest 900 percent for the year, and June and July played a large role in that run. However, the very first week in August saw SONS make its 52-week high and turn around fast and furiously. The stock immediately came under a great deal of pressure, creating a profitable opportunity for those traders prepared to pull the trigger on a falling stock. Since down moves usually happen faster than up moves, the potential profit on this trade was unbelievable. At both $82 and $74, SONS triggered a One Shot – One Kill short signal that really determined a meaningful reversal in trend, following a one-day reversal lower high, respectively. The stock ended up going all the way down below 20 before making a turnaround.

The next example of a parabolic rise is illustrated in Chart 6.4. Krispy Kreme (KKD) stock is a textbook image of what a short squeeze can do to any chart formation.

As the chart shows, KKD went on an explosive move from 15 to nearly 45 before pulling back. During the run, the short interest averaged nearly 50 percent. These parabolic runs can be a frightening prospect if you are on the other end of the move, but they can be very profitable if entered using the One Shot – One Kill Method. It is imperative that if you decide to short these stocks, you do so with the confirmation of a one-day reversal, overbought indicators from our technical arsenal, and viable Fibonacci expansion points, which increase the likelihood of the

CHART 6.3

Movement showing a huge parabolic run and a big retracement. Following a huge move up, or down, traders like to take profits. Commonly, a move can retrace as much as 62 percent of the rally, with the general trend still remaining intact.

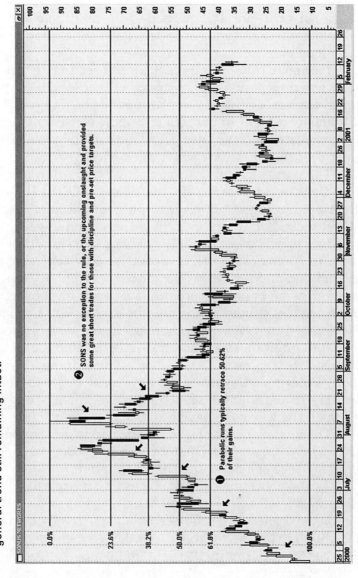

❷ SONS was no exception to the rule, or the upcoming onslaught and provided some great short trades for those with discipline and pre-set price targets.

❶ Parabolic runs typically retrace 50-62% of their gains.

CHART 6.4

Short squeezes can be exacerbated by a low float and high short interest. Stocks like Krispy Kreme (KKD) are punished shorts for being too overzealous.

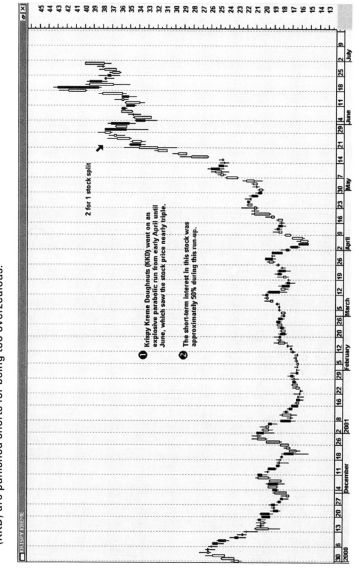

❶ Krispy Kreme Doughnuts (KKD) went on an explosive parabolic run from early April until June, which saw the stock price nearly triple.

❷ The short-term interest in this stock was approximately 50% during this run-up.

2 for 1 stock split

move being over. Otherwise, you can end up like many other traders who lose money repeatedly by countertrend trading.

Parabolic rises should trigger a mental alert in your mind to let you know that a likely shorting opportunity may be in its forming stages, that it could be time to quickly close out a long position, or both.

THE DEAD CAT BOUNCE

Playing the *dead cat bounce* is one way that institutions take advantage of unknowing investors and inexperienced traders. My reoccurring theme throughout this book is that the One Shot – One Kill Method looks to sell strength in down-trending markets and buy weakness in up-trending markets at predetermined price points, which create favorable risk-to-reward ratios. Looking to fade dead cat bounces is one way of doing so. This activity isn't rocket science. What you are essentially doing is reentering on a pullback, following a strong move down, instead of chasing a move down and putting yourself in a bad position.

But just what is a dead cat bounce? It can best be described in the following examples. Oftentimes, some fundamental catalyst will provide the reason for a stock to initially start to sell off. The stock is greeted with a huge amount of sellers and possibly a large gap down. The selling goes on for a protracted period of time and leads to conditions considered by many to be oversold. People who were short begin to take profits, which causes the selling pressure to abate; bargain hunters (inexperienced for the most part) begin to swarm in on the battered stock. They sense there is a fire sale going on and jump in with glazed eyes and dreams of making a killing. When the stock begins to rise without a catalyst driving it, take advantage of a great short opportunity.

You need to keep in mind the psychology that is taking place at this time. Many investors who went bottom fishing as the stock fell the first time promised themselves they would sell it back in a heartbeat if they could just get even. As the stock rises back up, it begins losing strength and heads back to the downside. Once again, watch for a move back to a shallow Fibonacci retracement, a pullback to a 15-period MA, a negative MACD pullback, and a Detrended Oscillator reading that shows the oversold condition is over. These indicators show that the oversold condition has worked its way off before going short.

As you will discover from observing the market, stocks generally provide multiple chances to make a good profit. In fact, if you study chart formations, you will be surprised at how often the second chance is actually more profitable and more reliable than the first entry.

Take a look at the moves on Vector Group, Ltd. (VGR) and Intel (INTC), which are illustrated in Charts 6.5 and 6.6.

These are excellent examples of dead cat bounces. They gave traders a good chance to get short or get out of long positions. When the companies came out with news that they would not make their numbers and would be laying people off, the stocks gapped down and people who were short started to cover their positions. The day following the news announcements, the stocks tried to run up in an attempt to fill their gaps. Shortly after their initial surges, however, the stocks started to weaken and began to head back toward their lows of the day. Then, in each instance, on the very next day, bargain hunters began buying what they then perceived to be cheap stocks. Try as they did, the bulls could only temporarily gain control, leading to short-term rallies. After those short flurries died out, the stocks started trending back down again, offering knowledgeable traders a chance to go short or add to their positions. All a trader had to do was execute on this information.

Playing dead cat bounces allows you to capitalize on other people's inability to trade wisely, as they amateurishly go after cheap stocks at the wrong time. Almost always, stocks are priced low for a reason—usually a very good reason. These types of stocks should be avoided in most instances as potential long setups. Understanding how to play violent contratrend rallies is something that should be left to a very skilled professional. Dead cat bounces usually don't last very long. If they do, they ain't dead cat bounces, baby!

Watch out for these types of formations, because they give you another chance to get back in a trade from the short side. Or they provide an opportunity to get out of a long position that went bad. Most dead cat bounces never make it through the first area of Fibonacci resistance at .382 of the recent decline. I like to

CHART 6.5

Watching the movement of Vector Group Ltd. (VGR), you need to understand that the first move is typically not the only move a trader will see. Knowing this is important, so that when it appears the market or stock has made up its mind as to which direction it wants to go, you are ready to act and be ready to pull the trigger on the first pullback. In the case of VGR, it gave multiple reentries on the bounce back into a declining 15-period MA.

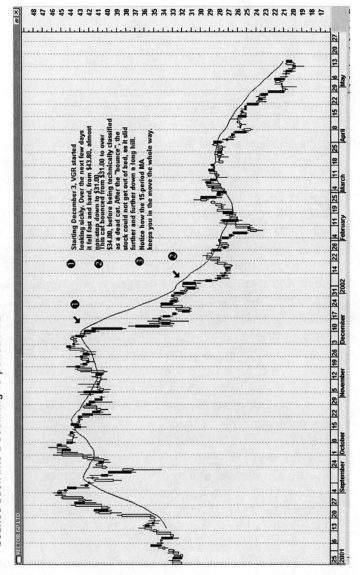

① Starting December 3, VGR started looking sickly. Over the next few days it fell fast and hard, from $43.80, almost non-stop down to $31.00.

② This cat bounced from $31.00 to over $34.00, before being technically classified as a dead cat. After the "bounce", the stock could not get out of bed, as it slid further and further down a long hill.

③ Notice how the 15-period MA keeps you in the move the whole way.

CHART 6.6

Intel (INTC) took a pretty good beating in 2000 and was a recipient of a nice gap down and got crushed hard over the next few days. I would never endorse a trading strategy that puts you in at such a hard spot. But do look for low-risk entries to the downside following this gap down.

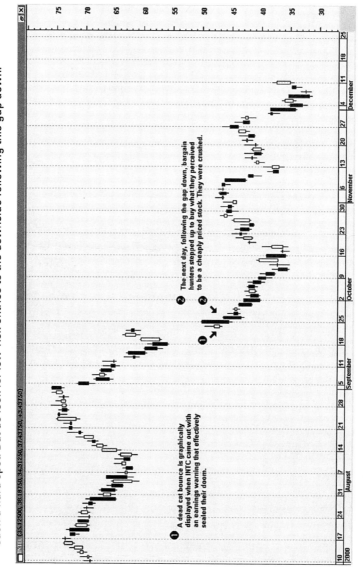

INTEL (35.12500, 38.18750, 34.31250, 37.43750, +3.43750)

❶ A dead cat bounce is graphically displayed when INTC came out with an earnings warning that effectively sealed their doom.

❷ The next day, following the gap down, bargain hunters stepped up to buy what they perceived to be a cheaply priced stock. They were crushed.

use a 15-period MA as a means of containing a dead cat bounce, as there is usually a great degree of exertion that precipitates the dead cat bounce. This situation makes the 15-period MA so effective at helping to gauge the strength of the move. If the market or a security rallies to the 15-period MA and rolls down, then that situation usually creates an opportunity to go short. Successful, well-prepared traders begin looking at these spots for the opportunity to get back in the trade on the short side.

Measuring the potential success of a dead cat bounce short trade should be done by using all of the factors of the One Shot – One Kill Method (for example, creating price targets based on Fibonacci numbers and historical support resistance) to assess risk-to-reward ratios, prior to entering the trade.

A natural function of human nature is to try and buy things cheaply, with the purchase of stocks being no exception to the rule. Those individuals with this propensity are usually the ones shouldering the burden just as major institutions and professionals are unloading the positions they could not sell during the initial downturn. This is a common practice among the pros. You should get comfortable with this section and the rest of this entire chapter, even if shorting and hedging is not something that you are naturally inclined to do. Understanding how shorting works can at least provide you with insight as to when to sell a long position that has gone against you and how to limit your damage.

BEARISH GAP DOWNS

Oftentimes, a stock will gap down in the morning and leave nervous traders wondering whether or not it is going to come back and fill the gap it created. These *bearish gap downs* are usually precipitated by unanticipated bad news a company puts out, which catches the market off guard. Fund managers never like being surprised with such news and do not want to hold onto losers in their portfolios.

It is precisely for this reason that, when trading in the gap, you need to watch the print (price and volume information of each trade), in order to get a good idea of whether the stock is going to make a rebound. If a stock comes out with bad news overnight, it will probably gap down in the morning. This gap down will naturally be met with a great deal of selling on the retail side of the trade. I would never short a mega–gap down at the open, as the risk-to-reward ratio is just horrible. However, if a number of trades are going off at just a few hundred shares, the market most likely has been expecting the news and is waiting to shake out those on the retail side who want to sell their positions. I am not suggesting that with the One Shot – One Kill Method you join the retail side in this type of trade, as this practice alone can be very hazardous to your wealth. However, stocks that experience a mega–gap down and don't recover can set up for nice shorting opportunities once the retail shakeout has happened. Once the stocks make a shallow intraday rally higher and subsequently moves lower, you are given a pivot from which to work—and a much better place to set your stop on the trade.

With that being said, if the news is met with large prints at the open, such as share sizes larger than 2500, then there is a good bet there is some force to the selling. As always, wait for the pullback and see how it responds. If the pullback is met with more selling, then get short and set your stop on part of your position 25 cents above the high of the day, and the other part above the most recent pivot high. This strategy will give you a good point to get short, with a low-risk basis, and should help prevent you from getting killed on any kind of countertrend rally.

Examine the move with International Rectifier Corporation (IRF), which is illustrated in Chart 6.7. You can see that just after the company announced it would not be making earnings, there was a tremendous amount of stock that was sold off.

When you see that type of situation arise, it's like seeing big tracks, which you should immediately follow all the way to the shorting window. Later that day, the stock tried to rally after the morning selloff, allowing smart traders an excellent opportunity to get short again with clearly defined risk. If the trend continued its downward movement from the morning, these savvy traders would then reap even greater rewards. The trend did

CHART 6.7

When a mega–gap down happens and the stock can't fight off the initial onslaught of sellers, it is a good sign that a sustained down trend will follow over the course of the next few days. International Rectifier Corporation (IRF) opened near the highs and closed near the lows, which suggested further weakness.

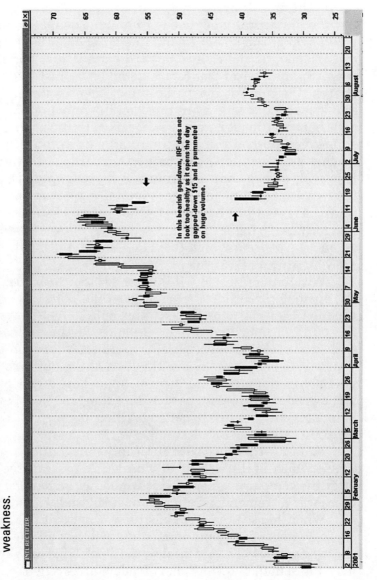

In this bearish gap-down, IRF does not look too healthy as it opens the day gapped-down $15 and is pummeled on huge volume.

continue and smart traders set their stop above the high of the day. These are the kinds of observations good traders make in stride with perfect execution.

Chart 6.8 is another example. Emulex Corporation (EMLX), one of the Nasdaq's biggest high flyers, came out with some less-than-flattering news for the Street.

The stock was crushed on a huge surge of volume. With this type of stock play, a more experienced short seller is required to enter. But anyone can use these tactics to unload a long position that has gone against her or him. The chart clearly shows that the public was obviously not expecting the news, and because of the inevitable selloff, this point looked to be a good place to get short. However, like all the other trades talked about, if you can't manage to get in the first move, don't chase the stock, as patience and discipline will usually reward you with a good second chance.

This strategy can also be used even if you are not comfortable shorting stock. If you own stock that gets hit with bad news, you have two options: Be like the rest of the sheep and sell at the open, and fight to get a decent fill on the trade, or see how the stock handles the pullback. If the stock manages to rally back near the open but begins to roll over, *that* is the point when you are usually best served to dump your shares. If you are a real trader and see all of this happening right in front of your eyes and still do nothing, then it is time for you to stop trading for yourself and invest your money in a respectable, high-yielding hedge fund. Until that time though, all trading decisions made by you, the trader, should be based solely on your own finding of facts, in which your emotions shouldn't play a part.

To summarize, for bearish gap downs do the following:

1. Watch gap down and print size to determine if there is force behind the selling during the first 30 minutes of trading.

2. Enter short after the first pullback fails and use 25 cents above the high of the day as a stop.

3. If you don't get into a trade today, watch and wait over the next few days to see if the weakness continues and allows you a second opportunity to get short.

CHART 6.8

From bad to worse: Investors wish they'd had stayed in bed as EMLX cruises through Fibonacci support and falls over 90 percent from its highs.

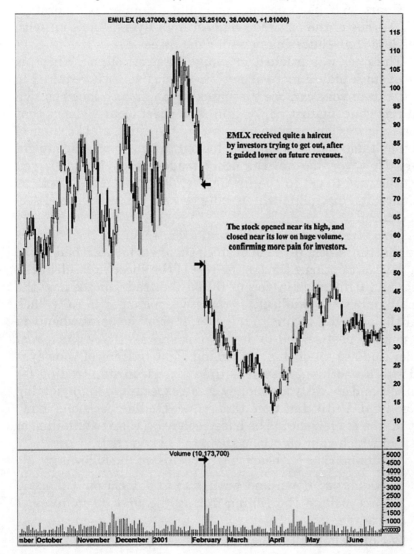

EMULEX (36.37000, 38.90000, 35.25100, 38.00000, +1.81000)

EMLX received quite a haircut by investors trying to get out, after it guided lower on future revenues.

The stock opened near its high, and closed near its low on huge volume, confirming more pain for investors.

Volume (10,173,700)

mber October   November   December 2001   February March   April   May   June

BEARISH GAP UPS

As fun as bearish gap downs can be, *bearish gap ups* are more my cup of tea, as over the years, fading retail order flow at the open has made many market makers and specialists enough dough to buy houses in the Hamptons.

Bearish gap ups provide yet another good shorting opportunity, often arising on an intraday basis. A stock that is in a prohibitive down trend tries to attract buyers who, early on, are doing some bargain hunting. The stock gaps up in the morning and tries to make a run up. However, as is usually the case with a bearish gap up, there is no real support for the move. The bears use the opportunity to sell into the rally. It is at this time that you should pay close attention to the action surrounding this stock. If after the first half hour of trading the stock has held onto its gains, then it appears there may be some legitimacy to the move. However, if the stock can't break above the open, then you can use this as an opportunity to short the stock and set the stop a 1/4 point above the high on the day.

In many instances, it is more profitable to get in if the gap up occurs at a major price target following a sustained rally higher. Often, following a rally over several days, the rest of the retail sheep get led to slaughter, as the market will look at a mega–gap up opening based on some economic news or that maybe Asia rallied strongly in the overnight session. The euphoria gets going and everyone is feeling good about owning stocks again. This is where you use your Fibonacci price targets and objective technical analysis to look for a good, low-risk entry point.

In situations like these, market makers expect the demand to be higher, due to market conditions, so the stock will gap up. However, for stocks in down trends, this point can be used as an excellent opportunity to short. The rules of entry are the same. Watch to see how the stock, the sector in which the stock trades, and the overall market handle the open. If these three things move in unison to the downside, and if the stock shows no ability to hold the open after the first 10 minutes, then aggressive traders may want to consider phasing in with one-third of their intended position, using the high of the day as a stop. More conservative traders can wait for the stock to fall once and then gauge the pullback to see how strong the trend is. Once the stock starts heading lower again, get in, and place the stop either above a pivot point or above the high of the day, depending on the time frame in which you are trading the stock.

The second, and most powerful of the types of bearish gap ups occurs following a three- to five-day rally, in which everyone is convinced the real move is on and doesn't want to be left out of the fun. The introduction of this book highlights that type of scenario. Akin to the first type of bearish gap up, the futures are bid up on relatively light volume and market makers do their best to knock out the illiquid ask orders on all the electronic communications networks (ECNs). They do so in order to get everyone hyped about the move higher, just before they fleece their waiting lambs and turn them into lamb chops.

The market will typically gap up, and hang out for a little while, before the music stops and there are not enough chairs for everyone to sit. The move down can set up a tremendous reversal. It is during this type of bearish gap up when the use of the TRI is critical in spotting divergences on the shorter time frame. If the gap up occurs at a major Fibonacci resistance point, then that situation adds even more fuel to the fire, as far as taking on a short position. Once you see the divergence and the market beginning to struggle, phase into the trade on the short side. The moving averages will have not caught up with the move yet, so set your stops above the high of the day, or the area of Fibonacci Friends. After you get short, watch the first bounce. If it makes a lower high, and rolls from there, then phase in with the rest of your position. Put your stop above the high of the day, and enjoy the ride. I have seen many bearish gap ups following huge runs, lead to two- to three-day reversals. Being aware of these opportunities can help greatly with your play selection and overall profitability.

Look at the situation with Qualcom (QCOM), which is illustrated in Chart 6.9. The stock had been on a phenomenal tear for all of 1999. Some positive analyst comments came out on the stock before the bell opened and the stock had a huge gap up. However, it was all downhill from there, as the gap up was met with sellers galore and the price of the stock was crushed.

As with a bearish gap down, you need to watch the volume on the stock, to see if the move up is making large prints on the

CHART 6.9

What are also known as rally killers are mega-gap up days following a prolonged move higher. This action sees the market open at highs and close near the lows of the day. These gap-up days are a warning sign to unload your long positions and look at some short-term short entries.

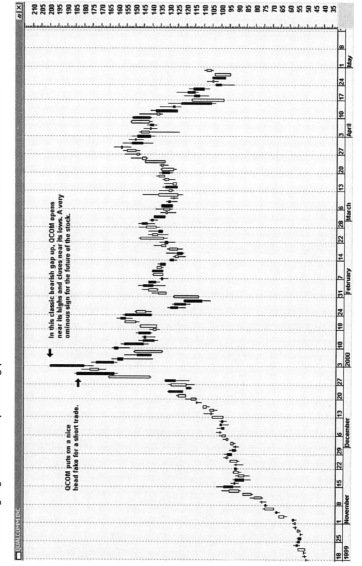

QUALCOMM INC

QCOM puts on a nice head fake for a short trade.

In this classic bearish gap up, QCOM opens near its highs and closes near its lows. A very ominous sign for the future of the stock.

147

buy side or if the large players are hitting the bid. If that is the case, I like to look for share size of more than 2500 shares. Most traders will tell you to watch block trades of only 10,000 or more shares; however, I think this maneuver is a mistake. A not uncommon tactic—in fact, one frequently used—is for institutions to route their orders in smaller chunks, for the sole purpose of hiding their intent. Therefore, I watch the speed of the time and sales as much as I watch the size of the volume.

Market makers and specialists are very skillful and adept at taking the retail traders' money, and they use gap ups and gap downs to accomplish this objective. The market makers have a very good understanding where the order flow is coming from and at what price there will be an equilibrium of buyers and sellers. For this reason, you would be much better off before making a trade under these conditions to wait for at least 10 minutes at the open and let the trend emerge. Picture yourself in this situation as acting like a sniper in a war zone, waiting patiently and watching as the setup unfolds, and then, and only then, quickly pulling the trigger.

Most investors spend their lives wishing for stocks to go in only one direction. I, on the contrary, whether as a result of my taking the road less traveled my whole life or realizing that winning short trades usually compounds my money faster than winning long trades, actually enjoy going short more than going long. Despite whatever preferences you may have, the best traders in the world can (and do) trade both ways. They are not caught up with their egos and about being right. They simply look at what the market is telling them and act on what is actually happening. If and when a trading situation presents itself, they attack. Period. Otherwise, there is just a lot of chart watching going on.

There is something to be said for profiting from a major downturn. It is similar to selling a stock and then watching it go down, but much more rewarding. If the market is going to go down (and, believe me, sooner or later it will) before rising and dropping and rising again, why not learn to profit from these regular occurrences? By employing the One Shot – One Kill Method, you will be prepared to profit from significant market moves, no matter the direction, exactly as many professional traders do every day.

Things to look for when playing a bearish gap up:

- A gap up following a 7-10 day move higher can signal the end to the move up
- Look for a Fibonacci price level or inflection point which may provide a good entry
- Enter on a shorter term bearish formation to at least put the short term trend on your side.

ENTRY TECHNIQUES FOR SHORTING

Every so often I like to remind myself of an old saying: "If you always do what you've always done, you'll always get what you've always got."

To do better, you must change what you are doing wrong and learn to step outside of your comfort zone. Keep in mind that fully half of every profit you make comes from your entry point. You certainly don't want to be told by anyone that you made a lousy entry into a position. Don't worry, you'll know, and you'll wind up getting what you have coming. The entry techniques for shorting used in this method will help stop a lot of the frustrations you have probably had immediately following your entry into short positions in the past.

The entry techniques I use for shorting stocks vary slightly from my entry techniques for going long. However, unlike going long, in which a trader can buy a stock on either an up tick or a down tick, at the time of the writing of this book, when shorting a stock, a trader is not allowed to go short on a down tick when trading equities. If you trade commodities or options, then this matter is not a concern for you, as you can get short on either an up tick or a down tick. As a result of the up-tick rule, situations may arise in which a stock sets up nicely for a shorting opportunity. However, once it starts falling, it may continue to fall a significant amount before getting a new up tick. Thereby it raises the risk-to-reward ratio, making the trade less desirable or even undesirable.

A common method used by hedge funds and institutions is to use *married puts* or *conversions*. These trading vehicles allow the trader to get short a stock on a down tick. Because many

retail traders or investors do not use married puts, it is imperative for you not to chase stocks down. A high percentage of stocks
that break down will attempt to retest their initial breakdown
level before the move down can begin in earnest. The subsequent failure of that retest provides the best opportunity for a
person to enter a short trade. As you learned in Chapter 3, one-
third of your Netto Number is derived from the formation of the
chart. Stocks that have broken down, retested their breakdown
points, and have started moving lower again receive the highest
Netto Number as a prospective short candidate, as they offer the
best chance to profit when shorting a stock.

The paragraphs that follow will take the same technical
indicators used in the One Shot – One Kill Method to go long,
and demonstrate how to use them to go short. When using the
One Shot – One Kill Method, these indicators are not intended
to be used individually, nor should they be. Rather they should
be used in collaboration with each other, to confirm that getting
short is, in fact, the right thing to do.

Chart 6.10 illustrates the Nasdaq 100 during the month of
February 2001.

The market had begun moving at a nice run after the Federal Reserve announced a surprise interest rate cut on the second trading day in January. The heavily oversold tech sector
managed to mount a nice oversold rally, which brought it up
through some significant resistance points. Traders who were
looking to go short on the oversold rally might have missed out
on the January up move, but they were finally rewarded for
their patience before February was complete. Chart 6.10 shows
that the Nasdaq 100 was coming into some significant Fibonacci
resistance areas that would truly test the legs of the then-cur-
rent rally. The market struggled to make it past those areas and
began to weaken near the end of the month.

During this time, many traders were asking themselves
whether or not the market was going to head back down and
retest its lows. In taking a good look at the indicators discussed
in Chapter 2, you could have determined that the chances of it
heading back down to retest its lows appeared to be the probable
scenario, as Chart 6.11 demonstrates.

CHART 6.10

A classic One Shot – One Kill short entry occurs in the case of the Nasdaq 100 when an oversold market rallies back into Fibonacci resistance and shows short-term overbought signals. This sets up the dynamics for a low-risk short entry to play to the downside.

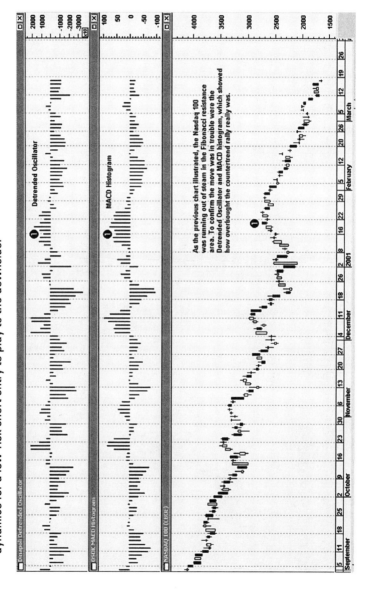

CHART 6.11

The most important part of the One Shot – One Kill method is to create solid price levels from which to work. When a number of Fibonacci Friends line up in the same area, the results can be powerful.

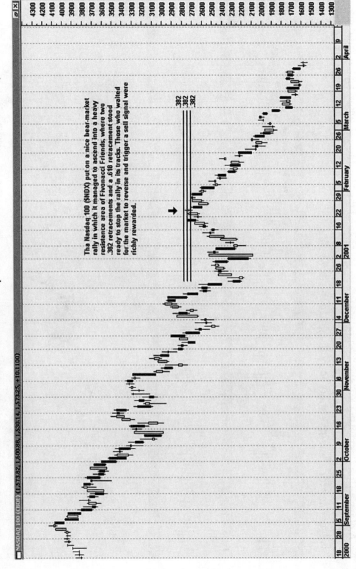

The Nasdaq 100 ($NDX) put on a nice bear-market rally in which it managed to ascend into a heavy resistance area of Fivonacci Friends, where two .382 retracements and a .618 retracement stood ready to stop the rally in its tracks. Those who waited for the market to reverse and trigger a sell signal were richly rewarded.

NASDAQ 100 (CBOE) (1,573.82, 1,600.88, 1,530.14, 1,573.25, +10.1100)

The MACD histogram, which had been positive all month, began to head back down again. This development suggested that, at the very best, the temporary up trend would go into consolidation or, more than likely, it would head back to the downside. The Vertical Horizontal Filter, which gauges the strength of a trend, also began to look weaker, giving further insight that the January rally was losing some of its legs. On a longer-term chart, the Nasdaq had not managed to take out December's high and was starting to set up from a pullback from the lows' scenario. The short play had begun to set itself up perfectly. That was the time to get into the trade, not the time for brow picking and second-guessing. Trust yourself fully with the method and you will begin to relish these situations, not get anxious.

On February 2, 2001 QQQ, an exchange traded fund representing 100 stocks traded on the Nasdaq, took out the low from January 31, which gave the signal to go short on the market. My reaction was to immediately set a disaster stop above the January high for half of my position, and set another stop above the 15-period simple moving average, which stood at 66 ¼, for the other half. The market tried to rally from that day but did not stop me out. The next day, after moving higher, the market succumbed to the weakness that my technical arsenal had been predicting. I watched the market move lower and lower over the course of the next two weeks. I used my price targets to let me know that the market was reaching a point to take logical profits, while I used the 15-day MA to add to my short-term position whenever the market pulled back.

Chapter 12 will walk you through a short trade and all the processes involved in making one. This chapter provides an overview of the dynamics of initiating a short position. Chapter 9, showing how to enter a trade, will provide a more thorough and precise explanation of short trading, including anecdotes.

Until you fully understand this method, it may seem complex, but it is not a hard process to follow. Traders using this method are simply looking to sell strength in declining markets, buy weakness in rising markets, enter trades with good risk-to-reward ratios, and take profits at predetermined profit targets. By following this simple strategy, over time you should see a dramatic improvement in your ability to spot market situations that repeat themselves. This acuity allows a good trader to profit over and over again. Being able to recognize and attack these situations is part of a strategy to creating wealth, without undue risk, that will help achieve your goals faster.

To summarize; while Chapter 9 will go into more details on the exact entry techniques to be used; entering short positions on stocks requires the benefit of an up tick. However, with that said, the classic One Shot – One Kill entry for shorting occurs after a stock has broken down from major support, rallied back to that support, and failed to advance past that point. From there, the stock takes out the low of the previous bar. That is the ideal spot on the chart, assuming there is a favorable risk-to-reward ratio to be had, for entering a trade with a short position.

HOW TO AVOID GETTING SQUEEZED TO DEATH

Being forced to buy back stock that you went short on during a violent and sharp rally is what many refer to as a *short squeeze*, and something that no trader wants to endure very long. It is akin to being a seven-year-old kid again and having your big Uncle Willie give you one of his really tight hugs and not let go. That general feeling of helplessness is what traders who are short feel, as their stock begins to rise without pulling back. Short squeezes happen regularly and are a fact of life. When you become free-thinking enough and willing enough to make profits while others remain stuck in the same old limiting investment methodology, that's when you will truly begin to maximize your potential income.

One of the most violent situations for a short squeeze happens when a down move is anticipated after the market has sold off on some pejorative news and closes on its lows and appears to be very weak. A number of hedge funds and retail traders pile on the shorts and carry the positions overnight. Many who do not, are looking for weakness the next morning. When the next day comes around, if the market manages to hold on its gains and not break down, weak shorts will begin to cover their positions on the failure of the follow-through or breakdown. This can also happen on an intraday basis, possibly following a poignant news announcement, like the Federal Reserve cutting 50 basis points in a surprise move. You can bet that along with people engaging in natural buying there are a number of nervous short sellers looking to get the hell out of their positions.

After looking through the chart formations in Chapters 3 and 6, you can clearly ascertain which formations are classic formations. But, obviously, trends reverse. At times these particularly bearish looking formations don't follow through. A double top, for example, which doesn't head lower but in fact breaks out to new highs is a classic case of short sellers helping push a stock higher. As I have said many times to students and other traders, having a trade that doesn't work out shouldn't be shameful, unless, of course, you fail to manage the risk behind it. If you cannot manage the risk or if you overleverage yourself, it can trap you. It will do so especially when a market that appears to be going straight down changes direction and swings into a huge, short-covering rally, while you do nothing but begin forming ulcers.

When you are able to switch your hat and recognize these situations, it can be a profitable disposition. You become part of the problem for the shorts and help add fuel to the fire by joining in with the buyers and being the *squeezer* instead of the *squeezee*.

If you enter a trade in which a bona fide short pattern does not follow through to the downside, as expected, it can cause a wave of buying by the people who originally initiated the short positions. When these shorts want to get out, the short squeeze can be a powerful process. To spot these situations takes time and experience. But having that ability can help you in these situations. If you are short yet can realize what is going on, you can turn a bad situation into a profitable war story.

It's true that you would have lost some money on the trade by getting stopped out of it, but if you cut your losses quickly, then you will not feel emotionally or financially battered following an inevitable short squeeze. What shouldn't happen is you panicking or worrying over the trade, because you should have learned never to get emotional about any trade you make. You should have had your stop-loss in place and executed on your plan of attack. In this particular instance, all you had to do was to blow out of your position. This is an ordinary part of a successful trader's life. To win big over the long haul, you must be prepared to walk away from many small losses along the way.

Short squeezes can also happen if the stock you are borrowing from your broker needs to be returned before you would like. The need to return the stock causes an increase in demand for the stock. This increase in demand can create a very frenetic situation.

Look for a couple of fundamental things when you are shorting a stock; spotting these developments may also help prevent you from being squeezed as well. Many stocks that go on parabolic runs do so because traders feel the stock is overvalued and decide to short it, despite the fact that there is no viable technical setup for the trade. When the stock pulls back, most of the traders will cover their position in order to get even in the trade. I advise you to be extra judicious when shorting stocks with greater than a 20 percent short interest and a relatively low float. This combination can be a lethal one to those who like to short stocks, as these stocks can be more easily manipulated. Short interest numbers are updated monthly and can be found on most financial Web sites.

A parabolic rise is shown in Chart 6.12, which involves Genesis Micro (GNSS). As shown in the chart, the rise begins to pull back and looks like it might be showing some mercy to the short sellers.

However, what appears to be a great shorting opportunity turned out not to be so great. This type of situation needs to be considered a normal occurrence in your mind if you are to ever become a successful trader. Learn to live with trades not going as you planned, because having trades not work out is part of life as a trader, whether you are shorting or going long. Stocks do move up as well as down. Many trades, which appear to be good shorts and are well calculated, may not work out. However, it does no good either, to make 19 out of 20 trades right and end up with a net gain of zero, just because of one trade in which you neglected your stop-loss and which ran against you big time.

What I am about to say next is so important, it overshadows all other trading errors by far and is the biggest reason in which traders fail. If I repeated these words on every page of this book, I would not be overstating their importance:

Never fail to manage risk.

CHART 6.12

Using trailing stops is important, as market reversals can quickly change a winning trade into a losing trade without the proper position management.

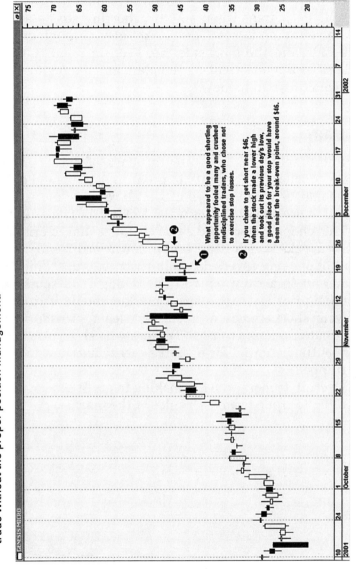

What appeared to be a good shorting opportunity fooled many and crushed undisciplined traders, who chose not to exercise stop losses.

If you chose to get short near $46, when the stock made a lower high and took out its previous day's low, a good place for your stop would have been near the break-even point, around $46.

157

If you are like the average trader, just following those simple words alone could potentially save you a lot of money and great emotional grief over the course of only five years. Think about it. Be patient when you are shorting stocks and *always* stick to your stop-losses. The market goes through gyrations to the upside and the downside. So, keep in mind that creating solid price targets, executing the plan, and managing risk is the key to making real money.

SUMMARY

Short selling is an integral part of most professional traders' arsenals. The ability to profit in both up and down markets should help enhance your overall returns and will provide you with more opportunities when looking for trades in the market. This chapter discussed some common characteristics found in most stocks which head into a downward trend. Being cognizant of one-day reversals, exhaustion gap-ups which can signal an end to a rally, as well as picking good spots based on Fibonacci price levels to short a market should help you better time your short entries, or at the very least, provide a good spot to exit out of a long position. Traders who short also need to be aware of the potential for a short squeeze and how to avoid getting trapped.

Overall, traders who are looking to profit consistently must be willing to trade from both sides of the market.

From Marksman to Expert

7

Trader Preparation: Using the One Shot– One Kill Method

As articulated numerous times throughout this book, the basis of the One Shot – One Kill Method is to buy weakness in rising markets, sell strength in falling markets, and take profits at predetermined price targets. Netto Numbers were created with the intent of quantifying this action and calculating good spots to enter in positions. The three components of a Netto Number are described in Chapters 2, 3, and 4 as technical indicators, chart formations, and Fibonacci levels with each comprising 10 of the 30 total points, respectively. This chapter will put together the components to create a Netto Number and lead into following chapters that will show you how to take this Netto Number and plan, enter, manage, and exit a trade based on it.

INTRODUCTION TO NETTO NUMBERS

In order to become a more effective trader, I decided early on that improvements needed to be made to the many trading systems and strategies being offered by successful (and not-so-successful) traders who thought they had a clue as to what they were doing. When I first started trading, I made numerous mistakes trying to micromanage positions, succumbing to emotions when trading, and always trying the newest method just as it was entering into a period of drawdown. With these methods, in just about every instance, I discovered a weakness that made them, although an improvement over trading like a craps shooter, either (a) too costly and difficult to learn, (b) missing many important aspects of a trading plan, (c) lacking consistency, or (d) all of the above. In short, some of these methods could help a person who invested the time to learn and implement them correctly and some of these methods left me scratching my head.

The development of the One Shot – One Kill Method and Netto Numbers sprang from the necessity to do better. Trading is an inherently difficult job that we as individuals make more difficult than need be. Time and again, I found myself being right about the market but getting in at bad spots, not properly managing winning positions, and changing my plan in midstream. This was both financially and emotionally destructive.

While Netto Numbers may initially come across as esoteric, the purpose of them is to offer confirmation when looking to enter a prevailing trend on pullbacks in good spots. I designed them to be simple and provide a quick reference point for helping a trader get into high-quality trades at good spots on the charts. Netto Numbers have two separate functions in the One Shot – One Kill Method. The first function of a Netto Number is to provide a score from 0 to 30 and serve as a means of assessing the quality of the trade. The closer the score to 30, the better the setup is and the better the chances for success.

The second and equally important function of Netto Numbers is to serve as the benchmark for the allocation of resources granted to these particular trades.

Netto Numbers serve as a helpful checklist for getting into trades. They help paint a clear, unbiased picture of where the bulls and the bears really are and calculate a defined value to place on your potential trading candidates. Proper implementation of them should allow you to substantially improve your ability to objectively analyze the market.

In order to understand Netto Numbers, you first *must* understand the material presented in the previous six chapters.

The process of deriving Netto Numbers is a simple and direct one, which is actually very enlightening, once you fully understand the steps you take to lead you to them. Without your understanding of this information, the successful application of Netto Numbers cannot be achieved.

When you are deciding which vehicle to trade, a search, based on the following criteria, will be necessary to help increase the odds of trading success. These criteria will give you a composite score, which will correlate to the Netto Number that will tell you exactly how much of your portfolio should be dedicated to the play. Strict adherence to money management principles is paramount for not getting wiped out. Some traders reel off an amazing number of winning trades, but because of greed and poor money management, they will often squander all their winnings on just a few trades. By using my method, and with the correct application of Netto Numbers, you will reduce the possibility of that happening, or so it is hoped.

The next function of a Netto Number is during the trade itself. A Netto Number helps calculate the overall portfolio exposure you can have during a particular move. This tool is incredibly powerful for determining where to take profit objectives and when to go the other direction. The Netto Number derives this exposure by finding agreement between a wide variety of things; to include price action in the underlying chart formation, Fibonacci Friends, major trend lines, the TRI, the Vertical Horizontal Filter, moving averages, MACD, as well as a Detrended Oscillator. This is obviously a very demanding set of criteria to meet, and it is why you will find that the quality of the trades you make should increase dramatically. You just have to make sure you detect the situation and act. You do this, once again, by taking a sniperlike posture and objective, by waiting and watching as your play sets up. If it does, you are ready to execute. If not, you go to Plan B.

CREATING YOUR PLAY LIST

For any trader or investor, there must exist a pool of potential investment vehicles that a trader can feel relatively comfortable trading. Creating your list of eligible candidates from which to trade will be done by creating a database composed of approximately 500 stocks from the S&P 500 Index. The remaining stocks you will choose will come from the Nasdaq 100, put together with another 150 stocks of your choosing. This will give you a database of about 750 stocks on which you will run a nightly scan. The 750 stocks you have will be made up of stocks from nine sectors on the S&P 500 Index as well as three sectors located within the technology field. These will include Basic Industry, Energy, Financial, Consumer Staples, Technology, Utilities, Consumer Services, Industrial, as well as the Semiconductor Index, Software Index, and Biotech Index. There naturally will be some redundancy between the stocks from some of these sectors. A complete list of these stocks can be found in Appendix B.

From these 750 stocks, you will run a scan looking for eligible candidates that show signs of achieving the highest bullish or bearish Netto Number. In order to find a bullish stock, you will run a very simple scan for stocks that are trading above their 18-period simple moving average, have closed below their four-period simple moving average and are positive on the MACD. To run a bearish scan, you will look for stocks that are trading below their 18-period MA, show a negative MACD, and closed above their four-period simple moving average.

The benefits from doing so are obvious. From reading about the application of the method earlier, you should have these two criteria met, before you even start the evaluation process. The point is to get you into stocks pulling back that have yet to resume their trend. While looking at the results of the scan, you must be able to envision what the chart will look like if the stock resumes the trend the next day. This visualization will help allow you to get a better entry. It will also give you a large number of high-quality plays from which to choose the next day. You will be able to assess and gain insight on things that are important to know, like sector rotation, because when one stock in a sector starts to rally, it might be a fluke, but when a number of stocks in a sector show these particular characteristics, there is a good chance you are looking directly at institutional hands rotating money in.

From the 750 stocks that were on your list, the stocks that meet the remaining requirements will shrink dramatically. As the number of stocks narrows down, you will see potential plays reveal themselves and be able to categorize them into your trading plan. This is one of the most exciting processes. It makes *you* the discoverer of what could be a really big strike and it's quite fun and exhilarating to uncover those sometimes well-hidden treasures. Of course, after discovering them, you need to be able to execute your trades correctly, to maximize your profits. When this topic is taught in One Shot – One Kill workshops, an entire day is devoted to this process alone because of its importance.

SCREENING FOR PLAYS

As discussed in the last section, three main criteria will be used to screen your plays. The first will be whether the stock is trading above or below its four-period simple moving average; the second, if it is positive or negative on the MACD; the third, if it is above or below its 18-period MA. These criteria are very simple; yet they serve as an effective way to filter out a number of the stocks in your database. If these criteria are met, then it is time to advance to the next step. For example, if you want to run a bullish scan, then you will run a scan for stocks that have closed above their 18-period MA, are positive on the MACD, and are below their four-period simple moving average. That last part may seem a little perplexing, but you want to find stocks that have pulled back from a run without breaking down. The opposite holds true for stocks that have closed below their 18-period MA, are negative on the MACD, and are above their four-period simple moving average. This will, once again, put you in good position with a stock, which has pulled back from its lows but not to the point of indicating a reversal.

As mentioned earlier, this process will sufficiently reduce the 750 stocks you selected. The next step will be to add the other factors into the equation. This will elevate your chances of making money on the trade from good to very good.

Once those first three criteria are established, it is time to move on to the others. The next requirement will be to view the chart formation. In this instance, you are looking for a chart formation that is bearish and coming off a rally but still on its way down. You are looking for the rally to fail, as you hope your instincts and analysis will be correct. A number of confirming technical indicators will give you the "all clear" to fire into the trade. However, finding the "perfect" setup, where all of the indicators are in alignment, is a rarity. The most important part of this process is to tip you off to the potential of a powerful move while still allowing you to get in at favorable risk-to-reward ratios. Any formation that shows you no advantage should be avoided. There are plenty of stocks out there. Settling for substandard criteria just to enter a trade is just a poor allocation of resources.

You need to develop the mentality of a sniper who is willing to wait for long periods of time on end, without ever firing a single shot, until the time is right. This discipline will help you see a marked difference in both the quality and quantity of your trades.

The next requirement is to determine where there is any significant Fibonacci resistance or support levels, which would either work in or out of your favor on the trade. Ideally, you want a group of Fibonacci Friends to be supporting you, at roughly the same spot the stock is. However, you must remember that trading on lower-volume, less-followed stocks will not produce the same kind of results with the application of Fibonacci analysis. For this reason, sticking to big-cap stocks, which are followed by numerous entities, is more conducive to profiting from Fibonacci Friends.

After you thoroughly assess where the Fibonacci levels are, it is now time to give a grade to them. An area that is replete with Fibonacci numbers in your favor earns a score of 9 or 10, out of 10 points, while an area with Fibonacci numbers working against you is probable cause for dismissal of the trade. Perhaps, though, upon further investigation, that score could be cause to go the other way. Patience, akin to a sniper's, is paramount in this business, and it is plainly evident and illustrated in my method. Most of what you will be doing is rejecting potential trades, akin to a Hollywood director at auditions screening actors for a starring role. You must be very demanding and particular and avoid bad trades, just as a director would avoid bad actors. For reasons other traders may consider nitpicky, you might dismiss a trade that does not meet specific criteria. Period. And remember, in the desire to make the most money you can, there is no need to overtrade. Using the One Shot – One Kill Method will help you find and evaluate, in a very thorough manner, the plays at which you should be looking. Then, you should use the techniques in my method to make good, sound trades.

The spotting of a significant trend line and trend channel is your next objective, confirming trend lines and trend channels, moving averages, Fibonacci ratios, and the rest of the tools in the trading war chest add more strength behind the firepower of these trading opportunities, which can quickly move in your favor.

The Vertical Horizontal Filter (VHF) comes in next. You will use it to determine whether a strong trend is just beginning or appears to be dying out. If a stock is moving up in a retracement and meets a solid wall of resistance filled with Fibonacci Friends, and if the VHF shows that the trend is dying out, then there stands a great chance that the stock will turn around in your favor. This ideal situation would earn another score of 1.

The Detrended Oscillator will come in next and tell you how oversold and/or overbought the stock is, and how likely a continued upward move is, based on the stock's movement in the past. You can tell if a rally is likely to fail when the stock has reached overbought levels, which have in the past been difficult to surpass, and suggest an impending pullback in price in this situation. However, the most important part of the Detrended Oscillator is to confirm that you are not entering into an extended position.

I suggest you repeat this process on all of the stocks you come up with in the initial scan you run. You will be surprised by your results. What is also important to note is that doing these scans will provide you with a very good sense of what the market is doing and better help you internalize what is going on. This nightly ritual will only become easier, as the price grids created on the initial scan can be easily updated once they are in place. Correct preparation can make it possible for you to win the battle before it is even fought. Chapter 12 walks you through a real-time trade and how to apply Netto Numbers from the first initial scan to booking your profits.

SHORTENING YOUR PLAY LIST

At first, the process of shortening your play list becomes particularly difficult, because after running your scans, you may begin

Factor	Points and Criteria
Formation	10 points — the cleaner the formation, the better
Fibonacci areas of support/resistance	10 points — you would like to see a set of Fibonacci Friends in your favor as you get in the trade
TRI –bullish/bearish divergence	2 points — you are looking for the possibility of finding either bullish or bearish divergence
Detrended Oscillator	1 point — as long as it doesn't suggest that the trade you are looking to get into is too extended, you will get full credit
Moving Averages	3 points—— you would like to have two of the three in your favor
Vertical Horizontal Filter	1 point — you are looking to avoid getting into positions that appear to be too extended
MACD	1 point—— you are looking like to have MACD in your favor
Trend channel and trend lines	2 points — you are looking to buy pullbacks of stocks in upward channels and sell rallies of stocks in downward channels

to think that most of your picks are winners. However, the method does not promote overtrading. It follows a set routine that focuses on involving yourself with only the most promising of the candidates and, through that process, producing winners. As your assessment continues, you will be calculating and applying Netto Numbers to each particular stock that makes the grade.

The stocks with the highest Netto Numbers for your bullish scan and the ones with the highest Netto Numbers for your bearish scan will be narrowed down to approximately 25 for each. This will give you an ample amount of targets to choose from for the next trading day. Using this method gives you an opportunity to choose from an array of high-probability trade setups. The other candidates will be listed, with alarms set, but not in view, as desktop real estate is expensive.

I highly recommended that all trading possibilities be recorded on a piece of paper, along with other pertinent information ascertained about the market from your research from the night before. Be sure to record support and resistance levels for the major markets (Nasdaq, S&P, Dow), Fibonacci areas, daily bias, leading and lagging sectors, as well as news or announcements that come out before, during, or after market hours. This piece of paper is called a *gouge sheet*. It is named after the piece of paper pilots carry with them in the cockpit of a jet, so, if they forget something in the heat of battle, their critical information is always readily available and at their disposal.

The importance of having both a list of bullish and bearish plays is that, should the markets or the sectors trend against you in the morning, you need to be able to go the other way with stocks that are already trending in that direction and stand the best chance of continuing that trend.

Shortening your play list, from what started at around 750 down to about 25, will give you the highest probability of success and, with it, the confidence you need. What you really have left is the cream of the crop, and sticking to your plan with such ripe candidates is what it takes to become a successful trader.

To do so, though, you need to study and understand the gouge sheet numbers and use alerts to notify you when stocks hit certain predetermined points.

ASSESSING MARKET CONDITIONS

When using the One Shot – One Kill Method, you will perform a nightly analysis on the market using Netto Numbers to qualify the monthly, weekly, and daily trend. By doing so, you will provide yourself with a perspective on which direction the market is most likely to move. The process for analyzing the markets varies only slightly from that for analyzing equities and sectors.

When using any one of the software programs mentioned in this book or one you are more comfortable using, the first thing you will do is to determine the monthly, weekly, and daily inflection points for the S&P 500 and the Nasdaq 100 indexes. This process will only have to be updated on a daily basis for the daily inflection points. The weekly and monthly inflection points will only have to be updated on their respective time frames. After determining the inflection points, you will write them down in your own gouge sheet, so that you will be ready for the next trading day.

The next function to perform is to determine if the market is in any bearish or bullish chart formation—for example, a double top, double bottom, or a ascending or descending triangle—or whether it has broken any significant support or resistance. If there is a prominent, clearly defined bullish or bearish chart pattern, then it may receive a Netto Number as high as 8 to 10 out of 10 possible points, as the chances of the market heading lower or higher off of these formations is very good.

Following your formation analyses, you will be creating areas of Fibonacci support and resistance on both of the markets, as having these numbers available to you will help you internalize and understand the ebb and flow of the market throughout the day. Using the techniques in Chapter 4 will give you the tools necessary to create areas of Fibonacci Friends and assign a point value to the markets. If the markets are pressing against an area of Fibonacci resistance, then it will receive a very low, bearish score of 0 to 1 out of 10 possible points. If it is sitting on an area of Fibonacci support, then it will receive a very bullish score of 9 to 10 out of 10 points.

Following the analysis of the formations, you will run the market through the five indicators from the war chest to make the final determination of how strong the trend is and how likely it is to continue.

All this activity may seem like an exhaustive process at first. But ask yourself: How much do I want to succeed? After a short period of time, many students find that looking at the market and deriving Netto Numbers becomes an intuitive part of their trading lives. The time spent deriving these numbers is very short in comparison to the rewards it yields.

After concluding your analysis, you will derive a score from 0 to 30, with the understanding that a market score of 30 supports, but does not require, an allocation of 3 percent of your portfolio to the trade. A score falling below 20 probably isn't worth your time. Using this information to go forward will be instrumental in determining how much you should allocate to each trade. If a trade is trending with the market, then you can allocate more of your capital, whereas a trade that is moving against the overall market trend should be avoided or, at the very least, should be made with a significantly smaller portion of risk from your total portfolio.

Utilizing this information, you will now perform a similar analysis on the sectors and stocks that come up in your nightly scan. As mentioned earlier, a good portion of the analyses that you perform will carry over to the next day of trading. For this reason, the first gouge sheet that you create will be the most difficult but also the most rewarding. Working smartly and using self-discipline does pay off in this business!

ASSESSING SECTOR CONDITIONS

As discussed earlier in this chapter, a trader using my method will break the sectors down into nine components of the S&P 500 Index, the Nasdaq 100 Index, as well as the software sector, semiconductor sector, and biotech sector. These 12 inevitably will have overlap and redundancy as you search through your database. As you spend more time as a trader, feel free to add more stocks to your database, paying particular attention to placing them in their correct sectors.

Using Netto Numbers in the same manner as you did with the S&P 500 and Nasdaq 100 indexes, go through the process to find out which are the strongest trending bullish and bearish sectors in the market. The results from this investigation can provide you with tremendous insight as to where the most fertile and profitable trades are located. Just as you will gain from reading this book, running this type of analysis is made much easier and more tenable with the use of stock analysis software such as MetaStock. After taking some time to learn the software, you'll find how easy and helpful it is. Being able to simply type in the symbol for an index or use any of many valuable tools instantly makes your time commitment less cumbersome. Nevertheless, don't allow this luxury to lessen your trading intensity or lull you into not using your best trading habits.

Choose the sector you wish to examine first, and then look at the chart pattern. The chart pattern provides the most important piece of information you can use in your trading strategy.

Based on the degree of bullish or bearish patterns talked about in Chapter 3, a score from 1 to 10 points is recorded.

The assessment of Fibonacci ratios comes next, with a group of Fibonacci ratios that sit in favor of the formation, giving the sector up to 5 points. If there are a number of Fibonacci numbers working against you, score a zero.

It is then time to run through the four technical indicators and two trend-following tools: the MACD, Detrended Oscillator, Vertical Horizontal Filter, and TRI as well as the 5-, 15-, 39-period MAs, and trend lines with trend channels. These are each given up to 2 points apiece.

After employing this strategy on all 12 sectors, you will be able to tell which sectors are trending up and which ones are trending down. From this vantage point you will be particularly keen to making plays within the strongest trending sectors. If you have a sector that is trending strongly with the market, pay attention to the sentimental favorites in that sector, as the odds are they are leading the market.

After the sector search is complete, you will compare the stocks that came out with the highest scores to the sectors that came out with the highest scores. As referenced previously, you will compile this information and make a gouge sheet to write it on. You should print this sheet and keep it accessible throughout each trading day. At the end of each day, you will place the gouge sheet in a folder that contains copies of all previous day's gouge sheets. Doing this will allow you to do two things. First, you will have on hand a record of stocks from previous trading sessions that were high-quality plays, in case they reappear as high-probability trades in the future. As a result of your nightly research, if they begin to break out, you will already have a well-defined strategy upon which to embark. Second, by performing this ritual every day you will begin to understand and internalize the market's movements in ways you never thought possible.

This initiative does require some work. Bear that in mind, because many times (and I'm more inclined to believe, from what I've witnessed, *most times)* traders don't do much, if any, effective homework. They may think they are doing it, perhaps, but, in truth, they aren't. Many people are too lazy to do the work required because they mistakenly think that a better life will just be magically bestowed upon them somehow. I tell traders whom I have trained in the past that trading is a job that is not cut out for a lot of people. It isn't because some people just don't have the self-discipline it takes to sit down for a few hours or so each day and do what is needed. Trading sure sounds glamorous; however, the truth is that, although it doesn't take a lot elbow grease to be a successful trader, it does take the effective use of specific knowledge. That knowledge, and a strong method in which to employ it, is what this book is attempting to teach you.

An example of my "Daily Battle Plan" for going into the trading day, and the information that it has on it. As with getting used to most things in life, the more you use your gouge sheet, the more you'll become accustomed to trading with it and you will soon be going to spots on it instinctively. Using Netto Numbers to trade the market is tenable for most, but it requires you to provide an investment of time, commitment to excellence, and a lot of enthusiasm for what you do.

Realize that you have the power to trade from anywhere in the world, with a powerful method. Many traders have discovered all that trading has to offer, but many of them are without a good plan to get any of it. You now have one.

ALLOCATING RESOURCES AND DETERMINING RISK

Just as every general must make decisions before going into battle, so must you, as a trader, decide how much to allocate to each trade that meets your criteria. Over the year or so from 2000 to 2001, traders would commonly say that the markets were some of the toughest ones they had ever lived through, and that making money had become much more difficult than ever before. What caused these difficulties was more of a result of traders being conditioned to watch stocks rise without ever seeming to fall. Traders who had been skillful enough to trade what was actually happening in the market, and not what they thought should happen in the market, did extremely well.

CHART 7.1

Intel looks very strong as it puts in a series of higher lows.

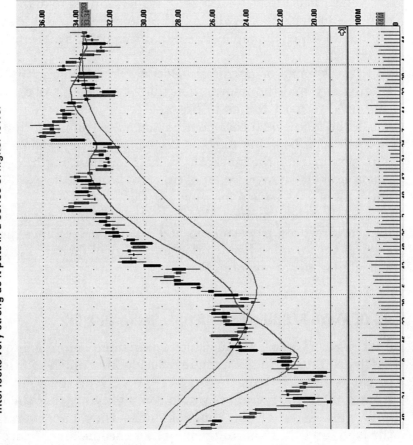

A number of variables come into play into how much of your capital you should put into any one trade. The first is the Netto Number that you have determined as a result of your nightly analysis. If the Netto Number is high (for example, from 25 to 30), you are looking to risk anywhere from 2.5 to 3 percent of the portfolio to the trade.

The next thing that you are going to do is to assess the strength of the sector in which the stock trades. If you trade futures, then your work is done and you can trade based solely off the Netto Number. If the sector you are trading is also trending strongly in the direction of your stock, then, this increases the amount of overall capital risk you may take as a result.

The last aspect to consider is the market itself. If the market supports your side of the trade as well, then you have a quasi-trading nirvana that allows you to allocate the most capital. Having the stock, sector, and market in your favor clearly creates the best advantage for being on the right side of the trend. It allows you to allocate the largest amount of capital toward the trade with the highest chances of success.

Charts 7.1 and 7.2 show Intel stock starting to break out to the upside as it makes a higher low on the daily chart, thereby suggesting you may have a tradable trend reversal. The Semiconductor Index ($SOX), the sector in which Intel trades, is also moving higher, combined with the Nasdaq 100 ($NDX) making a higher low as well, gives you a good trading opportunity, because you have all three parts of the market moving in your favor.

Some sectors carry a lower R-squared variable with the market and are not as important to have correlation (like the more defensive issues). However, if you have all three parts moving in your favor, you will substantially increase your odds of making successful trades.

SUMMARY

The Introduction to Netto Numbers is intended to provide you with a means of finding quality trades by using a combination of chart formations, Fibonacci price targets, and technical indicators to set up trades that allow you to buy weakness in rising

CHART 7.2

Understanding the correlation between a stock, its sector, and the market is very important. Stocks within a sector can oftentimes react in unison with their sector and the overall market.

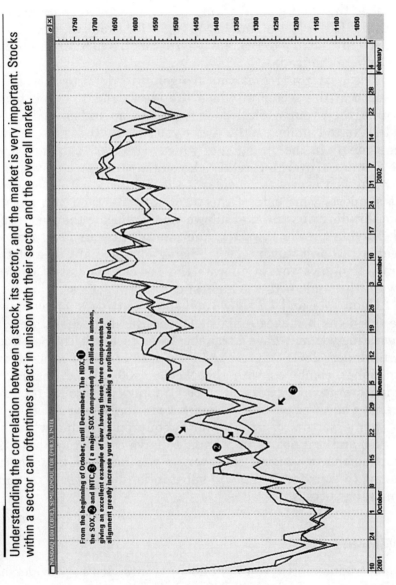

From the beginning of October, until December, The NDX, ➊ the SOX, ➋ and INTC, ➌ (a major SOX component) all rallied in unison, giving an excellent example of how having these three components in alignment greatly increase your chances of making a profitable trade.

NASDAQ 100 (CBOE), SEMICONDUCTOR (PHLX), INTEL

markets, sell strength in falling markets, and take profits at predetermined price points. A trade can score as high as a 30, with 10 points being given on the quality of a chart formation, 10 points being given for it's proximity to a solid Fibonacci level of support or resistance, and 10 points given for 6 different technical indicators. Trades that score between 25-30 points are the ones worth pursuing the most. After you run a scan of your trades, it is also important to perform the same function on the respective sector the stock is in, as well as the market it is in as well. If all three are suggesting the same thing, then the collaboration of information is even more powerful.

Through constant repetition of performing these scans and assigning Netto Numbers, you should be able to spot setups in stocks and potential trade candidates. After you have performed this, it will then be a question of execution which will be discussed in more detail in forthcoming chapters.

CHAPTER 8

Dynamics of a Trading Day: Where to Focus

In many battles, the final outcome is usually determined before the first shot is even fired. So it is with trading, where preparation and training before the actual event are the keys to success.

THE NIGHT BEFORE THE WAR

The night before the trading day, you need to spend time examining both the trades you made and the trades you didn't make that day. That night may also present you with an opportunity, because of late news that may have come out from a company that very day, to have an idea of what the market will do the following morning. The technical analysis techniques that are taught throughout this book are used to depict people's perceptions about the market. If there is a catalyst, it will either strengthen that perception or change it. Then, you must be ready act upon your plan accordingly.

For example, one day Cisco (CSCO) came out with positive comments after the bell and it was expected that the stock would gap up rather sharply in the morning. This information gave traders an idea of how the market would move and allowed them to devise a game plan for the day ahead. Knowing this news doesn't mean that you should buy at the open, but at least you have a chance to assess what the bias for the day might be. These types of news events can often cause a violent market reaction, to either the upside or the downside. By using Netto Numbers, you can stand to benefit from stocks that are in strong down trends that artificially gap up because of another event. This type of preparation through the previous night will also include updating your price targets, so you'll be ready for the next trading day.

If there are no newsworthy events, then simply keep an eye on the futures to see how things are going. But remember, while you need to understand where the futures are, as they can be easily manipulated on low volume and should not be taken as a guarantee as to where the market will ultimately head. I have seen too many uneducated traders lick their chops when they either bought a gap up or shorted a gap down in the morning, only to have that joyous feeling replaced, almost immediately, with one of being kicked in a tender spot, as the market sped quickly in the opposite direction. Don't follow in their misguided footsteps.

Another important thing to do when preparing a battle plan for the following day is to put together a couple of scenarios of what might happen that day. I try to have an up scenario and a down scenario with which to go into the day. If the market is going to head up, I try to map out where it might head and what kind of response this development might generate (for example, traders might sell into it because a spot might have been used as support a number of times). Conversely, if the market sells down, I try to determine from which spot I should be looking to take profits from a short. Then if it does bounce from the spot, I ask myself where the sellers are likely to step back and to resume the down trend. You need to do the same. Use your Fibonacci levels and price targets to help you put these scenarios together so that you are ready to attack in real time.

Trading is akin to playing chess in a game where the more advanced players usually think two to three steps ahead of the moves being played. Achieving this skill level takes some work, but it can be accomplished with smart work and dedication. Again, like I asked in the beginning of the book: How badly do you want it?

PREMARKET ACTION AND THE FUTURES

As you have diligently set up your trading plan for the trading day, use the premarket action and direction of the futures to guide you in the direction of your strategy. Clearly, you need to be circumspect in initiating positions in the premarket that are based on the futures action. However, the direction of the futures will guide you toward your bullish or bearish plan for the day. You have numerous possibilities for ways to play the open. The most important thing to understand is that you, the trader, the disciplined sniper, are the one who dictates the trade, not the other way around. For example, suppose the market is gapped up but not into a major resistance point. The situation does not make trading short worthwhile. But suppose, too, that the market is still too extended to take on a trade to the long side. Then you don't have to take a trade and can wait until things clear up. Remember, many trading opportunities arise on a daily basis. Because they do, you need to exercise patience and discipline.

As part of your analysis the night before a trading day, you calculate Netto Numbers for investment vehicles you plan to trade. You will always have the most bullish and most bearish indicators to use. If you watch the premarket action of a sector that is feeling the affects of an analyst's downgrade on a major stock, you will be guided to a more bearish posture throughout the day. The most bullish sectors in your report may be adversely affected by this news, thereby making plays in this sector no longer feasible. As long as you stick faithfully to your rules and entry techniques, you will not become involved with bad trades as frequently. And not being involved in mistakes is an important aim to achieve.

What I have noticed is that many traders don't fully appreciate the result of skipping the riskier plays. That's because they fail to recognize how *not* getting involved has saved them time, headaches, and, more than likely, money. When, because of your thorough due diligence, you are sharp enough to know what trades to dismiss, your bottom line will start to shine a lot brighter.

If you are relatively inexperienced, have little training, and are learning how to play a number of potential situations that can arise during the premarket, I advise you to first remain on the sidelines, to let the real trend emerge before attacking.

Inevitably, some traders will hear news and try to guess what the market will do with it. They are the ones who get in early on the premarket activity. But to do so and still walk away with more than 15 cents in your pocket requires a great deal of skill and expertise. For the most part, it is best to use the premarket and futures conditions to help you gauge market sentiment and where the market is likely to go.

THE OPEN: THE FIRST 10 MINUTES

During the first 10 minutes of just about every trading day, an exciting rush of action occurs, with many wild price moves. At this time, market makers are often trying to match up orders that have been sitting in the queue since the night before. As a result of this activity, the open flow can often have an imbalance. In order to fill all of the orders, many trades go off fast and furiously. Because they do, the opening activity doesn't always give a clear indication of what the *real* trend is.

One of the first rules most traders should follow is to watch from the sidelines as the first 10 minutes of action in the market unfolds. It is entirely possible that you may miss a substantive part of a move up or down while doing so. More importantly, however, you may also be prevented from getting head-faked into a trade that very quickly may cost you big money.

The first 10 minutes of the trading day also tends to reflect investors' reactions from recent news or economic events. These events can cause serious gyrations during the early minutes of the market. The things you should be looking for in the first 10 minutes are which stocks from your preselected list have broken out into clear trends and which ones are struggling to go in either direction. The stocks that don't move early need to be watched just as closely as the ones that are showing a clearly defined trend, because these other stocks are not frozen. Your research has revealed that these stocks are at a profitable junction and may move at any time. Although you may be acting on other trades, always keep a watchful eye to strike on a target that did not appear at first to be much of a killing. As long as you stay within your trading budget and personal trading ability and execute on your plan, don't pass up well-defined, highly probable profit-making trades. I have thus far never found a good reason for not doing so.

The two-minute chart is a very important tool to use during the first 10 minutes of the day. You should look for two trending-up bars that make higher lows and higher highs for stocks for which you are looking to go long (see Chart 8.1).

For stocks that are potential short candidates, a necessary prerequisite for consideration is two trending-down bars with them that make lower lows and lower highs (see Chart 8.2).

Not until your long setup breaks its previous day's high, however, should you enter; likewise a short setup needs to break its previous day's low. Getting into a short-term stock position before the end of the first 10 minutes is a very tricky proposition that requires more risk than is acceptable in the One Shot – One Kill Method. That being said, I have worked and trained some advanced traders who have accepted the higher levels of risk that associates itself with higher levels of profit, they were able to do so because of their truly expert and advanced abilities.

I hope all of you reading this book aspire to reach such a level of trading deftness and master all the conditions of the One Shot – One Kill Method set forth in this book. The key point to remember is that if you commit yourself before a meaningful trend has established itself; you will incur additional risk in your trading plan. Also, as you will see, if you are not adept at trading the open, your haste will only produce mixed results. Throughout the day, plenty of trading opportunities will arise with which you can make money. You do not need to take riskier-than-necessary chances to be successful in this business.

THE FIRST HOUR AND A HALF

The first hour and a half of the trading day is often marked with two powerful moves. The first is a move that has a great deal of energy behind it and takes the market in one direction. The second move is an attempt by either the bulls or the bears to regain some of the ground they lost in the first early morning battle.

CHART 8.1

Two-minute chart, showing two trending-up bars.

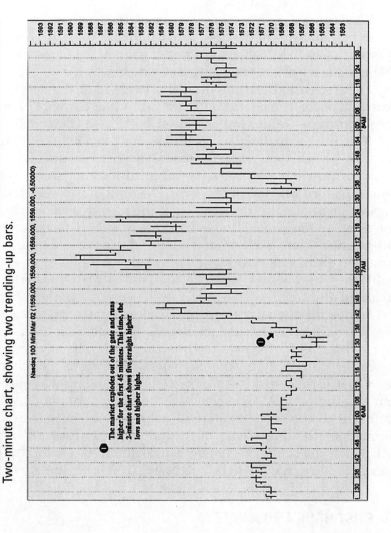

Nasdaq 100 Mini Mar 02 (1559.000, 1559.000, 1559.000, 1559.000, -6.50000)

The market explodes out of the gate and runs higher for the first 45 minutes. This time, the 2-minute chart shows five straight higher lows and higher highs.

CHART 8.2

Two trending-down bars—an indication that you might want to go short.

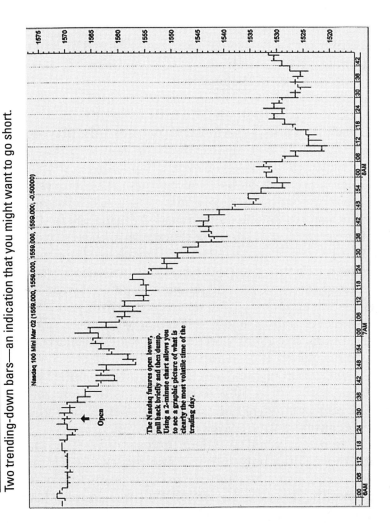

Nasdaq 100 Mini Mar 02 (1559.000, 1558.000, 1559.000, 1559.000, -0.50000)

Open

The Nasdaq futures open lower, pull back briefly and then dump. Using a 2-minute chart allows you to see a graphic picture of what is clearly the most volatile time of the trading day.

185

Traders who are experienced can play and profit from both of these moves, and although I won't analyze all the possible scenarios which may occur, it is important to understand that there are a number of entities pushing the market during the first hour and a half of the trading day.

Looking at the Nasdaq market (see Chart 8.3), you can see that it broke down straight out of the gate for a big loss during the first 45 minutes of the morning.

At about 10:45 A.M. Eastern Time, the market tries to rally, and it puts on a nice countertrend rally to move nearly 15 points off its lows. It takes experience to successfully play both the strong initial move and the less powerful countertrend rally.

The logic behind these two events happening is simple. Many professionals are both bullish and bearish. They understand the dynamics of the morning move and realize that 80 percent of the time a high or low for the day is reached during the first 90 minutes of the trading day. Aware of this pattern, those professionals begin to take profits once a substantial move has happened. After the professionals take profits the first time around, those who initially missed the move use the pullback to now get in on the right side of the trend. If the second move can't definitively break past the first move, then a likely relaxation will ensue. This countertrend relaxation usually occurs near some Fibonacci or other technical resistance. If no definitive movement in price occurs over a prolonged period of time, you should probably either exit your position or reduce it by 50 percent. It means that your entry did not work as you planned and you should either reload and strike at a more optimum time or look elsewhere.

I have recently had a student profess that he was making a career from trading only the first two moves of each morning! Within those moves, he captures enough profit to pay his bills for the month. However, the action that transpires is akin to a gunfight, with victory bestowed upon those who came to the battle prepared to fight. It is the noncompromising importance of this reason that I publish a daily, online report called *The Daily Battle Plan* (see Chart 8.4). I create and produce this daily plan for one reason and one reason alone—to keep subscribers informed of the ever-changing price targets in the market and the strength of those targets, in a timely fashion.

CHART 8.3

Classic early-morning down movement followed by late morning rally.

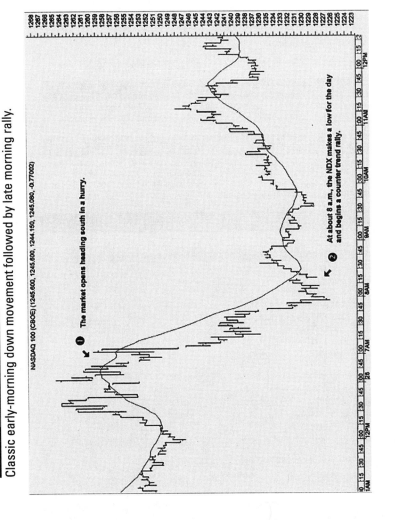

NASDAQ 100 (CBOE) (1245.600, 1245.600, 1244.150, 1245.080, -0.77002)

❶ The market opens heading south in a hurry.

❷ At about 8 a.m., the NDX makes a low for the day and begins a counter trend rally.

CHART 8.4

Sample page from the Daily Battle Plan.

Daily Battle Plan
SniperScope Trading Journal
Wednesday, October 29, 2003

Premarket Future's Values

NQZ3 – 1381   ESZ3 –1020   ZNZ3 112150

OSOK Key Short Setup For The Day

***1428 – There is quite a bit of resistance in here and any rally from yesterday should find resistance the first time through. I am looking for a 8-10 point pullback in here with a 4 point stop

OSOK Key Long Setup For The Day

***1390 This is a .618 RT from the pivot low from Oct 27 as well as . While we did break through this level on Friday, it served as the first breakout point in the rally over the last hour. A retest of this should give a tradable bounce. I will look to bid in around 1356 and have a stop around 1352.

Weekly Economic Calendar for October 27 – October 31

Date	ET	Release	For	Actual	Consensus	Prior	Revised From
Oct 28	08:30	Durable Orders	Sep	0.8%	1.0%	-0.1%	-1.1%
Oct 28	10:00	Consumer Confidence	Oct	81.1	79.3	77.0	76.8
Oct 28	14:15	FOMC Meeting					
Oct 30	08:30	Employment Cost Index	Q3		0.9%	0.9%	
Oct 30	08:30	GDP-Adv.	Q3		6.0%	3.3%	
Oct 30	08:30	Chain Deflator-Adv.	Q3		1.4%	1.0%	
Oct 30	08:30	Initial Claims	10/25		385K	386K	
Oct 30	14:00	FOMC Minutes					
Oct 31	08:30	Personal Income	Sep		0.2%	0.2%	
Oct 31	08:30	Personal Spending	Sep		-0.1%	0.8%	
Oct 31	09:45	Mich Sentiment-Rev.	Oct		89.5	89.4	
Oct 31	10:00	Help-Wanted Index	Sep		38	37	
Oct 31	10:00	Chicago PMI	Oct		55.4	51.2	

Market Summary from Tuesday, October 28, 2003

Put/Call Ratio:	.75
VIX OPENING VALUE:	17.79
VIX HIGH VALUE:	17.89
VIX LOW VALUE:	16.77
VIX CLOSING VALUE:	16.82

CHART 8.4

(Continued)

NQ Open Value:	1385
NQ High Value:	1421.5
NQ Low Value:	1383.5
NQ Close Value (4PM EST)	1421
NASDAQ Total Volume	2.09B
15 MA on Daily Chart	1401.53
39 MA on Daily Chart	1375.54
T-notes Open Value	1120.95
T-notes High Value	1130.95
T-notes Low Value	1120.30
T-notes Close Value	1130.60

Pre Market Analysis

A little bit of weakness early on following the tremendous run-up yesterday in to the close on both the 10 years and the equities. 1428 is going to be a key spot on the NQ chart as well as 1050 on the ES. A lot of people are going to be using that to assess the strength of this present move. On the support side, any action that stays above 1405 is still strong, if a pullback today takes us below that, then we have traded back into the neutral zone as far as the bias goes.

Netto Numbers – Key Support and Resistance

Up-scenario – NQ Z3

NQ holds all action above
Key Numbers NQ Z3:
1428
1440
1449-

Down-scenario – NQ Z3

NQ holds all action below
Key Numbers NQ Z3:

1405
1390 –
1383 –

Plan of Attack

I suspect today will be a day where the market digests things and any moves, both up or down will be ones which require traders to take profits quick. The 50-point up surge from yesterday has me ready to play the present move for a retest of the 1444 level in the NDX as once a move violates the .618 RT, it is suggestive we will move back to the former high. 1408 was the recent .618 so if we stay above that level, my longer term prospects are for a retest. A close below that level has me neutral again. Therefore, my lean is up and any long positions I get into, I will look to let half run until we retest presuming we don't close below 1408.

CHART 8.4

(Continued)

Daily Trading Journal			
Entry px	Exit px	Number of Contracts	Profit/Loss
		Cumulative Profit/Loss	

All of the foregoing is commentary for informational purposes only. All statements and expressions are the opinion of John Netto and are not meant to be a solicitation or recommendation to buy, sell, or hold securities. The information presented herein and on our related web site has been obtained from sources believed to be reliable, but its accuracy is not guaranteed. Estimates, assumptions and other forward-looking information are subject to the limits of forecasting. Actual future developments may differ materially due to many factors.

There are six sections to the Daily Battle Plan. The first is the economic calendar. Knowing what important announcements are coming out is very important, as the market tends to provide reactions to them.

The second section is a premarket analysis, which outlines what has happened over the past couple of days and where the market presently sits. This section also points out key technical levels at which the market is presently sitting; it serves as a lead to the forthcoming sections.

The third section is the up scenario for the market. This material goes over what course the market is likely to take if it heads up. I have at least three numbers, usually more, indicating some good spots at which to take profits or possibly put on some countertrend short trades, as the reaction from these numbers can be very powerful.

The fourth section of the Daily Battle Plan is the down scenario. The down scenario, much like the up scenario, puts together a sequence of movements in the market that shows which price points are likely to come about. Having these calculations allows a trader to have predetermined price points in mind before getting into the trade. It also allows traders to take on a countertrend long trade at these numbers once they have become adept enough at understanding how the market reacts to these numbers. However, with both the up and down scenarios, beginning traders, or more conservative traders, should not look to take on countertrend trades at first. Instead, they should simply look to use the numbers as places to book profits.

The fifth and most important section of the Daily Battle Plan is the Plan of Attack. The Plan of Attack outlines the contract allocation and how a trader should play the move if certain price points are hit to the upside or downside. For example, if the analysis shows 1220 as being a key pivot in the Nasdaq futures, then I might outline a scenario if the Nasdaq futures breakdown below that. If that happened, then I might be looking to offer into bounces once there was a clear break below this number, such as the market moving as low as 1216, until the downside target of the day, 1200, was hit.

The sixth and last section is Final Commentary. Final Commentary is what a trader uses to reflect on the market and the trades she or he made that day. It is a very useful tool to assess whether or not you were able to follow your plan of attack or if your Battle Plan was up to snuff. It serves as a great purpose for creating a trading journal. If you plan on doing more than just surviving as a trader—and, unfortunately, not everyone can enjoy the great lifestyles some traders live—you must be thoroughly prepared, mentally and physically, to do battle in the first hour and a half of the trading day.

The main point to remember is that the first 90 minutes of the trading of day are usually characterized by two definitive moves in one direction, followed by a countertrend move in the other direction that typically generates a nice 1×1 reflex bounce higher on lighter volume.

THE GRINDER

One of the tenets of using the One Shot – One Kill Method and successfully employing Netto Numbers is the precondition that you will be trading in trending markets with a great deal of energy. Trading in nontrending markets can easily lead to being whipsawed out of a number of trades, leaving you frustrated and lacking confidence as well as with reduced trading capital. Trading between 11:00 A.M. and 1:00 P.M. Eastern Time, during the time period known as *the grinder*, is usually a very tricky proposition. This is the time when the market settles down, so to speak, and gets ready for the afternoon session. Liquidity during this time is usually very thin. More importantly, between these hours the market typically does not tend to trend enough to make trading worthwhile. Many times, it is easy to get unsubstantiated moves and get whipped out on light volume. So unless you are in a rare situation, this is a good time to finalize your afternoon attack plans and relax a little.

For those on the West Coast, when studying the average market cycle throughout the day, it is clear that between 8:00 A.M. and 10:00 A.M. Pacific Time, there is normally not much going on. You should use this lull in the action to review notes from the morning and prepare yourself for the afternoon session. Using this method for day trading, you should have some free time every day to do things other than trading (if you can think of any). You should post a warning sign above your computer that denotes the grinder time period and reminds you to exercise caution before taking on any new positions.

The grinder segues nicely into that time of day that offers higher probabilities of witnessing a trending market—that is, the warm-up period. By exuding the qualities of self-discipline, patience, and personal control, you will save yourself a tremendous amount of money by not trading during the grinder time of the day. There are always those people who feel they must trade and feel compelled to always be in the action. I call them gamblers. In most cases, they lead themselves to excessive trading and accounts that dwindle, because of commissions and spreads, which eat them alive during the grinder.

As with any other time period, the *possibility* always exists that a definitive move may begin during the lunchtime hours on the East Coast. As you will find out, if you don't know already, traders who trade and make money during the grinder can be sneaky. Should a definitive move occur, and the move is for real, you need not feel pressured to jump in for fear of missing it. The majority of powerful moves usually pull back several times to give you a good opportunity to get in at a good price. Knowing this, good traders can be patient and disciplined not to chase moves, like many retail traders do. Every day thousands of opportunities will arise of which neither you nor I will be able to take advantage. Getting mad at yourself if you miss a move in the grinder is futile, and intelligent people should avoid feeling this way.

THE WARM-UP PERIOD

The *warm-up period* lasts from about 1:00 to 3:00 P.M. Eastern Time. This time often provides some good opportunities for moves for those who are ready to take advantage of them. During this period traders return from lunch and the bulls and the bears lace up their gloves for round two of the daily double feature in order to see who goes home the winner for the day.

If, during this time, you begin to see a market break through technical resistance or support, you should begin to consider phasing into a trade. No doubt you realize that the move will probably pull back, before the move can begin in earnest. Something also worth noting is that, while this period can produce some very profitable trades, it is not desirable for the market to get ahead of itself before 3:00 P.M., as that lessens the chances of the market following through in the final 60 minutes. An ideal situation would be that at about 2:00 P.M. Eastern Time the market begins to break in one direction for about 45 minutes, followed by a 15-minute respite, before making its final move into the close.

However, many important events happen during this period, such as the Federal Reserve Open Market Committee

(FOMC) meetings, which usually bring with them an increase in volatility. Also, there are additional news events or upgrades and downgrades by analysts, which may move the market. If you see a stock that you have been watching break out or break down during this time frame, by all means you should strongly consider executing the trade, as many powerful moves can and do materialize. This move can be substantiated even more, if the market or sector is able to break out to new highs or lows, as well.

Power Hour

Power hour begins at 3:00 P.M. Eastern Time. During this time of the day the market has had some time to establish itself and develop a number of intraday trends, with the last 60 minutes providing a viable barometer of the strength of the underlying trends. Also, keep in mind that during the last 60 minutes of the day the money from primarily professional investors and institutions flows, taking control of the market.

In institutional investor's parlance, *VWAP* (*volume-weighted average price*) is king. An in-depth explanation on VWAP is beyond the scope of this book. (To learn more, refer to *Stocks and Commodities Magazine* in October 2000). Nevertheless, what you need to understand is that VWAP is the real price at which many institutional investors are evaluated in regard to their trades. Because this is so, a number of trends that established themselves in the morning have a good possibility of reemerging in the afternoon. Institutions that bought in the morning to drive the price up wait for the midday pullback and often get back in for the ride in the afternoon. It is this ride that will often happen during the final hour, known by traders as the *power hour*. During this time frame, you need to pay close attention to the trending sectors of the day, because a trader who learns how to trade during this time frame can make a good living trading only one hour a day!

The same theory applies for a market that is down trending. Waiting for the market to retrace some of its losses can provide an excellent opportunity to get short. The last hour to hour and a half is much more likely to trend than the middle part of the day. The key behind the One Shot – One Kill Method is to try and put you into position to benefit from trending and energetic markets. These are the times a trader should focus on first, as they can be very profitable.

Trading during this time and during the first 90 minutes of the day is the most conducive way to let the markets come to you. Take a look at Chart 8.5. The S&P 500 trended strongly up during the morning and started to move again in the afternoon after failing to make new highs. The move in the last 90 minutes also gave a couple of short entries on bounces to the 15 period moving average.

I had been eyeing the play and knew that if the stock retested this level it would be in a prime position to make a run. It pulled back and formed a double bottom at about the start of power hour. The S&P 500 then started to run again. I got into the trade at the first breakout, while waiting to scale into the position on the first pullback. The S&P 500 reflected the early morning trend, as the volume was surging, tipping me off that there was some force behind the move.

The trade was much more translucent because during power hour you have the benefit of not having to outguess the market. Spot the trend, if there is one, and go with it when it matches up with your analysis from the night before. You should be just like a sniper sitting in a tree waiting for the enemy, so that you have the cleanest shot at making a profit.

This type of trading opportunity arises almost daily, and it just takes a small series of solid trades to really make a noticeable difference in your portfolio's bottom line. It also just takes a few sloppy trades to make a noticeable difference in your account. As my father used to say, "it's better to do it right the first time than the fifth time." It's more profitable too, I might add.

SUMMARY

As important as it is to know what and how to trade, it also critical to know when to trade. Chapter 8 goes over the dynamics of a trading day from the opening 10 minutes, which usually sets a frenetic pace for the morning, up to the finale of the trading day during power hour. Most professional traders are looking to put

CHART 8.5

S&P 500 trending in the morning and rallying in the afternoon.

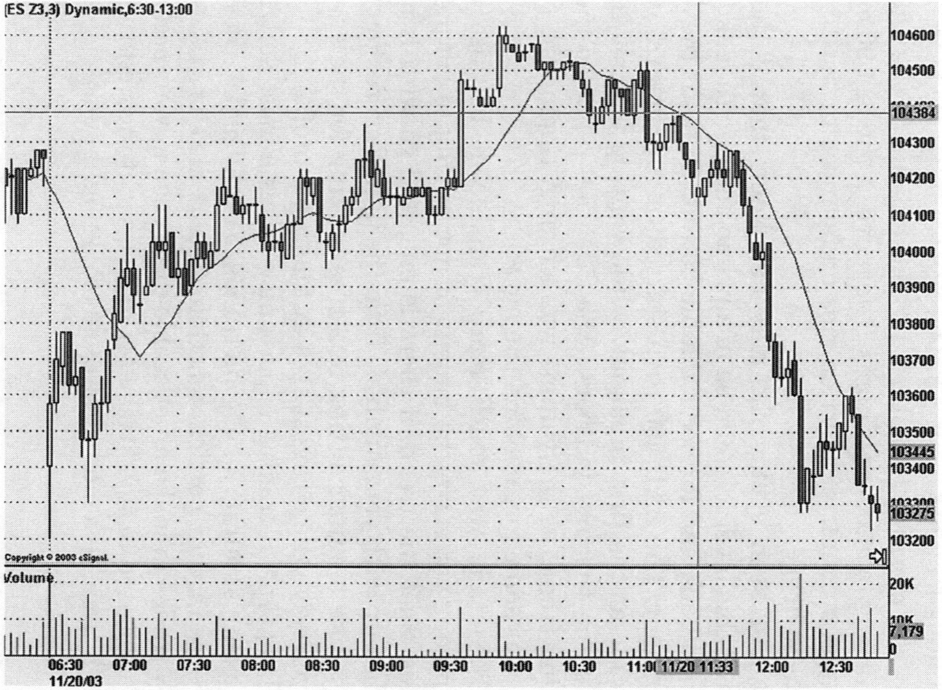

[ES Z3,3] Dynamic,6:30-13:00

Copyright © 2003 eSignal.

Volume

positions on in the first 90 minutes and the last 90 minutes of the day. This is not to say that the middle part of the day doesn't present opportunities, however, it is important to be more selective during these times as liquidity has a tendency to dry up and make trading more difficult.

CHAPTER 9

Entry Techniques:
Knowing When to Strike

The first eight chapters of this book have shown you what to look for before initiating any positions, as well as what not to look for. The remaining chapters are going to help you put these ideas into practice, so that you will be able to successfully apply what you are learning and make your trading education a profitable one.

While reading the remaining chapters, it is advised to use the first eight chapters as a reference for questions, which may arise over the remainder of the book.

As you read through Chapters 9 and 10, please consider the material presented in these two chapters to be as one. Many of the techniques that are discussed to enter a position can also be applied to exiting one as well. Chapter 9 focuses on scaling in and out of positions, using the previous day's high and low, Fibonacci price points, and other indicators for entry, and addresses some of the important psychological aspects of trading—the most important one being the ability to step outside your comfort zone when trying to pull the trigger on a trade. Chapter 10 addresses how to use more technical factors like moving averages, Fibonacci price targets, and support and resistance, as a means of exiting, while wrapping it up with an introduction to the OSOK Money Management Matrix that is designed to incorporate the concepts of the book at a cursory level to give you an idea of how you might play a run in the market while only risking a small amount of your account.

This and the next chapter were written to compliment the two most important aspects of trading: the entry and the exit. This is the cradle of trading civilization and the topic is worth a lot of attention. While these next two chapters go over a number of possible scenarios in both the entry and the exit, it is beyond the scope of this book to discuss every "what-if" scenario that may arise, and therefore the best teacher to a student is to combine the methods in this book with real-life trading experience.

ALIGNING YOUR SIGHTS FOR PROFITS

Part of the reason for the title of this book being One Shot – One Kill is that it is the mantra of the U.S. Marine Corps' marksmanship training. A key component to being a good sniper is the ability to wait. In some cases, that means you must wait for extended periods of time until you have negotiated yourself into a position where you can take one clean shot. In most instances, this effort requires a large amount of self-discipline, which, quite frankly, most people simply don't have.

During the course of the trading day, the market has a propensity to emit what can be perplexing signals, which can cause quite a number of traders, including myself, to be confused as to what the market is trying to say. At these times that I will not be making any trades—nor should you be. That is not part of this method. Too many traders act without ensuring that the probability of a successful trade is on their side. This action is akin to taking unnecessary potshots, with nothing more than hope in the rifle's sights. I will not take a shot unless the odds are clearly in my favor. At times, this predilection has caused me to go days on end, or even longer, without making a single trade. Successfully battling my yearning to overtrade was one of the biggest hurdles to becoming a successful trader.

This chapter deals with different strategies on getting into trades. It is broken down into four sections that teach traders what they should be thinking as they get ready to pull the trigger. The first and obvious concept at this point in time is the fact that traders are waiting for a pullback to get into a position, as they are looking to buy weakness in rising markets and sell strength in falling markets. Chapter 9 goes over that basic concept. Then the chapter moves on to a discussion of a more tactical way of entering positions—by waiting for the market to provide confirmation a trader steps into a trade by taking out the high or low of the previous bar. The chapter also discusses how to scale into entries based on the price targets that have been generated and anticipating future price movement before it has occurred in order to get a better-than-average price on a trade. The One Shot – One Kill Method stems from the strong belief that a combination of both anticipatory and confirming signals should be used when making an entry and this chapter shows you how to put that into practice.

Every trader and investor has a different threshold for risk. However, the One Shot – One Kill Method will serve most trading styles, from the most aggressive to the more conservative. Diligently study and then apply the techniques involved, as they should save you time and money over the course of your trading career. Timing is such a crucial factor in any investment decision, and strategic timing, coupled with the proper application and execution of these techniques, should enable you to execute your trades with the skills and confidence necessary to succeed.

PLAYING THE PULLBACK

In trading and investing, you will sometimes see a stock take off into the stratosphere before you buy it, leaving you to question yourself as to why you just didn't buy it at the right time. You also might see a situation where a stock you just sold begins a meteoric rise—right after you get stopped out. You can trade these positions with confidence and a high degree of success using a strategy called *playing the pullback*. This strategy has been around for years, but the exact means of ascertaining both whether a move is a pullback and by what means to enter is a cause of great debate and why a market exists.

As has been mentioned repeatedly, the One Shot – One Kill Method is predicated upon buying weakness in rising markets,

selling strength in falling markets, and taking profits at predetermined price points. Trading pullbacks embody this mantra.
They are a natural occurrence in the rise or fall of every traded
vehicle, as the market will typically retrace a certain portion of
its gains or losses before gathering more steam and resuming
the current trend.

Playing the pullback is one of the many successful aspects
of the One Shot – One Kill Method. But simply playing the pullback is not enough. You also *must* ascertain that the weapons of
war, your technical analysis tools, are telling you that what you
are seeing is in fact a pullback and not a reversal. In Chapters 3
and 6, you saw numerous examples of one-day reversals and
parabolic runs that almost religiously gave back a tremendous
amount of their gains. You will want to be wary of entering
trades with these types of patterns.

Chart 9.1 shows the move of Ciena (CIEN), which was
trending very nicely when it pulled back to support, at an area
of Fibonacci Friends.

Having the price targets generated from Fibonacci support
gives you a better sense of where a stock could potentially
reverse.

These types of patterns are very profitable. They allow you
to get back into positions, because they have a very strong
underlying trend, which supports the move the stock is making.
Almost always, it has only pulled back to find its legs again, and,
more than likely, so have many of the One Shot – One Kill indicators supporting it. This situation permits you to get into the
trade with a much better risk-to-reward ratio than if you simply
chased the stock on its way up while trying to fight for a good fill
from your broker.

Many of us, when we first became traders, had a bad habit
of buying stocks that were overextended to the upside or shorting stocks that were overextended to the downside. This tendency left us in a position for our trades to go against us initially.
This setback made us get out of the position because we were
forced to trade with too wide a stop and couldn't stomach the
move against us. This lack of discipline and patience was something I had to overcome. Eventually I transitioned myself from
being a trader who would be right about the move and not make

CHART 9.1

At point 2 on the chart, Ciena (CIEN) gives an excellent opportunity to get long at some Fibonacci support and a rising trend line. From there, CIEN heads back to retest its old highs.

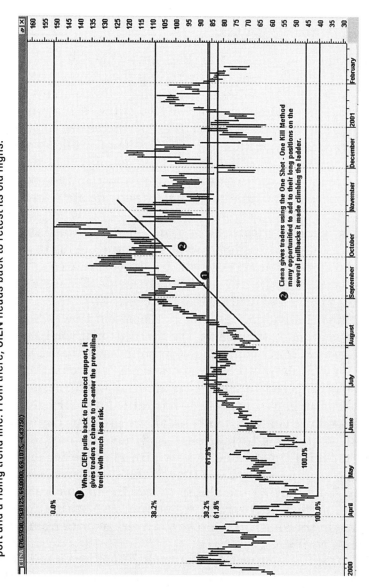

CIENA (70.55938, 79.8125, 69.00000, 69.1875, -4.93750)

① When CIEN pulls back to Fibonacci support, it gives traders a chance to re-enter the prevailing trend with much less risk.

② Ciena gives traders using the One Shot - One Kill Method many opportunities to add to their long positions on the several pullbacks it made climbing the ladder.

203

any money to being a trader who might be wrong about the move but in a position to get out relatively cheaply.

CONFIRMATION SIGNALS

Within many aspects of the One Shot – One Kill Method, having a defined entry is critical for pulling the trigger when the time comes. I am a big advocate of scaling into positions in halves, thirds, or even quarters. One of two entry techniques I use for doing so is to witness the market either taking out the high of the previous bar, if I am looking to go long, or taking out the low of the previous bar, if I am looking to go short. Many of the setups that you see in this book, from a swing trade perspective, receive their confirmation signals when the stock in consideration takes out its previous day's high or low. When this activity occurs, usually a rash of buy or sell orders hits the market, because most professional traders who are looking to get long, or possibly, cover a short position, are using this area as a place for their stop, and vice-versa on the downside. This is a fact of life that traders must deal with and accept.

Most individuals are not in a position to watch their positions on a tick-by-tick basis. For this reason if you have the ability to watch your swing trades on an intraday basis, you may be able to wait for a pullback on a shorter-term chart on which to enter as opposed to getting in at what might be an extended spot. For example, if the stock has rallied five straight bars on a three-minute chart to finally break the previous day's high, then I will wait for it to pull back and buy the next dip on that shorter-term time frame to help give me a better entry on my longer-term position. Even though the stock isn't extended on a daily chart, having the ability to buy the dip on a shorter time frame, or to sell the rally when you are looking to go short, should in the long run improve the average price from which you enter a position.

If you cannot watch your trade, then, if you are looking to go long, you must put your buy-stop order for the stock at 20 cents above the previous day's high, or, if you are looking to go short, 20 cents below the previous day's low.

As discussed in the beginning of this chapter. I believe in combining a method of entry that allows a trader to anticipate and confirm her or his position before getting in. Since traders using the One Shot – One Kill Method have the benefit of creating price targets based on Fibonacci ratios, which have the potential to generate incredible movement off of them, they should then try to capitalize on this advantage and enter at those spots on the charts.

Chart 9.2 shows Applied Micro (AMCC) when it starts to pull back and then break out to new highs in early August of 2000.

After watching for the pullback, you should get back in when the stock starts to break the previous day's high. By doing so, you are putting both shorter- term and longer-term momentum on your side.

Use of this entry technique is a most effective way to get into pullbacks from highs and lows, but it is much less effective when you are looking to get into a prevailing trend. For example, if a stock has broken its previous day's low for five straight days, then a wise move would not be to initiate a short position on the sixth day of the stock breaking down. It wouldn't be because the point where you have to put your stop on the trade is so far away, relative to your price target, that you wouldn't get a favorable risk-to-reward ratio. The One Shot – One Kill Method tries to provide you with entry techniques that will allow you to be in a favorable position once you enter a trade. You will thereby be allowed to be more relaxed because you are profitable in the position from the beginning.

At this stage of the game, you have seen a chart formation of a stock and feel comfortable that this is the time to get into the trade. As you do so, you will, in essence, have your sight alignment aimed for a direct hit through the crosshairs on your trading rifle.

Let's look at a real-life example. The stock you are looking at playing, Quest Diagnostics (DGX), just broke out of its ascending triangle formation in early March 2003 (see Chart 9.3).

In this situation, you need to have, not only the formation supporting you in the trade, but also a strong price target created,

CHART 9.2

There are a couple of different ways to get into a stock that is in an up trend. After it has pulled back and for at least three bars and stays above its respective rising moving averages, a trader can enter the position when it takes out the high of the previous bar.

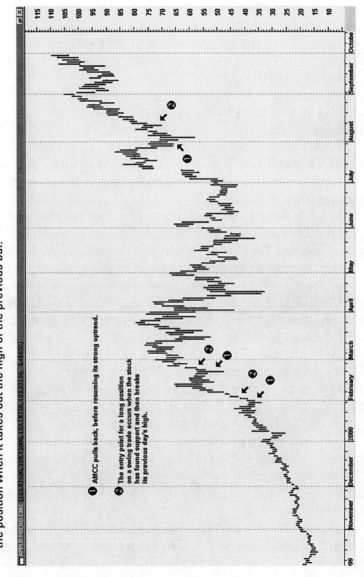

APPLD MICRO CIRC (105.07500, 105.87500, 103.75000, 105.18750, 105.53136, -2.46850)

1 AMCC pulls back, before resuming its strong uptrend.

2 The entry point for a long position on a swing trade occurs when the stock has found support and then breaks its previous day's high.

CHART 9.3

Movement of Quest Diagnostics (DGX), showing classic breakout from an ascending triangle formation.

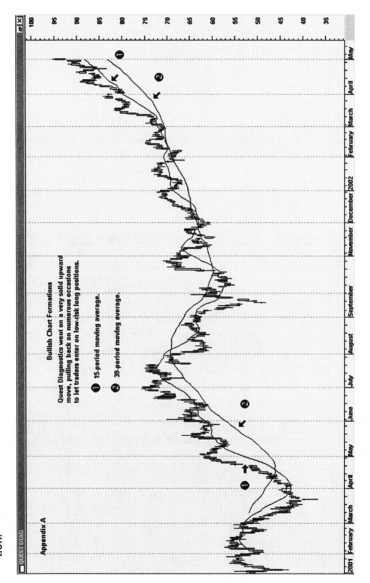

so as to help you assess the risk-to-reward ratio. This price target is the first confirmation signal you need to have in place before you make a trade. You need to see, from the Vertical Horizontal Indicator, that the trend is not losing strength, thereby increasing the probability that the trend is still in place.

The last thing that provides confirmation in this trade is when there are no Fibonacci areas of resistance in front of any move up (or at least a logical distance away), so as to not interfere with your profit.

This confluence of indicators and price targets gives you the confidence of knowing that the probability of making a successful trade is on your side. Now, you simply have to wait for the stock to take out the previous day's high to get long, or the previous day's low to get short, and you will be ready to go.

ANTICIPATING PRICE ACTION BY SCALING YOUR ENTRY

Use of the break of the previous day's high or low to enter a long or short position, assuming it has a good Netto Number, is one way of entering a position. However, I have found that combining that method of entry with either bidding into pullbacks in rising markets or offering into rallies in declining markets is a good way to improve the average price of entry on a trade.

Typically, most traders wait for the market to break down below the previous day's low to short. But because One Shot – One Kill traders have the tools to create sophisticated price targets, use of a combination of the two methods of entry can often achieve better average prices on positions. What typically happens with me is that by the time the market or stock hits my target, reverses, and goes the other way, it is at a less desirable price than I would have had if I would have scaled into the position. Understandably, most people can't offer into a stock that is in a short-term trend up while remaining in a long-term trend down. Nevertheless, if you can overcome this fear and get in for at least half the position, you should help improve the average price on your entries.

One very good way to enter a trade is to do what is called *scaling into a position*. The purpose of scaling into a position is so you can enjoy a large piece of the run, without having to commit your entire size, before finding out how right you are.

Scaling into a position might be appropriate in a number of circumstances. The first one would be if a market, after rallying, is pulling back to some Fibonacci support, has a rising 15-period MA, and has had a third straight down day but appears to still be in a strong trend. By scaling into only part of the position, I can effectively buy the dips of the move and add the rest of the position when the stock resumes its up trend in earnest. This maneuver will usually result in a better-than-average price. If the stock breaks below key technical support levels, then I will blow out of the position and lose only one-quarter to one-third of what a normal trade would cost.

The second circumstance where it would be smart to scale into a position is to play a runaway short squeeze, or big surge, that doesn't want to pull back. Usually, in such a situation I will bid into a shallow pullback with the understanding that if it continues to pull back, I will be okay because I can trade with a looser stop, and if it keeps going, then I can add to it. While I would never commit a full position to this type of impulse move up, trading smaller size by bidding into a shallow retracement can help you still catch a runaway move without chasing it higher.

I remember when the market rallied on news that the Fed would keep interest rates idle. I wanted to get a piece of this move but did not want to chase the futures and get in at a bad price. I had all the technical indicators supporting my entry, with a clear up trend on a 13- and 60-minute chart as well as a strong daily trend. But I did not want to get in the market for too much, so I took a partial position on the first shallow pullback when the market was still coming down. You need to have this kind of flexibility so that when there is strong exertion on the move, it can be fast and furious, which is why playing a shallow pullback on a dip can let you get a piece of it without getting smoked on a nasty retracement. I will typically set my stop below the 15-period MA of whatever period I am trading, as even if I am wrong after buying the dip, the 15-period MA will provide a stop for the market to bounce and let me get out without getting smoked on the pullback.

The next example is of a short trade into which I scaled. QUALCOMM Inc. (QCOM) broke down from a continuation pattern (see Chart 9.4).

CHART 9.4

In either direction, when the market begins to move solidly in one direction, there are usually multiple reentries to get in on the move. QUALCOMM Inc. (QCOM) provided a couple of spots to get back into short positions after it broke down to new lows.

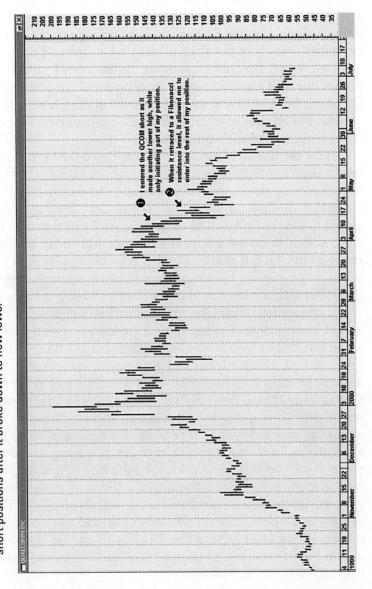

① I entered the QCOM short as it made another lower high, while only initiating part of my position.

② When it retraced to a Fibonacci resistance level, it allowed me to enter into the rest of my position.

I got into the first part of my short position when it bounced up from support, using the countertrend rally to offer into the move as a means of anticipating where the stock would go. I understood that once it took out previous day's low on the daily chart, I would hit it with the other half of the shares. If the down move went as the Netto Numbers foretold, then I would add to my shorts on the pullback to the original breakdown point. During this pullback many investors get faked out and end up taking smaller profits than they should settle for. In this particular situation, many people who went short on the initial breakdown all set their stops to break even and the market did its best to take them out before QCOM would roll south in earnest. Therefore, they were covering their shorts just as the pullback was ending. Other traders who sold out went long again, thinking it was a viable reversal. In some circumstances it would be, but when a pullback comes back and hits a Fibonacci area of resistance and is looking weak, it is time to load the boat and ante up more to the short side. Then, I slammed that trade and scaled into my position more, with total confidence as the stock continued to roll over. As I expected, QCOM dumped, and I closed out half my position at the next Fibonacci support level, while letting the other half run.

That is classic One Shot – One Kill Trading, and it brings tears to my eyes when I see students trade in this manner. Keep in mind that while this trade did go in my favor, in the past and in the future, trades like this will go against me, carrying with them the possibility to reduce my total profit from the trade from adding to the position. For this reason, you must have a complete understanding of the One Shot – One Kill Method as well as an unyielding discipline to manage risk.

Chart 9.4 showed how to scale into a short position. Chart 9.5, pertaining to L-3 Communications Holdings Inc. (LLL), shows how to scale into a long position at a key trend-line support and Fibonacci Friends.

LLL is pulling back to both a spot of Fibonacci support and a strong up-trending line. As mentioned earlier, scaling in at these spots on a chart, before the stock has broken previous day's high, is a good way to lower the cost basis and enter strongly trending stocks with minimal risk. One clear benefit of

CHART 9.5

L-3 Communications (LLL) pulls back to a rising trend line and some Fibonacci Friends at the same spot near 37.

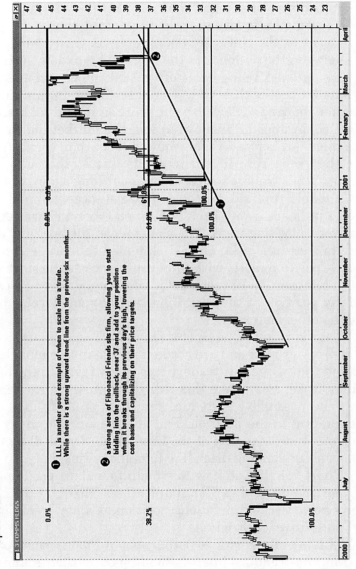

① LLL is another good example of when to scale into a trade. While there is a strong upward trend line from the previos six months...

② a strong area of Fibonacci Friends sits firm, allowing you to start bidding into the pullback, near 37 and add to your position when it breaks through its previous day's high, lowering the cost basis and capitalizing on their price targets.

this method is that, if you scale into a position and the trade goes against you, the use of a stop-loss, which gets hit, limits your losses and overall risk.

By scaling into a position, you give yourself a good chance to get into the initial move during the first shallow pullback and then catch the rest of the move when the stock resumes its up trend. Remember, poor judgment and greed causes traders to chase moves and load the boat before it is time. I have been there and made that mistake more times than I would care to admit. Stay professional and follow the One Shot – One Kill Method and you should be around to enjoy the big days, even when you have an inevitable losing streak.

PULLING THE TRIGGER

The One Shot – One Kill Method was built to provide a method that will allow individuals to put the odds in their favor on an ongoing basis. For traders who have the discipline to step outside their comfort zone and pull the trigger. When I first started trading, the size of the stock being traded was my hubris, which had me convinced that I was a stock prodigy and I could never lose. Therefore, I felt justified by taking on excessive risk. However, after getting whacked a number of times, I, like many other traders, went through a period where I would carry negative baggage with me before executing a trade.

Those losses open up personal inferiority complexes that we all carry around with us. The only way I could get past that baggage and make my way to the next level as a trader was to force myself to step outside my comfort zone in my trading. This effort usually meant trying something new or taking a loss of larger size. As crazy as it sounds, what helped me more than anything in my development as a trader was what I learned from my losses. A humbling loss was usually the catalyst that helped me start my next winning streak, because it seemed to focus me on my trading even more. Complacency could not set in, which is very easy to do if you are "comfortable."

Mark Douglas's book on trading psychology, *Trading in the Zone* (Prentice Hall, 2001), is a great read and really delves into a number of the psychological rigors that traders must endure. I continually force myself to try to achieve better results and challenge the traders around me to do the same. Pulling the trigger on a trade is something that you should try to make as automatic as possible. But we are all human as well, so you may find yourself on occasion justifying to yourself why you shouldn't take on a position when the method says you should. I certainly do. Reaching your full potential as a trader is an ongoing process that requires hard work and dedication.

Say that the signals you have been waiting for have now come into play. For those who are trading off a daily chart, once you are comfortable with the prospects for the trade, it is time to execute. As mentioned earlier, I use a combination of anticipation and confirmation methods to enter a position. However, there are a number of intraday dynamics that may affect this rule, so some discretion is needed when the time comes. As mentioned in the last section, my method combines these entry tactics to achieve a better-than-average price point. It incorporates the price targets on the pullbacks with the market, telling you it is time by breaking below the previous day's high or low.

A look at Chart 9.6 of the QQQ (the tracking stock for the Nasdaq 100) shows that traders were trying to short a market, which was rallying for six straight days, and as such, got crushed.

During this time, the market never once broke the previous day's lows, thereby not triggering a bona fide reversal pattern, which allowed a trader to commit a full position size. It was not until the market took out the previous day's lows that it actually pulled back enough to provide some money on the short side.

While using this one entry tactic alone will not allow you to commit your entire position to short at the top or buy at the bottom, this technique, coupled with the other tools in the One Shot – One Kill Method, allows you to intelligently and systematically enter trades with clearly defined risk-to-reward ratios.

SUMMARY

Taking on entries for trades in good spots is critical to making money. By using a combination of pullbacks to the 15 and 39

CHART 9.6

The Nasdaq 100 shows some solid strength and never breaks the previous day's low over a stretch of seven days.

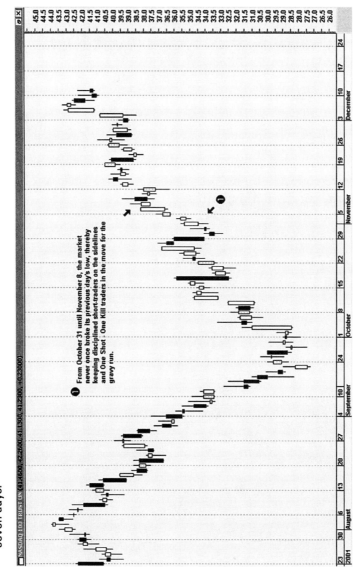

From October 31 until November 8, the market never once broke its previous day's low, thereby keeping disciplined short-traders on the sidelines and One Shot - One Kill traders in the move for the gravy run.

215

period moving averages, Fibonacci price points, trend lines and channels, as well as retests of former spots of support and resistance, you will be giving yourself the best chance to make money by entering at solid spots. The idea being that if you use these spots to enter on pullbacks, you should get enough of a bounce to at least cover the cost of the trade in most cases. If you do get stopped out, it's because the trend has probably reversed and not because you got in at a bad spot and were shaken out of the position prematurely.

The most important point that can be stressed in this chapter is to be patient, as succumbing to our impulses when it comes to taking on trades can get all of us in trouble. The collaboration of the above mentioned indicators should help improve your timing on your trades and help prevent bad impulsive trading from happening.

10

How to Exit a Trade, Lock in Profits, and Limit Losses

As discussed in Chapter 9, an amazing number of people have no problem whatsoever getting into a trade. They shine at that endeavor; it's the getting out that gives them fits. Having a smart, well-defined exit strategy is an integral part of the One Shot – One Kill Method.

This chapter will cover both the psychological and tactical hurdles inherent in exiting a position.

OVERVIEW OF EXITING A TRADE

In most normal markets, there is a natural order to how stocks and indexes move. Some people who trade for a living believe in letting their winners run. This is one approach that in a trending market can reward a trader handsomely. But it requires a higher degree of maintenance on your position in the form of lowering stops to trail the market. Other traders like to hold onto winners until they get up a certain percentage, then they take profits. The One Shot – One Kill Method incorporates both ideas. This topic is discussed in more detail on the One Shot –

One Kill Money Management Matrix at the end of this chapter, which will summarize some of the key points with regards to entering and exiting positions, using the tools you have learned to that point.

Throughout this book, the importance of price targets has been stressed. Taking your profits at predetermined points will greatly enhance your mindset and should increase the number of wins in your win-loss record. Getting into a trade with a clear understanding of where you will get out is crucial.

Because there are many criteria for exiting a trade, you need to remember when you enter a trade to make sure that a number of indicators are not already near the levels in which you would exit. If they are, your Netto Number should not be very strong. A better option would be to pass on the trade for the time being until it sets up better.

Having a good sense to exit a trade is something that will show up in the creation of your price targets, or Fibonacci grids, weapons of war, as well as the experience of trading. Simply reading a book and learning everything a trader needs to remember in order to trade successfully is very difficult, if not impossible. An individual must put forth his or her own best effort and time into the chosen endeavor to be successful.

I have mentored a number of students, who, through their actions, or lack thereof, have questioned whether or not they really need to put in the time and effort in order to be successful. They often ask if some software program is available that can do everything for them. With today's technological advances, software can help reduce time spent on the tasks quite a bit, but if successful trading were actually that easy, don't you think everybody would have found out by now? Trust me, there is no free lunch. However, some of us do pay a lot less for the same meal.

The best traders in the world have worked hard to get where they are today. They have also learned not to board the emotional roller coaster ride that the market and trading are. Instead, they take an unemotional sniper's-eye view with a figurative rifle in hand and take one shot to make one kill. This style seasons a trader for a lifetime of successful trading combat.

METHODS OF EXITING

There are a number of ways to exit a position that is going your way, or going against you—in the case of the latter, the sooner the better. The first part of this section is going to address how you can take profits from a position that is going your way. As you enter a trade, to some extent, you are also entering a battle of will with yourself, to control your emotional balance between greed and fear. This battle becomes more difficult to deal with when a position you take goes either in or out of your favor, much sooner or much greater than you expected, or both,

My first goal in a trade is to get the cost of the trade out of the way. There is a saying on Wall Street: "Bears make money. Bulls make money—and the pigs get slaughtered." I couldn't agree more, and the truthfulness of this statement is one of the reasons that I like to take the cost of the trade out, understanding that I will be getting back in on the next bounce. If the position continues to go my way, fine. However, maintaining consistent profits is the goal of this method.

Some traders who get blown out of a position at a major Fibonacci price target and watch it keep on going would feel the need to chase it. I actually get excited when this happens, because I understand that on the next bounce I am going to offer in more aggressively. For example, let's say you have a price target at a major level of Fibonacci support. The market sells down right through that level and keeps on falling. Some traders might feel upset that they covered half their position and couldn't enjoy the whole move down. I feel happy because the market is telling us that there is some strong underlying price movement—stronger than I initially anticipated—thereby allowing me to sell into the subsequent bounce more aggressively. The market will always give you a second chance. The real question is whether or not we as traders will be ready to execute on the opportunity.

The One Shot – One Kill Money Management Matrix, provides a base from which to work on how to scale in and out of positions. How successful the endeavor is ultimately comes down to the discretion and ability of the person trading the account. So, take the time to thoroughly comprehend the lessons in this book so you can take advantage of the daily plethora of profitable trading scenarios.

The next situation common to traders is getting into a trade that is unprofitable. If you follow the method of entry—scaling in at good spots and getting out when the position doesn't work out for you immediately—then in most cases you should have a chance to get out on a subsequent bounce.

For example, say I am looking to get long the Nasdaq futures after a rally from 945 to 970 by bidding into the move at 965, a spot where a rising 15-period MA is sitting on a three-minute chart. I get filled at 965 and put my stop at 958. The market doesn't have the legs to put in a bounce around the area of my entry, and it keeps going down to 960, with my stop only a few points away. After a 10-point pullback from either highs or lows, late retail traders come in and try to get part of the move. So on cue, the market will probably bounce to shake those guys out and take the move back to an area near my initial entry, around 963 to 965.

At this point in time, because I bid into the move and got a good price, I would consider blowing out of my position because even if it kept going higher, the fact that it didn't bounce where I wanted it to on my initial entry, in this case a rising 15-period MA, signifies that there might be a trend reversal. I can't say clearly if we are coming up to make a higher low or if we are going to challenge highs again. And since I don't have an ego when I trade, it makes more sense for me to blow out of it. If I sell into the bounce and it keeps going up, there is nothing lost, because I will probably have a chance to bid into the next pullback again at around the same price I offered into the move. This is how I manage positions if I have anticipated the move and bid into a pullback from highs or offered into a pullback from lows.

Suppose I get into a trade by waiting for it to take out the high of the bar. If it immediately works against me without being stopped out, then I am more inclined to let that one work for me and continue to follow my plan of attack. Of course, I would assume that I had a high Netto Number before getting into the trade. Getting whipsawed happens to even the best traders in the world. Managing risk should be your ultimate concern! And doing so correctly will effectively eliminate what I call *financial mood swings*.

Never worry about the direction of the market. It has never done me any good to do so. I focus only on my trades. Some of my most profitable trades have started out with me being in some serious pain, but since I was never stopped out, I stuck to my plan. Say you are in a trade in which your time frame is three to five days and after two days it is not profitable. Many traders get impatient and blow out of it before it was time. I encourage you to be patient and to follow your plan of attack. It is important to let these things develop.

SUPPORT AND RESISTANCE

Many different means can be used to determine when to exit a trade. Historical *support and resistance lines* can be very useful in the process of creating price targets. The One Shot – One Kill Method qualifies support and resistance in a couple of ways, with the first being an area where the stock has shown a tendency to consolidate in the past before breaking up or down. When stocks return to these areas, the likelihood exists that what was once resistance to an upward move is now support for a downward move.

While these points don't have as much significance as Fibonacci levels, many times there will be a confluence between historical support and Fibonacci support. If that is the case, then the movement of the stock may likely stall or reverse. Keep in mind that as a trader you want to be the like the "house" and keep the odds in your favor. If you observe and act upon these situations, by taking a series of predetermined profits based on sophisticated price targets, you will allow the big trades to eventually fall into your lap. On the other hand, if you are always trying to hit home runs, you will often strike out before even hitting a single. Look at Chart 10.1 and you will see that the Dow Jones Industrial Average bounced down from the 11,000 mark six times over an eight-month period before finally closing over 11,000.

When a level like 11,000 is continually being used as a point to turn away a market, a trader should take notice and possibly use this as a point to exit a trade. Even if you exit at a major his-

CHART 10.1

Key areas of support and resistance are great spots on the charts to take profits until they are finally broken through. They are also good spots to go long when they come back for a retest after breaking out to the upside and to go short when they come back after breaking down lower.

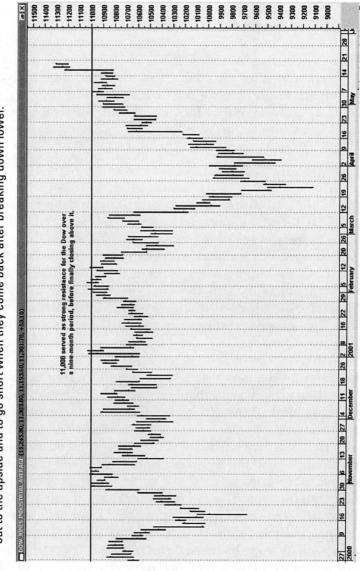

DOW JONES INDUSTRIAL AVERAGE (1) 245.80, 11,303.80, 11,193.60, 11,301.70, +53.10)

11,000 served as strong resistance for the Dow over a nine-month period, before finally closing above it.

torical support or resistance level and the market keeps moving in your favor but you have taken profits, there is no need to feel bad, as the market will probably pull back to that level one more time before making the next move up. Historical points of support and resistance can be very useful, especially if they coincide with Fibonacci support and resistance points.

FIBONACCI LEVELS AS EXIT POINTS

Fibonacci levels are specific points that highlight a likely area for the market to stall or reverse direction, as Chapter 4 detailed. Before getting into a trade, making yourself aware of strong areas of Fibonacci support or resistance. Taking a proactive approach and creating price targets is necessary for your success with the One Shot – One Kill Method, to make and take profits before your stock goes through a natural retracement.

In an earlier explanation of Fibonacci retracement and expansion analysis, you found that you should be looking for an area of Fibonacci Friends to appear *before* you take part or all of your profits. As you become more aware of Fibonacci resistance and support levels, you will find yourself competing for fills in ways that you are not used to. However, the market dynamics will go a long way in determining how much of the position you decide to take off the table.

In Chart 10.2, the stock for Taro Pharmaceutical (TARO) presented a great shorting opportunity, when it started to weaken after it made a lower high and took out the previous day's low, near the end of August.

The short-sell entry point was triggered at 42, with a protective stop sitting above 45. The stock followed suit and fell for the next 11 days before coming up to meet a bunch of Fibonacci Friends. The Fibonacci Friends were formed by an AB = CD expansion move down, and a .618 retracement from a previous move up. These two points sat within $1 of each other, and traders using the One Shot – One Kill Method were aware of these targets before they even initiated the short trade. The One Shot – One Kill method is based on putting together a roadmap of the investment vehicle you are trading so that you have

CHART 10.2

Patience is often the key to getting into good trades. Taro pulls back nicely off of its highs before rallying into a Fibonacci .618 retracement. This bounce provides a low-risk spot to get short and look to play the move down to the 27 area.

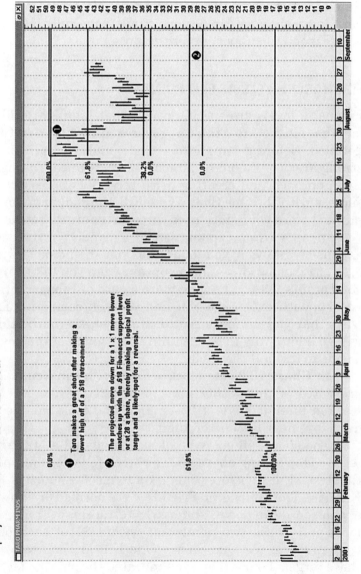

clearly defined risk parameters and price targets when entering a trade. Once you gain confidence in these targets, it becomes much easier to initiate exit strategies, as you are more aware of the probabilities of a reversal.

Wherever Fibonacci Friends meet, it is likely to be an important area and an important time to lock in some, if not all, of your profits. As a trader employing the One Shot – One Kill Method, you should have the understanding that these areas of Fibonacci Friends can lead to explosive, contramoves in the present trend. It is for this reason that using Fibonacci levels is one of the most proactive approaches to taking profits in trading. Being able to intelligently understand what is taking place, by observing and respecting these levels, will help keep you one step ahead of the market, and make your wallet heavier to lift.

HOW MOVING AVERAGES PLAY A ROLE IN TRADING

In trending markets, moving averages do a great job of keeping you in a trade for the bulk of most moves. As mentioned in Chapter 2, the 5-, 15-, and 39-period simple moving averages do a great job on any time frame of keeping you in a trade without being prematurely stopped out. However, as with all moving averages, there is a lag time for generating the signal. As a result, it has been my practice not to initiate a first position on the breakdown or breakout of any of these averages. Instead, I use it as a means of measuring the trend and keeping me in the trade once the move gets going.

Many people have heard the old trading maxim "cut your losers and add to your winners." The exact method to do this is still somewhat of a mystery to most people. Many traders I know who have tried this style of trading, only adding to their winners, discovered that, before they knew it, their winning trades had turned into losing trades because of how they added into the trade. The 15-period MA, coupled with a conglomeration of Fibonacci Friends, offers a low-risk area to add to a winning position. In my experience, I have found that if a move continues to go through the 15-period simple moving average, then there exists a strong possibility that a short-term trend reversal is in place. At that point, I need to get out of the position.

The worst discovery traders can make is to get into a trade and get stopped out only to find out that they were right. Be aware that no method is perfect at determining, in real time, whether a trend you are seeing is a trend reversal or a pullback. You need to put parameters in place so that you get stopped out of a trade only as a result of being wrong about the trade, not because you exposed too much risk with your stop. If the latter reason applies, it means you micromanaged your way out of the trade before it was time to do so.

As discussed in Chapter 2, the 39-period MA is very useful to quantify the longer-term trend in the time period that you are trading. When you are position trading something—that is, owning it for one to three weeks—you need to see where the daily 39-period MA is and keep a decent perspective on how things are shaping up. When day trading, you should always be aware of where the 39-period MA sits for the sector and market on an hourly basis. To recognize a trend change to the up side, watch for the vehicle to have two successive higher closes than the moving average; to recognize the down side, watch for two successive lower closes. If the move does not do this, then consider the trend to still be in play until it reaches its price targets. By using this objective means of assessing your positions, you can eliminate emotion from the equation and allow yourself to increase your profits in a very logical, systematic way.

Take a look at Chart 10.3, which shows movement of the Nasdaq 100 from April to October 2001. Using a 39-period MA, a trader trading with a short bias on a daily chart would have managed to prosper from the down trend that began on June 11.

This powerful, yet simple means of determining what the longer-term trend is serves as a powerful starting point before you embark on the trading day. Before implementing this kind of entry-and-exit strategy, you need to completely familiarize yourself with ways to implement this kind of trading comfortably. It recommend that you take your trading slowly at first while you become familiar and comfortable with the One Shot – One Kill Method. Once you gain confidence, you will be able to better manage your winning and losing trades.

CHART 10.3

Unlike the 15-period MA, which keeps you close to the action, the 39-period MA does a good job of keeping deeper pullbacks in check. It also often allows for a better assessment of the longer-term trend.

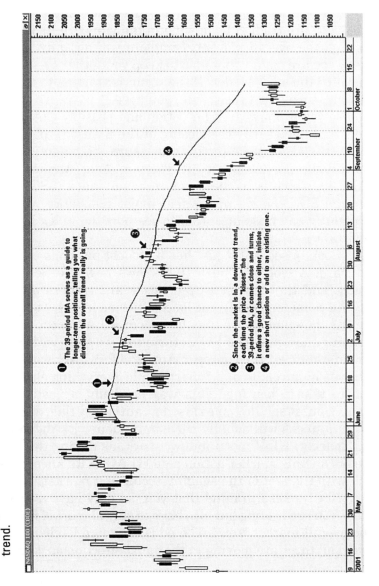

1 The 39-period MA serves as a guide to longer-term positions, telling you what direction the overall trend really is going.

2 Since the market is in a downward trend, each time the price "kisses" the

3 39-period MA, or comes close and turns, it offers a good chance to either, initiate

4 a new short position or add to an existing one.

227

EXITING BASED ON SECTOR AND MARKET CONDITIONS

The saying "a rising tide lifts all boats" is definitely applicable to the world of trading stocks. It is extremely important that the stock you are trading be moving in tandem with its industry sector and the overall market. I implore you not only to watch the stock you are trading but also to keep your other eye on the sector in which the stock trades. If the sector is starting to roll over, or if it comes up against resistance, you need to be aware of this situation so you are prepared for action and possibly exiting the position. (not necessarily the closing of the position). In general, the market is also a good proxy to measure the potential of a trend continuing. For example, if you are long Applied Materials (AMAT), which is in the Semiconductor Index ($SOX), and you see the SOX coming up against major resistance, you ought to prudently pay close attention to see how the index handles that resistance.

Look to see it if it just has a modest pullback or if it is sold off hard. A look at Chart 10.4 shows how the Semiconductor Index and the market tipped observant traders off that they should consider closing out long positions in order to protect the profits they had before they lost them. KLA-Tencor (KLAC) was rallying, however, the SOX started to weaken with the rest of the market over the course of April 2002. KLAC was still sitting near its highs on its daily chart, while everything else was starting to take a beating. This was no doubt a positive sign for KLAC, but it should have raised a cautionary flag, as most of the big-cap stocks will usually move in tandem with their sector and the market. KLAC soon followed suit, as during the next three weeks anemic market action sent KLAC to its knees, in sympathy with the rest of the sagging sector and market.

Always keep in mind that you not only have to monitor the stock you are trading but also have to stay abreast of its sector and the overall market trend. The odds are more likely in your favor when all three are moving in the same direction as your trade.

SETTING STOP-LOSSES

Every great general in combat is always aware of the risks before entering a battle. Again, let me stress: You, as a general of

CHART 10.4

A classic example of the importance of the correlation between the stock, its sector, and the overall market. KLA-Tencor (KLAC) was holding its own, until the weight of the overall market ultimately brought it down.

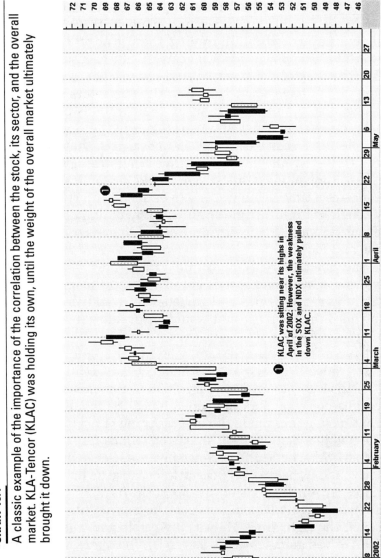

1 KLAC was sitting near its highs in April of 2002. However, the weakness in the SOX and NDX ultimately pulled down KLAC.

your capital, must *always* take a proactive approach to managing the risk behind both your positions and the exposure of your overall trading capital. Not setting your stop-losses (and immediately executing your trading plan once they are hit) is just as serious financially as you playing Russian roulette with yourself. That oversight is never worth it. In trading, there is no other safeguard as powerful at stopping a financial catastrophe as a stop-loss.

During the years I have covered the market, the most distressing thing I have heard from countless investors is that they don't have a stop-loss in place when their trade is being made. Now, there are as many trading strategies in the world as there are people, and this variability is one aspect that makes us unique. However, any trading or investing strategy without a viable risk control measure—for example, a stop-loss built into the trade—is a time bomb waiting to happen. Unfortunately, too many people get into a trade or an investment and do not have a predetermined loss limit they are willing to endure before they concede and move on.

A sad but true real-life example illustrates what happens when a risk control measure is not in place. Although this trading tale might seem wild and unbelievable, and that someone trading his or her own account would never allow this to happen to them, I assure you, it is true.

I have a friend named Sam, who in my opinion is not the greatest trader in the world, although he's a really nice guy. Back on the last day of February 2000 (I remember the exact day because of what has happened since) Sam called me and said that he had just made the biggest trade of his life.

He had just bought 2000 shares of Tellabs Inc. (TLAB) at a price of 457/8ths, or $45.875. Nowadays we use decimals.

On that day, he was very ecstatic, because he had bought all his shares within 15 cents of the low of the day.

He was bragging about how good he was at pulling the trigger at just the right time. He was invincible and was convinced that TLAB was going to go to $90 to $100 a share. Well, I told him that it might, and on that trade, he had made a good entry, a very good entry. The stock had hit close to a temporary bottom and, whether he knew it or not, the stock was about to move up very quickly.

Two trading days later he called me to let me know he was already up almost $7 a share. It didn't stop there. About a week later he called to let me know he was up over $11 a share, and a week after that, he was up almost $20 a share! He told me that although he had already made a lot of money on the trade it wasn't too late for me to get a piece of the action. The stock was now at almost $65 and he was convinced it was still moving up. I told him I'd sit this one out and wished him all the luck in the world. I didn't speak with him again till the beginning of summer that year and he told me he was still up in the trade and happy. I had no idea that he had not taken any profit from the trade as of yet. Over Christmas and New Year's, he still carried on about his stock.

In February 2001, coincidentally almost one year to the day after he made the trade, Sam moved. I didn't hear from him until a recent email he sent me in which he said he had never taken a penny's profit from the trade, nor did he ever have a stop-loss in place. At one time the stock was worth over $76 a share. At the time of this writing, because he had no stop-loss or clear profit objective in mind, Sam still owns the stock; however, now it is worth less than $10 a share. At least he didn't add to his position while the stock was falling.

I implore you to learn from his mistake before you learn from your own. Always immediately set your stop-losses with a clear profit objective in mind. *Always*. If you fail to do so, you should not allow yourself to trade your own account.

Stop-losses are what keep you in the game. No plan, system, or person is perfect when it comes to market prognostication. This occasional fallibility can be overcome with a system that keeps losses to a minimum, before they get out of control, and allows you to be around when times come for the big runs. There are a number of different ways, contingent upon the risk you are willing to endure and the time frame that you are trading under, that will help determine where you place your sell stop. The same techniques that got you into the trade are also going to be a factor in telling you where to get out. Setting appropriate stop-losses takes experience and practice. A lesson learned without the loss of capital puts you way ahead of the game.

The first rule, which has saved me during inevitable drawdown periods, is the *3 percent rule.* This holds that a trader should never risk more than 3 percent of the total value of the portfolio that he or she has. For example, if my portfolio is worth $50,000, I will set my stop-loss so that I can never lose any more than $1500 on any one given trade. This rule comes in very handy, as I, like all other traders, have gone through times of losing several trades in a row. The main reason I and many other experienced traders can trade for a living is that we keep our losses to a minimum, so that during our bad streaks we don't get wiped out.

Never get into a trade where the stop-loss is more than 3 percent of your portfolio. If this makes the stop too tight, then you need to lower your share size, so that you do not get knocked out of the game before you get started.

Always use the 3 percent rule. It will help you keep your portfolio diversified and prevent you from becoming married to a position because it takes up so much of your account. You will be able to cut your losses faster, if they never get that big to begin with. If the techniques in this book are properly applied, then protracted periods of drawdown will most likely be an infrequent occurrence. However, the inability to properly manage money leads to the quickest demise of new and experienced traders.

There are many more sophisticated money management strategies that are beyond the scope of this book. For some further information, I recommend reading a book by Josh Lukeman, called *The Market Maker's Edge.* (McGraw-Hill, 2000) and one by Ryan Jones called *The Trading Game: Playing by the Numbers to Make Millions* (Wiley, 1999).

MANAGEMENT MATRIX FOR WINNING AND LOSING POSITIONS

There are as many theories and styles in the trading world as there are traders. While many of these systems seem to make sense intuitively, they fall short when it comes to the bottom line. They also leave a vacuum of information on how to translate good theory into profitable trading. Up until this point, you have learned about Netto Numbers, Fibonacci Friends, moving averages, the TRI, and a whole host of other indicators, which can help you increase the profitability in your trading. However, it is the implementation of the One Shot – One Kill Money Management Matrix that should help you execute on the maxim "cut your losers as soon as they penetrate their limit, and not only ride your winners but add to them systematically as they continue to exhibit the tendencies which led you to trade them in the first place." This is extremely important part of the One Shot – One Kill Method. You really need to learn how to implement this matrix into your trading, to avoid poor execution of the plan. After all, poor execution of a good plan is about as useful as the good execution of a bad plan.

This book has discussed the necessity of creating highly probabilistic price targets, which will allow you to book your profits at points where the market stands to turn around. The One Shot – One Kill Money Management Matrix will provide you with an objective way to capitalize on both directions of a strongly trending market. It does so by having you enter relatively small positions, thereby risking a small percentage of the account, with the intent of taking on much larger size without ever risking more than the initial amount. If you have any questions about the method, please visit the One Shot – One Kill Trading Web site, at www.oneshotonekilltrading.com, for some further information. But first, you need to thoroughly familiarize yourself with the matrix and how it works. So, read the following paragraphs carefully. Having a strong knowledge is imperative in understanding how to correctly implement the matrix.

The matrix is based on being able to move in and out of a position in quarters. With that being said, since most of the book has focused on Nasdaq stocks, or the NDX itself, I will use the Nasdaq E-mini to illustrate how the matrix would be applied to managing positions.

Since you are going to work in and out of the positions in quarters, for the sake of this explanation, you will use four contracts, which at the time of this writing is equivalent to 3200 shares of the QQQ, the tracking stock for the Nasdaq 100, as the base for your positions, moving the contract size up as you go. This matrix can apply to any number of investment vehicles. For example, instead of using 4 contracts, you can trade 400 shares, or 4000 shares. You can even trade 200 shares of a stock and divide by a quarter, to move in and out of 50 shares per trade. The idea is to take on trades with a limited amount of your portfolio exposed, with the potential of catching a strong trend and realize appreciable gains.

Let's assume that you have a $40,000 futures account. At the time of this writing, this would allow you to carry about nine contracts overnight, and day trade about 18 contracts with an initial margin of roughly $4100 for an overnight position and $2050 for a day trade.

Initiating the First Position

Upon receiving the first buy signal, you would initiate a long trade for four contracts at 1600 on the Nasdaq 100 E-mini futures (NQ), as shown in Chart 10.5. On this trade, you would risk no more than 5 points, or $400, being that one point on a Nasdaq E-mini is equivalent to $20 ($4 \times 5 \times 20 = 400$), or approximately 1 percent of the $40,000 account. If the position goes against you and you lose 5 points, then you get stopped out, take your loss, and move on. This is actually the simplest and fastest scenario, with the possibilities only getting more involved and complex from here.

If the position goes your way 5 points, then you will cut the first contract at 1605 and raise your stop to breakeven—that is, 1600—as this will allow you to book a partial profit. Really, you are letting the position work for you and give you the peace of mind of knowing that in most cases the worst you can do is make a little money on the trade. The next step, after cutting a quarter of the position and raising the stop to breakeven, is to ready yourself to sell half of your position, two contracts, or two-thirds of your remaining position, at your profit target. In this case, you had a predetermined profit target of 1615. The market hits 1615 and you clean out the other two positions and have now realized a profit of $100 on the first contract and $600 on the other two contracts, and you are still letting one position run, which has an unrealized gain of $300.

CHART 10.5

The first part of the One Shot – One Kill Money Management Matrix calls for you to initiate your first position with a 4 lot and lock in some profits after you get a move in your favor.

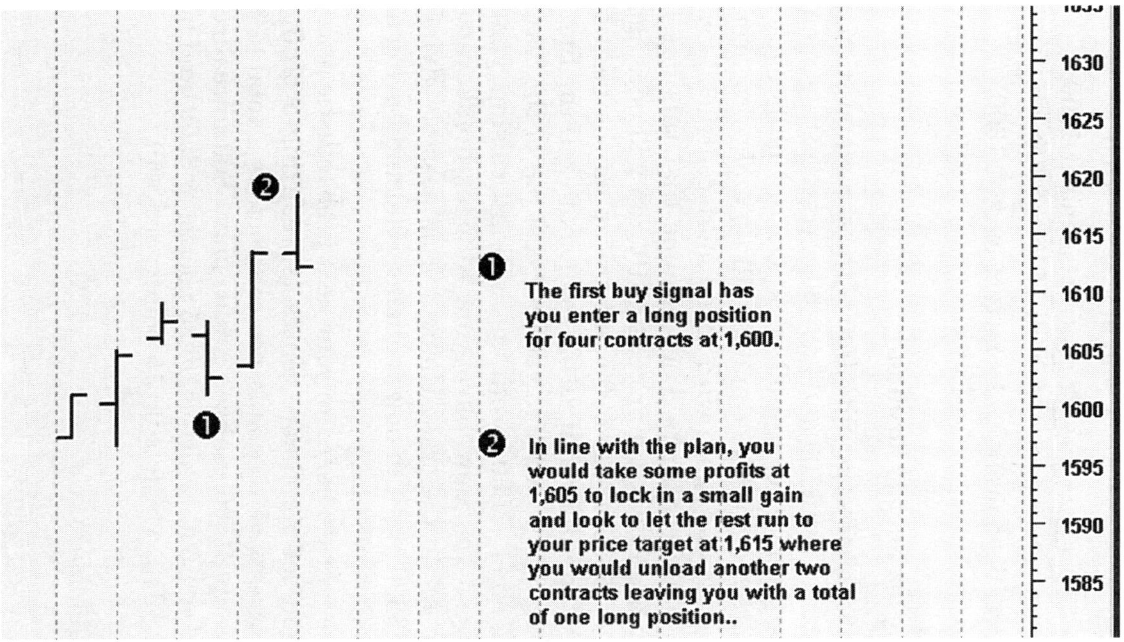

❶ The first buy signal has you enter a long position for four contracts at 1,600.

❷ In line with the plan, you would take some profits at 1,605 to lock in a small gain and look to let the rest run to your price target at 1,615 where you would unload another two contracts leaving you with a total of one long position...

SHORT SUMMARY

Realized profit   1 contract long at 1600,
                       sold at 1605 = $100
                       2 contracts long at 1600,
                       sold at 1615 = $600
Unrealized profit   1 contract long at 1600

Initiating the Second Position

Chart 10.6 shows the initiation of the second position. Now that you have booked $700 and have a contract sitting open, you will wait for the market to pull back. Once it pulls back and your indicators tell you the trend is still up and to reenter, you will hit the long side again with seven more contracts, giving you a total of eight contracts. Let's assume that this has happened and you are filled at a price of 1610. You will once again risk 5 points, or $800 of the $900 you are up on the position to that point. After entering at 1610, you look to sell the first two contracts at 1615 in order to get your cost out of the way. You also book a quick $200 profit as well as raising your stop to breakeven. You now have your stop at breakeven, and the prospective on the trade changes from possibly giving up $800 of your $900 profit to now realizing $900 and having an unrealized profit of $800.

The market heads to your next probabilistic price target of 1625. You sell four more contracts, realizing a profit on those four contracts of 15 points per contract, or a total of $600. You are now up $1500 realized profit, plus $800 unrealized (long 1 contract at 1600, which is up 25 points, or $500, and long 1 contract at 1610, which is up 15 points, or $300).

SHORT SUMMARY

Realized profit
First Leg
        1 contract long at 1600, sold at 1605 = $100
        2 contracts long at 1600, sold at 1615 = $600

CHART 10.6

As you continue to add to your winning positions on successive pullbacks, the final target occurs as you then clean out your slate of positions.

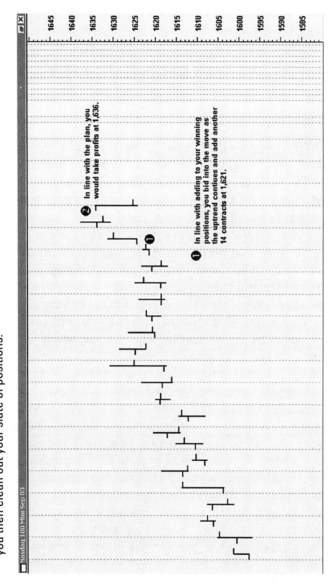

Nasdaq 100 Mini Sep 03

2 In line with the plan, you would take profits at 1,636.

1 In line with adding to your winning positions, you bid into the move as the uptrend contiues and add another 14 contracts at 1,621.

1645
1640
1635
1630
1625
1620
1615
1610
1605
1600
1595
1590
1585

Second Leg
>   2 contracts long at 1610, sold at 1615 = $200
>   4 contracts long at 1610, sold at 1625 = $1200

Unrealized profit
>   1 contract long at 1600 = +$500
>   1 contract long at 1610 = +$300

Initiating the Third Position

Chart 10.7 shows the initiation of the third position. You have now booked $2100 and have $800 in unrealized profits sitting on the table. There have been two nice moves up, and you are going to let this run its course until your indicators tell you the time has reversed. Remember, it is not the purpose of this section to explain all of the indicators but rather to provide a good working knowledge of how the numbers work. You can then understand the concept behind booking some of your winnings while letting some of your position ride.

Once again, you will wait for a pullback to your support levels before really gauging whether or not you will hit this big—with an additional 14 contracts—thereby allowing you to have 16 contracts on the long side.

The market does pull back and gives you another buy signal, allowing you to enter the order for 14 contracts at 1621, with a profit target at 1636. You have a 5-point stop and are presently up $2100 unrealized and $640 realized, thereby making a total of $2740. Upon entering, you put your stop 5 points below your entry, thereby risking $1600 of your $2740. Many people are uncomfortable doing this, as the prospect of surrendering that much of their gains causes them to lose sleep. This disinclination is natural, as most people have a hard time letting their winners work for them. The temptation to book quick cash from a trade that is working and let a losing trade run takes to heart our most innate human emotions. However, keep in mind that you will only do this if the One Shot – One Kill Method says the trend is still strongly in place.

As with the first two legs, you will take out a quarter of the position at the breakeven point at 1626, and most people can

CHART 10.7

In line with the maxim of adding to your winners, after you blow out of the trade the first time, you then wait to reload when the market pulls back, get long again with the same idea as the first trade.

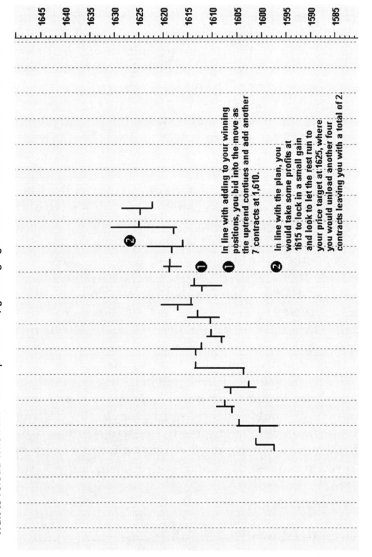

❶ In line with adding to your winning positions, you bid into the move as the uptrend contiues and add another 7 contracts at 1,610.

❷ In line with the plan, you would take some profits at 1615 to lock in a small gain and look to let the rest run to your price target at 1625, where you would unload another four contracts leaving you with a total of 2.

breath a sigh of relief, because they know that this is where it gets really fun. With this profit, you have now booked another $400 bringing your total realized profit to $3140 and unrealized to $1840. You will set your order to sell the remaining 12 contracts at your price target of 1636. If this target is reached, then you will take all of your profits at that point. Should this scenario come to fruition, this account would realize a total of $6740, or nearly 17 percent of its portfolio, while risking only 1 percent at the onset of the initial trade. Knowing this has helped me and other One Shot – One Kill traders stay out of losing trades and let winning trades work for us. We normally don't press our luck after three moves, unless there is a major surge in the market. However, after a move like this, you would typically begin to look the other way for a more defined pullback.

This is a hypothetical situation intended for you to understand the tenets of the One Shot – One Kill Money Management Matrix. There are, of course, many times when you would not add on 12 contracts to the final leg, but would only find it suitable to add on another four to eight, as the move may have become really extended and a deeper pullback is more plausible. This move started at 1600 on the Nasdaq futures and pulled back three times on its way to 1636, a nice 36-point move. Properly managed, it could have allowed you to increase your account by nearly 17 percent while only risking 1 percent. This is the power of leverage, when it is used correctly and responsibly.

Many people use leverage when they first get into a position and are biting their nails, hoping the position works out. Margin is a double-edged sword, which has destroyed many traders whom did not respect it, nor had a coherent plan to use it. If you only use margin to help capitalize on winning positions, then you stand less of a chance of suffering a major setback.

SHORT SUMMARY

Realized profit

First Leg   1 contract long at 1600,
sold at 1605 = $100

2 contracts long at 1600,
sold at 1615 = $600

Second leg   2 contracts long at 1610,
                  sold at 1615 = $200

                  4 contracts long at 1610,
                  sold at 1625 = $1200

Third Leg   4 contracts long at 1621,
                  sold at 1626 = $400

                  10 contracts long at 1621,
                  sold at 1636 = $3000

Contracts from Previous Two Legs

1 contract long at 1600, +$720
1 contract long at 1610, +$520

	Contracts	Open	Close	Profit
First leg	4	4		
Positive 5 pts.			1	$100
At price target			2	$600
Second Leg	8			
Positive 5 pts.				$200
At price target				$1,200
Third leg	16	14		
Positive 5 pts.			4	$400
At price target			12	$4,240
Total Profit				**$6,740**

Total profit from trade: $6740 before commissions and slippage.

This is a hypothetical situation intended for you to grasp a basic feel of the One Shot – One Kill Money Management Matrix. Use of the indicators and techniques in the One Shot – One Kill Method will tell you whether or not the pullback you are seeing is a reversal or a relaxation in the present trend.

From this example, it is easy to see the power of letting good positions work for you while getting rid of losers fast. As your familiarity with the One Shot – One Kill Money Management Matrix increases, you can get into more sophisticated money management strategies, incorporating things like sector strength, how broad the rally is, and other indicators that tell you how aggressive to be when adding to positions. But this simple-yet-effective means of entering positions should help you effectively manage your winners while keeping losers to a minimum.

SUMMARY

The method of exiting positions carries with it a number of similarities as entering positions do. Using Fibonacci price points, retests of support and resistance, as well as extreme levels of overbought when you are long, and oversold when you are short, provide good spots to take profits from your respective long and short positions in the market. While it is great to book profits at these levels, the possibility of getting stopped out of positions exists as well. For this reason, it is imperative that you never forget that first and foremost you must manage risk as a trader; failure to do so can be devastating. This chapter also went over the Money Management Matrix, which provides a means of using a solidly trending market to enter and exit positions at key spots, while using the profits from the previous trades, to lay into the next trades with larger position size, thereby effectively using one solid move to reap tremendous profits. While these setups don't come everyday, being ready for them when volatility increases can have a tremendous impact on a trader's profit and loss statement.

CHAPTER 11

The Importance of Eliminating Mistakes

Let's start out this section with a reality check on why it is important to be just a little bit better than the next person at what you do. To illustrate the point, let's look at baseball. In baseball, being a .200 hitter means that every 10 times you are up at bat, you get two hits. Three hits out of 10 makes you a .300 hitter. In the big leagues, just as in life, there is a big difference between a .200 hitter and a .300 hitter. In Major League Baseball, a .300 hitter gets paid about $5 million a year to play and deal with the hassles of being a megastar, whereas a .200 hitter is either playing on some farm team in Duluth, for lunch money, or making a hard and fast self-realization about his ability and moving on to a more suited career, like selling insurance. All this fuss because of the difference of just one hit in every 10 at bats. You, no doubt, truly want to be a good trader who turns learning how to trade successfully into a great way of life, not settling for being a .200 hitter.

If I thought that goal was unattainable, I never would have begun the task of writing this book and sharing the information within its pages. Anyone can learn to use the One Shot – One Kill method. But the lack of discipline in using it often causes a trader's downfall. You would probably agree that a big mistake would be for you to begin trading at all without a sound game plan. And, if you decided on a plan but refused to stick to it, you would also be making a mistake. Likewise, if you have a poor plan and a strong conviction to it, you are making yet another mistake. The odds can seem to be against you right from the start.

The essence of this section is to convince you that, in order to trade profitably, you must eliminate as many mistakes from your plan as you can. You must understand that mistakes are too easy to come by in this business. So, don't plan on lackadaisically riding shotgun. You must be sober and in the driver's seat, ready to hit the gas or the brakes at any moment. This is not to say that if you are in a losing trade, you must have made a mistake to get there. But you must, upon entering a trade, even at a bad entry point, *proactively* manage your position correctly.

I and every good trader I know have made all of these mistakes at least once and, in most cases, a lot more than once. There is no shame in doing so, as I believe a right of passage to becoming a truly great trader is to feel pain from your mistakes. The hubris of most individuals usually puts them at a disadvantage when they try to trade the markets profitably. However, I encourage you to relax a little when reading this chapter and think about your own experiences and anecdotes while listening to my mistakes.

Other than that, fending off mistakes that drift into your mind is not a hard feat to overcome. A very strong trading method is developed in this book, and your job is to follow and eventually master it. (If you can do that, as a rule, you will not make mistakes.) You will always be able to spot a potential mistake beforehand and, by following your plan, you will know what is the right thing to do. What you actually choose to do at that point is what will ultimately define your success as a trader.

FIGHTING THE TREND

Some successful contrarian traders out there do make money fading the market and going against the crowd over short periods of time. Since *trend* is a relative term contingent upon what time frame you are using, it is important that you have the trend in your favor before you get started. Fighting the trend is akin to stepping in front of a freight train coming at you at 100 miles per hour. I sure as heck don't want to get in the way.

Intel Corporation (INTC) was caught in a nasty down trend from September through October 2000 (see Chart 11.1). The stock kept moving lower.

Some of my less-experienced trader friends began buying the stock based on the daily charts, telling themselves that it just *had* to go back up. They completely disregarded the underlying trend for the daily chart, the time frame that they were trading on. The stock kept moving down until after hours the company came out with a report that they were going to miss earnings, causing the stock to gap down $11 the morning after the announcement. It was ugly. My mother gave me a call that day and told me of the bad news of her "investment" that she had made just two days earlier. She had told me she had bought INTC at 66 just two days earlier, and now with it trading at 48, she didn't know what to do. She could not believe that she could lose her money that fast. I felt sorry for her and told her to dump it and cut her losses and consider it a lesson learned.

In April 2000, the Nasdaq took one of its largest haircuts ever. People were fighting with each other to get out of the door (see Chart 11.2). I ran into people who were accustomed to "buying the dip." These people either had ignored or just didn't understand the signals that the market was giving off at the time. People had taken out second mortgages on their homes to buy more stock as the market fell.

Nonetheless, the numbers indicated that this might be the start of a more substantive down trend. Needless to say, it ended up that many people who had made a ton of money from the previous years had lost all of that and then some during that ominous April, because they ignored the underlying trend.

In December 1999, a number of traders thought the market could not continue with its November pace and decided that they were going to short the market (see Chart 11.3). The rationale for their decision was that the market was overbought and it had to come back down again. These traders got greedy, as whatever

CHART 11.1

Intel (INTC) gets hit with some quite violent selling as bargain hunters who came in got beat up pretty good.

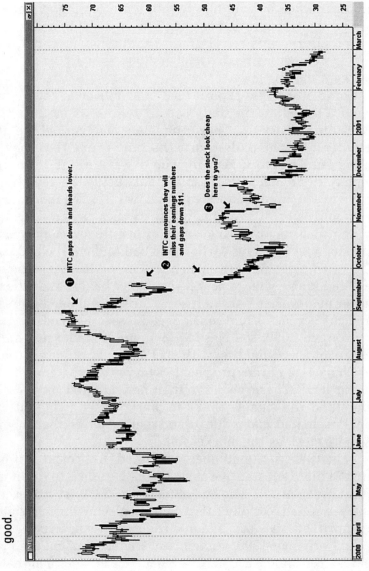

1. INTC gaps down and heads lower.

2. INTC announces they will miss their earnings numbers and gaps down $11.

3. Does the stock look cheap here to you?

CHART 11.2

The importance of avoiding mistakes as a trader can't be stressed enough. In the case of this chart, many people who tried to fight the down trend got crushed.

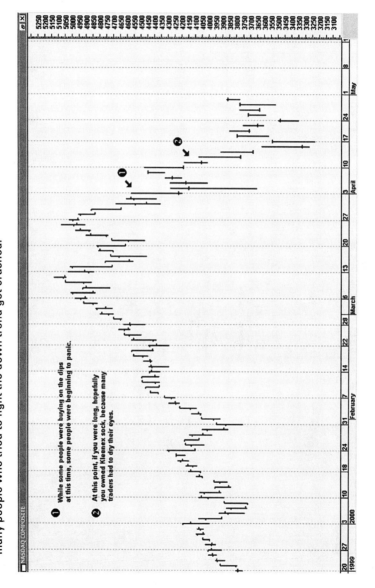

❶ While some people were buying on the dips at this time, some people were beginning to panic.

❷ At this point, if you were long, hopefully you owned Kleenex sock, because many traders had to dry their eyes.

CHART 11.3

Possibly the most difficult part of trading is the seductive nature of calling a top or calling a bottom. Leaving your emotions at the door is very important.

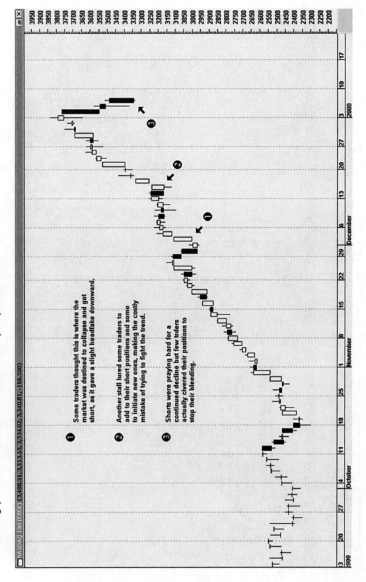

1. Some traders thought this is where the market was destined to collapse and got short, as it gave a slight headfake downward.

2. Another stall lured some traders to add to their short positions and some to initiate new ones, making the costly mistake of trying to fight the trend.

3. Shorts were praying hard for a continued decline but few traders actually covered their positions to stop their bleeding.

went up had to come down, according to them. Unfortunately for them and for the rest of us, the market doesn't care what any of us think; it is going to do what it wants.

Fighting a strong underlying trend in the time frame that you are trading is a very difficult way to make a living. This is not to say that you cannot play reversals. You have been given the tools in the last 10 chapters to help you distinguish between a trend that has truly reversed and one that is still strong.

At the risk of oversimplifying this matter, a good rule of thumb to use when attempting to ascertain the trend in whatever time period you are trading is to see where the underlying trading vehicle is relative to its 5-, 15-, and 39-period MAs. If it is sitting above all of those, then the trend is probably up and shorting should be kept to a minimum. The opposite should happen for a market moving down. The bottom line is that there are cases to be made for taking on countertrend trades. But the skill and experience necessary to pull them off makes them difficult to play. For trading stocks, see where the respective sector is sitting relative to its 5-, 15-, and 39-period MAs as well as to the overall market. That's a quick and easy way to see how things are stacking up.

LOVING YOUR LOSERS

Every investor and trader has made losing investments and losing trades at one time or another, and the smart ones know they will make losing ventures in the future, as well. It's a hard fact in every trader's life. No system, method, style, strategy, or trading tactic can keep you immune. The One Shot – One Kill Method, if followed correctly, will not allow you to sink your ship or become devastated by a single loss. A losing trade should be looked at as just another cost of doing business, because that's what it truly is. However, once you determine that you are wrong about a trade, don't get the idea of greedily adding more to your position to "better" your average entry price. At times scaling into a position, based on certain setups, can enhance a trader's returns; however, the majority of investors do not have the skill or discipline to consistently profit from doing this. There is a sound reason why this method does not partake in this practice. It's a simple, yet powerful premise, which needs to be discussed here and soon become part of your trading regimen.

Let's start by saying that a necessary and important distinction must first be made. Sending a specified amount of money off to a mutual fund every month is completely different than speculating that a stock will go up after it has already gone down. Why would you decide that it would be a smart action to buy more? Just to lower your overall cost? Too often it's an emotional problem without logic becoming involved.

A trader friend of mine (who now carries a much lighter wallet) used the good old "Fire Sale" logic to make a trade in CMGI, Inc. (CMGI). Take a look at Chart 11.4. This stock would eventually fall off of its horse, from about $160 per share to about a price of just $2.

At first glance, the Fire Sale logic might seem to be correct. If something was priced 10 or 20 times higher just a few months before and is now "on sale" at ridiculous lows, then why not step in at such an opportune time and make a sizable investment? It just seems so right. As you will hopefully learn from reading this book, stocks that halve can halve again and again. You need to have much more than a bargain hunter's mentality behind a decision for buying a stock.

Getting back to my friend, this was just the first bad part of his trade. He initially went long in the stock at 32. The trade immediately moved against him and fell to 28, as he did nothing. Then, a few weeks later it fell further, to 25. He had no stop-loss in place and no clear time frame as to when or how he would get out of the trade. He just thought the stock was going to rise.

He decided that since the stock couldn't go any lower (akin to fighting the trend), he would buy more of the stock on margin. The stock dropped to 20. He bought more on margin. A few weeks later the stock dropped to 17. He loaded up again, truly believing that this was the only way he could save himself. The 3 percent rule had now turned into the 30 percent rule. A few weeks later, the stock was trading at 12. Of course, *at this price* he just *had* to buy more. It was screaming, Buy right now! There was no way this stock could fall any further. To make matters worse, he saw an analyst on CNBC say that CMGI could be trading at $100 a

CHART 11.4

CMGI was another nightmare that never ended for a lot of people.

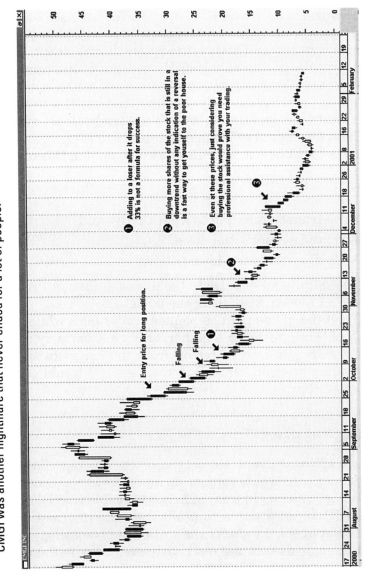

① Adding to a loser after it drops 33% is not a formula for success.

② Buying more shares of the stock that is still in a downtrend without any indication of a reversal is a fast way to get youself to the poor house.

③ Even at these prices, just considering buying the stock would prove you need professional assistance with your trading.

Entry price for long position.

Falling

Falling

CMGI INC

251

share in a year or so. So he bought more. The stock went down to $8 a share and, as I had been doing since the stock was at 22, I pleaded with him to, if not sell everything, substantially reduce his exposure.

This unbridled trading binge, on one stock alone, turned a one-time nice guy and buddy into an emotional wreck. His relationships with people changed. He became a different person. This "Trader's Tuition," to some extent, is a necessary rite of passage for most people who become traders. His lesson from this educational experience, on this one trade alone, could have paid for a four-year Ivy League degree.

Let's count how many rules he broke on just this one trade:

1. He fought the trend.
2. He added to his loser.
3. He traded according to what CNBC said.
4. He did not set a stop-loss.
5. He did not control his emotions.

These are a lot of rules to break during five *full seasons* of trading, let alone just chasing one trade!

Trust me, if you plan on being a trader for a while and you put all of those mistakes together, or even separately into your trading plan, you'd be better off from the get-go to stick with only trading baseball cards. But, then again, I wouldn't even be sure about that.

TRADING THE NEWS

As part of the current stereotype of the average day trader, many Americans would conjure up an image of someone fraught with anxiety, sitting in front of her or his cable television watching CNBC, in an attempt to profit from the information being spewed out about the stocks the station is presenting.

Economic data comes out nearly every day in the markets. Before a number comes out there is usually an expected number. For example, the ISM Index comes out with an expected number of 52. Whether the news appears to be good or not should have little concern to you as a trader, as many times the price action following that would not seem "logical" based on how the number either beat or fell short of expectations. In fact, if the numbers should lead to a healthy rally after coming in stronger than expected, and they don't, that can serve as a head's up for a potential reversal. As a trader, you need to focus on the price action, as markets can rally on bad news or good news, or sell on bad news or good news. The main thing this method is looking for following a news announcement is for an underlying trend to emerge—if it is down, sell the rallies; if it is up, buy the dips. Keeping things that simple provides clarity in the field of battle and makes executing that much easier.

Stock recommendations are another thing with which traders and investors alike can get caught up after they watch various market pundits spout their knowledge. Understand that buying a stock recommendation based on what a guest on TV or radio says can be a very dangerous propensity. Doing so is akin to buying a stock because a friend tells you his sister is dating a guy who sits in the next cubicle from a guy who knows something fantastic about the stock that nobody is supposed to know but, whatever it is, it's good news, and everybody "in the know" is buying big.

This example may seem far-fetched, but situations like this happen every day across America. Television networks are usually very explicit in telling their viewers to do their own research before making any investment decision, but many people still end up making trades without thoroughly checking them out correctly. And, of the ones who do, many do not follow a proven trading method while in the trade.

Traders need to keep in perspective while trading the markets throughout the day is that much of what news stations report and present is from a fundamental analysis perspective. Fundamental catalysts move the market. But the techniques presented in the One Shot – One Kill Method are going to give you the tools to be a free-thinking trader, one who can independently analyze the market and act on those analyses. It's always best to understand both sides of a trading opportunity, and it never hurts to get another perspective, but the sole place to get an opinion is not from some market expert—or anyone else, for that matter. Only after doing your own analysis and applying it to your method should you ever enter a trade, because ultimately *you* are the responsible party.

A number of news stations and journals, in April 2000, paraded analysts and fund managers on their show, who told everyone to buy on the dips and stated that the current selloff was just normal market behavior. They were saying this while the volume showed that clearly institutional selling was going on and the chart formation clearly showed a double top, both of which are incredibly negative. Caveat Emptor always applies when it comes to the financial markets, so be aware and be cautious whenever you hear a tip from anyone. By using the method in this book, you will be able to ascertain for yourself how viable an investment opportunity really is. I hope you will live long enough to discover what all those who make it as traders have already discovered, that a well-thought-out plan of attack is crucial and the charts usually don't lie.

CHASING STOCKS

One of the mistakes that novice traders and even seasoned professionals make is chasing stocks that are moving up very quickly and entering the trade but not at the right time. It can be extremely frustrating when a trader wants to go long on a stock and, for some reason, can't get filled. As the stock price continues to rise, the traders' frustration grows and they begin to up their bid for the stock, feeling that the stock will not ever come back down. Keep this in mind, if you should be so lucky as to be in this situation. Good stocks are like good women or men; more than likely they will come back and give you a second chance to make good. So, be prepared. Stocks don't go from 30 to 100 in one day. A stock that is going to make that kind of huge move will usually run for a while, pull back, consolidate, and then run again.

Chasing after stocks can be very hazardous to your profitability in that, by the time most people decide they will buy a stock, the intermediate run is usually over with. Use the indicators presented in this book to determine whether or not the stock is overbought before you enter. Or take the more advisable route and watch the pullback and see just how much strength the upward movement on the stock has. Using the One Shot – One Kill Method will help prevent you from chasing overbought stocks and give you the chance to get in on the meat of the trend.

At times, of course, not chasing a stock will cause you to miss out on a huge run. But being successful at trading requires an incredible amount of patience and discipline, as well as the knowledge of knowing that these situations regularly occur and are all part of the big picture of a trader's world. Every day, you will miss thousands of money-making opportunities, but if you become a good trader, you will still find enough of those good trades every day to retire in style.

NOT SETTING STOP-LOSSES

You would be very foolish if during any trading you failed to set even one stop-loss. After getting into a trade, there is no escaping the fact that you must immediately become a risk manager. Your job as a risk manager has only one duty, one responsibility. It demands that you protect your troops in battle. Failure to set stop-losses and limit exposure can have serious consequences to a trader and usually happens sooner rather than later.

Contrary to what you may have been told by some self-proclaimed stock market gurus, there is no such thing as a perfect system. So, everybody at some time is going to be wrong with a portion of his or her trades. Without a stop-loss in place, you could win 19 out of 20 trades and still be down money. That would be an unfortunate occurrence, but one with a recognizable cause. It happens simply because, as a rule, bad traders do not take seriously enough, nor do they completely understand, the importance of setting a stop-loss.

I have recently been in several heated debates with money managers, who, in my opinion, use some of the most flawed risk management logic I have ever heard. I posed a question to a number of money managers and brokers during a recent investment symposium and asked this question, "If your clients would have bought Microsoft at $120 a share, at what point in time would you have told them to get out?" I even gave these professionals the benefit of hindsight, to help them out, in order to see what kind of risk managers they were with their clients' accounts. A number of them said that they would hold on to the stock because it was a good company and admitted that they wouldn't have put any stop-loss in place. This strategy seems intuitive to most people who follow the market. However, what the managers didn't address in their answer is that Microsoft, which had fallen off its high of 120, and was currently trading around 60, would need to earn approximately 20 percent, compounded annually for almost four years, just to get their clients' initial invest back! Twenty percent would be a healthy move for a company with as big a market capitalization as a Microsoft.

The point is that failure to take proper risk control tactics can have drastic consequences. It always seems we hear about the other guy who bought a stock at its high and now is trading it for one-tenth of its purchase price. He does so probably because he did a poor job of risk control and did nothing from letting a bad situation get worse. If you take only one thing from this book, let that be to *aggressively manage your risk*. That does not mean you need to hypertrade; it just means you should set reasonable stop-losses based on the techniques in this book and stick to them. You will notice drastic differences by getting rid of your losing trades quickly, before they become huge loss anecdotes that make for frustrating memories.

With the discipline to exercise proper money management, you can make money regularly. Always remember that the number-one reason that traders lose small and large fortunes is because they do nothing in the face of danger. They don't act or react like trading soldiers of war. Soon, each open trade becomes like a cancer that is too big to carry in their stomachs any longer, and at great cost it must be cast away.

The following bears repeating: One of the biggest reasons traders go broke is because they fail to manage risk on every trade—and because they fail to act if their stop-loss is hit. The way to prevent this from happening to you is actually quite easy. You simply never trade without putting a stop-loss in place as soon as you enter a trade. If and when a stop-loss triggers an alarm, don't reset the alarm to a new price and hope the stock doesn't move closer to it. Rid yourself of the position and move on.

TRADING DURING CONSOLIDATION

For the One Shot – One Kill Method, *consolidation* is defined as sideways movement of greater than eight bars. During this time, if a trend has not emerged, then an indefinite period of time may elapse before anything ever emerges. And which way it eventually will emerge is truly a crapshoot. Using the One Shot – One Kill Method you will not feel the need to force trades, which will lead you to trade into consolidation. Always stay with trending markets and get out of trades that consolidate six to eight periods, so that they don't have time to go against you. The purpose of using my method is to put the odds in your favor, and consolidating stocks offers only a 1 out of 3 chance of success. Those odds are never in your favor, and that is why the trading-in-consolidation philosophy is not part of my method.

As a manager of money in the market, you need to understand that the probability of your stock's moving further in your favor is only 1 out of 3. Playing the trend is the best way to profit from the market on a consistent basis. There are, of course, successful contrarian investors out there, who pick and choose their spots to fade the short-term trend.

Trading in consolidation is not conducive to creating financial wealth. After factoring in commissions and slippage, overall, trading in consolidation can be difficult to profit in. Take a look at the daily chart for General Electric (see Chart 11.5).

An attempt to guess the direction of future movement from the daily chart is not the kind of high-probability trading the One Shot – One Kill Method espouses. There are a number of reasons why this is so. For one, it costs you time, by tying your money up. Remember, your stock is currently in consolidation, and you don't know how long it is going to stay that way. For another, and more importantly, it costs you money. It does so because, while your money is just sitting in consolidation in some ho-hum stock, you could have had it hard at work for you in other strongly trending stocks.

CHART 11.5

Trading during times of consolidation can be very difficult in getting a sense of where things are going and should be avoided until the energy returns to the market.

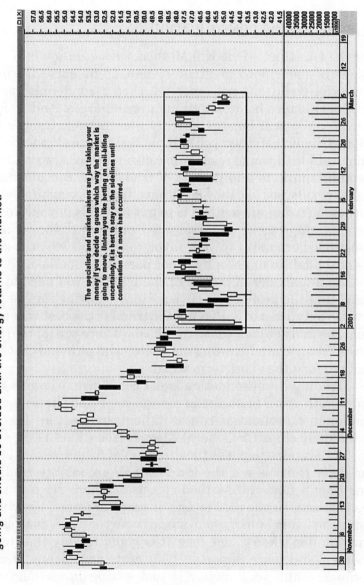

The specialists and market makers are just taking your money if you decide to guess which way the market is going to move. Unless you like betting on nail-biting uncertainty, it is best to stay on the sidelines until confirmation of a move has occurred.

Chart 11.6 is another example showing a choppy Nasdaq market.

NOT CONTROLLING EMOTIONS

Every good publication on trading stocks I have read addresses the importance of a person's psychology when she or he makes a trading decision. That topic has been covered well in other chapters of this book. But I firmly believe there is one lasting derivative a trader must live with *after* making every trade, aside from the hard money earned or lost, and that is her or his ongoing emotional mindset. I urge you to read this chapter with the utmost seriousness and regard its lesson with reverence. Maintaining an even keel, whether you experience a huge win or loss, is such an important part of trading, that I implore you to always keep yourself in emotional check.

The essence of buying and selling stocks is the understanding of the brutal relationship between greed and fear. That truly is the underlying reason stock prices move as they do. An ability to remove yourself from the fog of war and think clearly and intelligently, based on the study you have done and the training you have received, will give you a decided edge in the combat arena of the financial markets. I have seen far too many traders act like they were "golden" when they hit a few good trades in a row. Likewise, I saw others who beat themselves up for losing a few in a row, and sometimes for even losing one trade alone! You need to realize that you have to live with yourself before, during, and after each trade. The only time I want you to beat yourself up is when you fail to use a well-thought-out trading plan. Not doing so, especially when you know as much as you do now, is just plain dumb.

Feeling happy about making a good trade is to be expected, but don't mistake yourself for being an unbeatable trading wizard. And conversely, you are not expected to jump up and down with joy after each losing trade. Study and learn from your losing trades, but just as vigorously, study your winning trades. There is a lot to be said for getting a good night's sleep, and you want to make sure you are never losing sleep over your trading. Failure

CHART 11.6

An example of a choppy Nasdaq market.

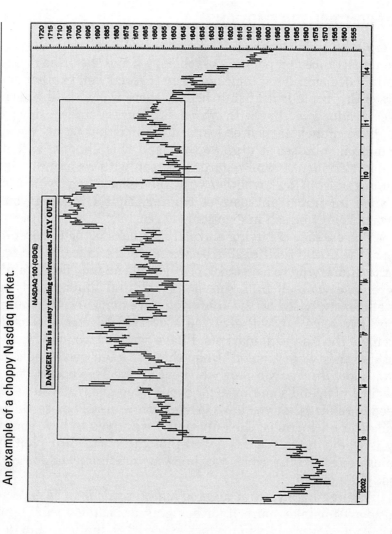

to control your emotions, and succumbing to acting on greed or fear and not on a proven method, can cause a trader to make catastrophic mistakes, resulting in debilitating losses. These losses can be very difficult to overcome. Other than loss of sleep, these occurrences have been known to cause some unprepared traders to lose their homes and break up their families.

This chapter has attempted to isolate most traders' major pitfalls, which I have found to be at the root of most traders' problems. Without a doubt, not controlling emotions has the most profound of all effects on a trader's psychological well-being. It can paralyze you when your stop-loss is hit (if you have one in place to begin with), which effectively cripples you as a good trader and defines you as being a poor one.

But, whether you're chasing stocks, listening to news stations for trading advice, not setting stop-losses, or doing lazy analytics, these problems can always be traced back to a lack of personal control. They are always actions of personal choice that are likely to be repeated if they are not corrected. The aftermath of each trade is something every trader lives through, and you would certainly not be following *my* method of trading if you could not enjoy your life and remain mentally healthy during your time spent as a trader. However, more so than following any method or tactic, not succumbing to your emotions will be the biggest thing you can do for the profitability of your portfolio.

While a comprehensive examination of trading psychology is beyond the scope of this book, I highly encourage you to look back and review your trades on a regular basis. Take notes whenever you make trades, based on your feelings and reasons for making the trade. The truer you are to yourself, the sooner you will become a sniper of the financial markets, unflappable by events, willing to take losses in stride as a business expense, while viewing each victory as a just reward for a job well done. Taking control of your emotions is unquestionably a critical step to becoming a consistently profitable trader.

SUMMARY

The mistakes that have been outlined in this chapter are ones that I took from my own trading experience and passed them on to you with the hopes you can learn from them for a much less expensive price. At the root of most trading mistakes is succumbing to the emotional impetus of the moment, i.e. getting caught up in the last trade and putting undo pressure on ourselves which usually takes us away from our objective mindset and puts us in a sense of desperation.

Things like not setting stop-losses, chasing moves, and fighting the trend are usually the result of taking a few bad beats on the trades right before that and as a result often trying to make back lost money while foregoing discipline and patience. It's hard to be immune from this, but being aware of it can serve as a way to prevent it from happening. In the end, you are ultimately responsible for how you control your mistakes and trade. As experience is the best teacher, learning from mistakes made by you, or someone else, has the potential to enhance your bottom line.

PHASE

Locked and Loaded

CHAPTER 12

Making a Real-Time Trade One Shot – One Kill: From Chalkboard to Battlefield

If you have made it this far, you are to be commended. However, from this point on, only a modest percentage of people who want to become traders fully immerse themselves into what they are doing, and of those who do, only a fraction of them do so skillfully. This is not to say they cannot or will not become successful traders; it is simply an observation that most trader wannabes do not do what is necessary to become successful. The same goes for you. Just because you read a book and sort of grasp the idea behind it doesn't mean you are a successful trader. Remember how having a little knowledge can be a dangerous weapon?

Trading is like football, in that it offers participants the chance to adjust their strategies as the game is being played. In fact, every time a quarterback goes into a huddle, he is modifying his game plan to improve his team's chances for victory, based on knowledge acquired during the game, as it unfolds.

However, before any games are played, there is practice, practice, and more practice. At this time the chalkboard is used extensively, to experiment with different scenarios, study past performances, and illustrate how future plays should be executed. The chalkboard is a crucial element of the learning cycle.

During practice, coaches and players work on strategies and test them out in scrimmages during the week, so they will be ready by game day during the weekend. Those practice scrimmages are the closest the players will get to really playing a game, and they are being played for only one reason: to win games.

Your trading practice is played when the markets are closed. You are your own team, and you play in the National Trading League (NTL). Your computer is your chalkboard and your trading software is your chalk. You are the coach, quarterback, and mascot of your team. This is the time when you hone your skills and test your theories. These experiences can be eye opening as well as profit inspiring. Profit inspiring but not profit producing. Profits in this business are produced only one way, by trading when the market is open, with real money.

Now it is time for you to make first contact. Most of what this book has talked about thus far is a sound trading method that will provide positive results for those who choose to follow it. But enough talk. It is time to trade.

Whether the game you are playing is football or trading, once you sense victory, you quickly gain confidence and feel strong and in control. But, if you sense defeat, you lose your confidence and almost wait to be beaten. In trading, a financial beating can hurt more than a hard kick to the groin and be just as life changing. That is one of the reasons why it is so important for you not to become a wounded statistic.

From 9:30 A.M. until 4:00 p.m. Eastern Time, every Monday through Friday, there is a war going on and there is no time whatsoever for chalkboards. This is the time when blank ammunition is switched for live rounds and when you can get hurt, if you are on the battlefield. All the talk is over and now is the time to put up or shut up. This is when everything you have studied and practiced either works as you had planned or needs dismantling. It is not a "frantic time" filled with chaos, because you have reviewed and rehearsed, and you are armed with intelligence and confidence.

All speculation must stop at this point, as shots are now being fired and you are in gunfire range. Risk management (your protection) and your battle plan are the only two things you have to get you through. This is the time when you take all theories and put them into real, live practice. You can never allow yourself to become gun shy, because, once you are, you cannot be a sharpshooter. Your ability to keep yourself on track and within yourself will ultimately determine your fate, as it has for many others.

FINDING THE SETUP

Ever since Chapter 2, I have reiterated in one way or another that the most important factor in the One Shot – One Kill Method is the price action of the underlying investment vehicle you are planning to trade. This is depicted in the form of the chart pattern. From this chart pattern, you can expect to ascertain who is in control, the buyers or the sellers. After your determination is made, it is now time to execute. Just as I do every night, you will run through a series of charts of the major market indexes, attempting to distinguish any clear setups that may tip you off to the future direction of the market. By doing this every night, over time you will gain experience and develop a feel and understanding for where the market is moving.

In Chapter 3 showed you how to evaluate different chart formations that fit into one of the categories from that chapter (for example, double top, double bottom, ascending and descending triangle, or breakouts from consolidation). For the first real-time trade in this chapter, you will go back to the middle of August 2001, where the Nasdaq 100 was forming a descending triangle pattern (see Chart 12.1) with a base in the 1600 area.

As mentioned in Chapter 2, most breakouts (or breakdowns) have a proclivity to return back to their breakout or breakdown point before heading lower or higher in earnest. It is on this subsequent failure that the best shot for a winning trade is probabilistically offered—and the most ideal risk-to-reward ratio.

The Nasdaq broke down from this descending triangle. From doing your Fibonacci projections, you estimate that between 1450 and 1462 is an area that would allow the breakdown point of 1600 to serve as an area of Fibonacci Friends. This is where you probabilistically expect the first move to go, before retracing to retest the original breakdown point of 1600. It will

CHART 12.1

As with every trade in the One Shot – One Kill methodology, you need to create a price target of where you expect the market to go, in order to take logical profits. In this case with the Nasdaq, a downward target of 1450 has a number of Fibonacci support.

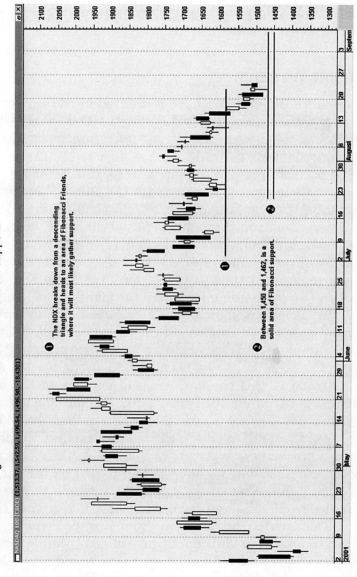

NASDAQ 100 (CBOE) (1,513.37, 1,542.59, 1,496.64, 1,496.96, -18.4301)

① The NDX breaks down from a descending triangle and heads to an area of Fibonacci Friends, where it will most likely gather support.

② Between 1,450 and 1,462, is a solid area of Fibonacci support.

also give you confirmation that the breakdown was a meaningful one and the retest is likely to fail. Whereas, if this breakdown never reached your projection point, it would send an alert to you that there was not enough thrust behind the move to allow the subsequent retest of the 1600 level to fail.

The Nasdaq moved to a low of 1467, which was 5 points above the top portion of your 12-point range, and then began a retracement back toward the initial breakdown point near 1600 (see Chart 12.2). After retesting the 1600 level and putting in a doji at an area of Fibonacci Friends, the index began to look heavy.

The first thing you look for in a setup is the cleanliness of the formation. A number of things are working for this formation as a possible short trade. The first is a descending triangle pattern, which has broken down and come back to retest its breakdown point. The second thing is an area of Fibonacci Friends, which is holding the present rally at bay against the 1600 area. There is a .382 resistance, which lies at 1584, and a .618 retracement, which lies at 1592. The 15-period MA, which does a great job of keeping tabs on the trend, serves as a great stop from a further advance for the move higher.

The Detrended Oscillator shows a slightly overbought condition, thereby eliminating the fear that you are chasing an oversold condition down. Also, the Vertical Horizontal Filter shows no signs of the underlying downtrend topping out. These all stack up very favorably. These indicators should be more of a redundant feature than a telltale sign of what is out there, as the formation and Fibonacci levels are the two most important aspects of the trade.

This particular formation showed a bearish bias, with a descending triangle and a retest of that level. With that said, you are now looking at the indicators from a bearish bias. That is, if the indicators support the formation, they will get a positive number; if they do not, they will get a negative number. Since the formation is a nearly perfect descending triangle, which has returned to its base, it would rate a score of 10 out of 10. The area of Fibonacci Friends as resistance gives you 9 out of 10, with an area of Fibonacci Friends sitting above it the present move. The Detrended Oscillator will give you 1 out of 1 point;

CHART 12.2

Before getting into a trade, you should have as many technical indicators as possible in your favor. With a declining 15-period MA, there is a retest of support, which is now resistance, and supporting ancillary indicators, there is a textbook One Shot – One Kill short setup at point 3.

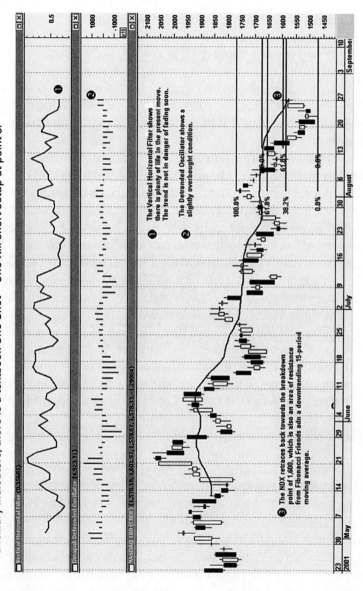

Vertical Horizontal Filter (0.35665)

Disnapoli Detrended Oscillator (-6.92371)

NASDAQ 100 (CBOE) (1,576.18, 1,601.97, 1,559.67, 1,578.33, -1.29004)

1. The Vertical Horizontal Filter shows there is plenty of life in the present move. The trend is not in danger of fading soon.

2. The Detrended Oscillator shows a slightly overbought condition.

3. The NDX retraces back towards the breakdown point of 1,600, which is also an area of resistance from Fibonacci Friends adn a downtrending 15-period moving average.

100.0%   61.8%   38.2%   0.0%

0.0%   61.8%   0.0%

the Vertical Horizontal Filter will give you 2 out of 2, because the trend hasn't exhausted itself.

You will also get 2 out of 3 points, since the Nasdaq is below the 15-period and 39-period MA, while above the 5-period MA. You receive nothing out of 1 point for a positive MACD. The TRI (not pictured) showed no bearish or bullish divergence; thereby indicating that the present trend was likely to continue. The last indicator at which I look for the Netto Number is the trend channels and trend lines. In this case since the Nasdaq is in a negative trend channel it will get 2 our of 2. The amount of points for this trade is shown in Table 12.1.

After tallying all of the points, which gave you your Netto Number of 27, you can now allocate 2.7 percent of your portfolio to a short trade that is dedicated to the Nasdaq, or to the proxy of it, the QQQ (the Nasdaq 100 tracking stock). This process repeats itself for the sectors and stocks you are looking to trade as well. If the overall market, sector, and stock line up in one direction, it is time to get ready to go to combat. The process of computing a Netto Number takes a little time and practice, but once mastered, it adds a shield of protection and calculated aggressiveness to your trading tactics. Over time, it adds up to big numbers in the final tally.

Table 12.1

Netto Number for the Setup Points

Formation	10/10–clean formation and subsequent failure Fibonacci areas of support/resistance 9/10–a .382 and a .618 resistance held formation back at first attempt
TRI –bullish/bearish divergence	2/2 –lower low in both price and the indicator
Detrended Oscillator	1/1–slightly overbought on a bearish formation
Moving Averages	2/3–below 15- and 39-period MA, above 5-period MA
Vertical Horizontal Filter	1/1–showing no loss of trend strength
MACD	0/1–a positive MACD, hence the reason for no points
Trend channel and trend lines	2/2 - caught in a negative trend channel
Total points	27/30

CREATING PRICE TARGETS AND RISK-TO-REWARD RATIOS

Without having favorable risk-to-reward ratios and an idea of
where the market is heading, the story of your trading could end
up being titled *One Shot–Got Killed*. At any rate, as you have
learned from the previous chapters, you incorporate Fibonacci
retracements and expansions, historical support and resistance
points, and the other indicators to help you identify where the
market will go. In this example, if in fact your assessment for
downward movement on the Nasdaq is correct, you will look to
enter a trade on the Nasdaq once it breaks its previous day's low
of 1559, by 5 points. Then you are in on the short side and will
set your stop above the high of the doji, which is at 1600, giving
you a risk of about 50 points, factoring in slippage and commissions on the trade.

Now that you have identified your risk, you must project
where the Nasdaq can go and make the determination as to
whether it is worth risking your money on the trade. The first
thing that needs to be done is to create a Fibonacci price target.
You do so by projecting down a natural 1×1 expansion on the
daily chart, from 1672 down to 1467, or 205 points, and project
that off of 1601, to give you a target of 1396. You also do a 161.8
Fibonacci expansion off of the 1672 pivot point, down to the 1467
high, and it creates a target near 1340, which is also in the area
of the 52-week low on the Nasdaq, or approximately 210 points
away from your potential entry. You are now beginning to create
a price grid with an expectation that if the Nasdaq takes out the
low resting at 1560, it will move to a minimum of 1400 on the
downside. But a retest of the 52-week low near 1348 is also
likely. As such, you have provided yourself with sufficient information as to where you will be looking to take profits when the
setup triggers.

With approximately a 50-point risk, after slippage and commissions, you can conservatively say you stand to make a 150-
point gain, if the stock falls from 1560 to 1400, or more
aggressively, a 220-point gain, if the market falls from 1560 to
1340. Either way, you are looking at a very appealing 3-to-1 to 4-
to-1 risk-to-reward ratio; based on the price targets you created
using some simple Fibonacci price projections and historical

support levels. Keep in mind that these assumptions do not include adding to your winning positions on pullbacks during this move, should the opportunity emerge.

Since you had a Netto Number of 27 out of 30 on this setup, you can risk 2.7 percent of the portfolio on this trade. You will assume for this trade that you are trading with a $100,000 account and can risk $2600 on the initial entry. This does not address how you can add to the winning position; instead, it addresses just your initial entry. Since you can risk $2600 on the trade (about three contracts of the NQ, or Nasdaq e-mini contract traded on the Chicago Mercantile Exchange), which, at the time of this writing, is 2400 shares of the QQQ, this would leave you risking about 50 points per contract, or a total of $3000. This is an acceptable threshold, despite being slightly higher than the amount allotted.

After entering a short position on this trade, you could expect to make anywhere from $9000 to $12,000, if your price targets are hit. Now, there are clearly a number of scenarios that could take place along the way, which would affect your expected return. However, this book will deal with the trade itself and how it should be handled using the One Shot – One Kill Method.

EXECUTING AND MANAGING THE TRADE

To this point, you have found the setup, calculated a Netto Number, created a risk-to-reward ratio based on price targets, and allocated a position size, if the signal is triggered. Moving forward, you see the next day that the Nasdaq takes out the low from the previous day and you get short three contracts (NQ U1, NQ is the root for the futures symbol representing the Nasdaq 100 emini contract, U is the month designator for September and 1 is the year designator for 2001 hence NQ U1 is the September 2001 contract for the Nasdaq Emini) at 1555. You immediately set your stop at 1605, thereby minimizing your loss to 50 points, or $3000 (50 × $20/point × 3 = $3000). As you enter your position, your first objective is to take some size off once you hit your breakeven point, near 1505. This will allow you to book some early profits as well as lower your stop-loss to your entry point, which is a few ticks above the previous day's high on August 29 (see Chart 12.3). All this gives you some breathing room and flexibility, knowing that, barring a major gap up, the worst you can do is earn $1000 on one contract and break even on the other two.

A natural question to ask at this point would be, if you are booking one-third of your profit when you hit your breakeven point, doesn't that affect your risk-to-reward ratio? I wish the answer to this question were as simple as yes or no. However, if the trade is working for you, you have the option of adding to your position on pullbacks and on further continuations of the current movement. Because of this option, your risk-to-reward ratio can have a variable range, which is ultimately decided upon by you, so stay within your boundaries. Remember, the idea behind creating a solid and profitable risk-to-reward ratio is that you want to make sure you have a favorable expected return going into the trade. This gives you a tool to assess whether or not the trade is worth the risk. In this example, even if you were to cut one contract off at the breakeven point, you would still be set up for a 2.33-to-1 risk-to-reward ratio on the trade.

With that said, though, it has been my experience that very few trades go in a straight line to a price target. More customarily, a move pulls back numerous times along the way. It is during these pullbacks that you can add back in—not only the initial contract you took off but also, depending on how aggressive you are, even more contracts.

By taking part of your position off the table and getting your cost out of the way, you remove a good degree of pressure from your shoulders. You know that you just need to *manage* the trade correctly from here on out and you will most likely walk away with a profit. A loss is *unlikely* at this point and your confidence is high.

You have now taken profits from one contract and are sitting pretty well in the trade. With the swift fall and being up nicely in the trade, most people would be looking to take profits now and wait to reload later. However, the Nasdaq has not shown any convincing signs of slowing down, so why change your plan? The huge mistake most traders make on a regular basis is to change their plan once they are making money. For

CHART 12.3

The price targets for this down move suggest that 1400 and 1340 are very likely candidates for spots at which to take profits. As the Nasdaq continues to trade, more Fibonacci ratios will emerge, thereby providing a clearer picture as to which number is more viable.

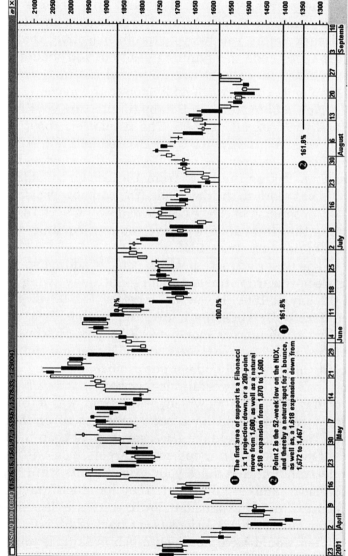

❶ The first area of support is a Fibonacci 1 x 1 projection down, or a 200-point move from 1,600, as well as a natural 1.618 expansion from 1,870 to 1,600;

❷ Point 2 is the 52-week low on the NDX, and thereby a natural spot for a bounce, as well as, a 1.618 expansion down from 1,672 to 1,467.

example, they may book their winners too early and not let them ever arrive at their calculated price targets. Or worse, they may let their losers run.

Please respect your plan, and only change it when the Netto Numbers don't add up. Nevertheless, should the market pull back before you hit your profit objective, that would be a great spot to add to a winning position. You should do so only if the market stays below the 15-period MA and other indicators also support the tactic of adding on to the move.

Now add to your position by reinitiating your first contract, which you took off at 1505. The revelation about this move is that, with the new pivot point created at 1502, it has provided you with a clearer picture of where the market is ultimately heading. Taking the move from 1601 down to 1438 gives you a 160-point move to the downside. You can now project a Fibonacci 1×1 expansion or AB = CD move down. Chart 12.4 shows that taking that from 1505 will give you confirmation of one of your initial price targets at 1340.

The first contract, in which you are adding on, has a 1.8-to-1 risk-to-reward ratio, as the large intraday swing put the high of the day at 1500. If you had a better risk-to-reward ratio, you could actually consider adding more than one contract and really let the house's money work for you. However, being that you are short two contracts at 1555, you are not complaining about the swift and sudden down move. You may also notice, if you look at the powerful one-day bar, that the Nasdaq hit an intraday high of 1500, which, at the time, was a three-day high. Many traders would have been forced to cover their positions there, and that would not necessarily have been the best move.

Once you begin using price targets, you will benefit from understanding that since your price targets were not hit to the downside, and a failure at 1500 produced another 1×1 Fibonacci price expansion down, you are less likely to get shaken out of your positions (see Chart 12.5).

You would have not been much at fault if you would have covered your positions, because in real time you can never be sure whether a move is a reversal or just a hiccup along the way. In my second book, I will discuss ways to trade around positions using different option strategies. However, the purpose of this

CHART 12.4

The market rolls from your spot and begins to progress towards your price targets. After getting a nice move in the trade, you would be wise to take some profits off the table and give yourself the added flexibility of adding back in on a bounce or adjusting the stop.

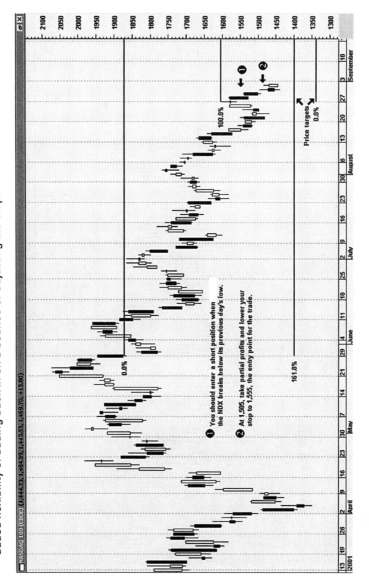

① You should enter a short position when the NDX breaks below its previous day's low.

② At 1,505, take partial profits and lower your stop to 1,555, the entry point for the trade.

CHART 12.5

With a Fibonacci 1 × 1 expansion resting at 1340, as well as the 52-week low at that point in time, this becomes the trade's prime profit target.

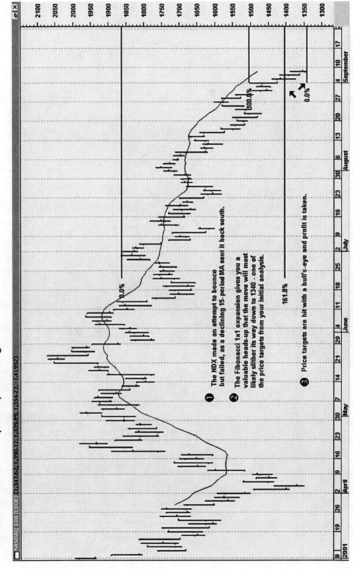

NASDAQ 100 (CBOE) (1,347.62, 1,390.12, 1,339.89, 1,354.27, -7.41992)

1. The NDX made an attempt to bounce but failed, as a declining 15-period MA sent it back south.

2. The Fibonacci 1x1 expansion gives you a valuable heads-up that the move will most likely slither its way down to 1340 – one of the price targets from your initial analysis.

3. Price targets are hit with a bull's-eye and profit is taken.

book is for you understand the fundamentals behind this method. Once you understand how price targets are created, you will be prevented from getting shaken out very often. However, nothing is perfect and getting shaken out is merely a cost of doing business.

Exiting the Trade

Over the next three days, the market heads lower and hits your target of 1340. At this point, it is time to clean out the shelves of your short positions and take all of your profits. For this reason, creating price targets and establishing risk-to-reward ratios is paramount to properly utilizing and implementing the One Shot – One Kill Method successfully. This trade worked out well, as many do. But at times trading can be more difficult. The afore-mentioned trade is not intended to give you the impression that things always work out the way they were scripted. Be aware that trades don't all go your way. The idea of this walk-through is to give you an idea of what to look for when managing a trade. Once again, I must reiterate that to be a successful trader you must have a coherent plan of attack and execute it as planned.

COMBINING THE 15-PERIOD MA AND FIBONACCI EXPANSIONS TO PROFIT

Many traders often ask themselves, what is the best way to enter a position that is in a trending market? Over the years of trading, one of the most powerful tools of the One Shot – One Kill Method has been the combination of a 15-period simple moving average with a Fibonacci 1 × 1 expansion. This section will provide you with a real-life example of how to use the 15-period simple moving average to enter positions in a low-risk, high-reward manner, and how to exit at highly probabilistic pre-determined profit points, through the use of a 1 × 1 Fibonacci expansion.

Let us first begin with the 15-period MA, which, as you know from reading throughout this book, can be calculated on any time frame. It has an uncanny ability to keep a trader in on a move of a strongly trending market, whether that be for a 3-minute, 13-minute, 60-minute, or daily chart. Most traders get very anxious when they see a market that is running either up or down and they are not in the move. As such, they "chase" after the move and enter in spots where the move is too extended and likely to pull back. Either that, or they enter at a spot where they have to put a stop so far away from the money that it causes them stress and they can't effectively manage the position. By using the 15-period MA as a means of entering a trade, the risk-to-reward ratio is much greater. Because it is, the overall performance of the trader should increase accordingly.

Charts 12.6 to 12.9 give an example of how to use the 15-period MA, which occurs on a daily basis with the Nasdaq 100 Index during November 2000.

The market had been in a protracted down trend. Most traders wanted to get short the market but would have gotten shaken out of the position because every little rally appeared to be a reversal. Yet those who applied the simple, yet very effective tool of a 15-period MA were able to enter the move with a very low risk trade. Point number 1 in Chart 12.6 shows that the Nasdaq has rallied to the 15-period MA at 3676 and then fails. I like to build my short positions at the 15-period MA as it is a great spot to get into a low-risk short trade in a declining market. This is point one and two in Chart 12.6. It does so the next day and allows you to get short the market and place your stop above the high at 3725. The Nasdaq ran as low as 2850 from that move.

On November 8, we see the market but in an ominous down candle on November 8, 2000. point 3 on Chart 12.6) . The Nasdaq has fallen below the 15-period MA and taken out the low from the previous day at 3217, but this is not the best entry for this trade as you may need to find an hourly chart; Instead, point 4 offers a much cleaner short entry as the market breaks down and makes a new 11 period low, bounces back to a declining 15 period MA and allows you a spot to get short there. Therefore, it provides a great short entry for at least a partial position when the Nasdaq breaks the previous day's low at 3001 the other half of the short trade is entered. This setup occurs on November 27, 2000 (point 5 on Chart 12.6), when the Nasdaq

CHART 12.6

Looking to the 15-period MA to reenter trends is a safe way to get into low-risk trades to both the upside and the downside.

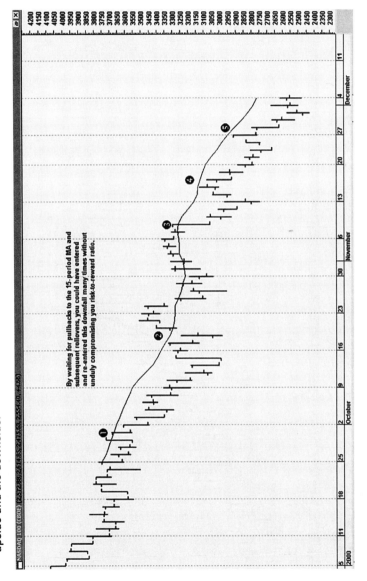

By waiting for pullbacks to the 15-period MA and subsequent rollovers, you could have entered and re-entered this downfall many times without unduly compromising your risk-to-reward ratio.

CHART 12.7

Working a Fibonacci 1 × 1 expansion in tandem with the 15-period MA is a very powerful combination.

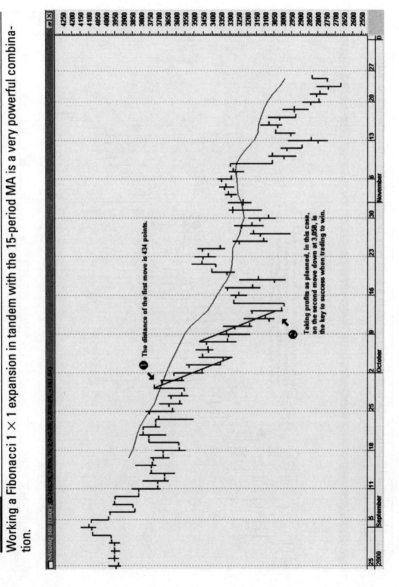

① The distance of the first move is 434 points.

② Taking profits as planned, in this case, on the second move down at 3,059, is the key to success when trading to win.

CHART 12.8

On the above move lower by the Nasdaq, a number of times the market respected both the 15-period MA and the Fibonacci 1 × 1 expansions.

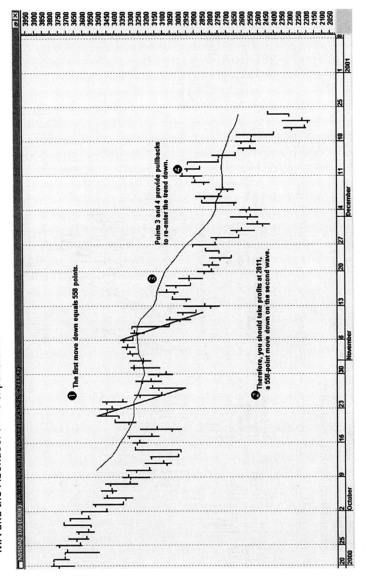

❶ The first move down equals 558 points.

❷ Therefore, you should take profits at 2811, a 558-point move down on the second wave.

❸

❹ Points 3 and 4 provide pullbacks to re-enter the trend down.

CHART 12.9

When multiple Fibonacci 1 × 1 expansions set up in the same area, this is a prime spot to play a low-risk countertrend move in the other direction. In the case of the Nasdaq, a robust 500-point rally ensued from a prime reversal spot.

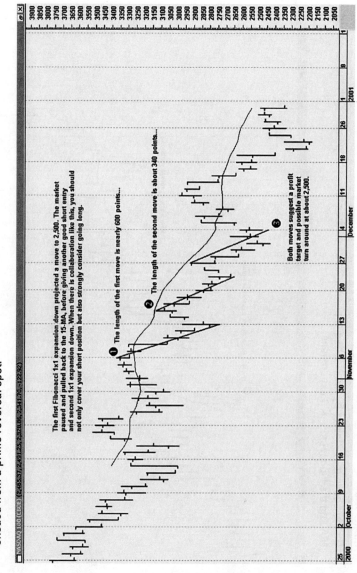

The first Fibonacci 1x1 expansion down projected a move to 2,500. The market paused and pulled back to the 15-MA, before giving another good short entry and second 1x1 expansion down. When there is collaboration like this, you should not only cover your short position but also strongly consider going long.

① The length of the first move is nearly 600 points....

② The length of the second move is about 340 points....

③ Both moves suggest a profit target and possible market turn around at about 2,500.

made an intraday high near the 15-period MA. Its failure to close near there set up for the possibility of another entry point.

The next day the market presented the opportunity by breaking the previous day's low at 2759, allowing another confirmation of a short signal, setting the stop at above the previous day's high of 2913. These setups emerge in all markets and reward those with patience. Using the 15-period MA to reenter prevailing trends and bankroll large trades is just one of many parts of the One Shot – One Kill trading method.

The 15-period MA is great for entering positions, or reloading on winners that have pulled back, but the use of the 1×1 Fibonacci expansion ratio is what can really enhance your overall profitability. It allows you to take profits at price targets without having to surrender sizable amounts of your gains.

Up to this point, I have displayed four different entry points to get in the market. It is now incumbent to display four points from which to exit the Nasdaq 100. The first entry point came from a breakdown below the 15-period MA. It requires that you use a close above the previous day's high as a means for exiting the position until you make a second pivot point from which to measure a Fibonacci 1×1 expansion down.

On October 5, the market made another higher low and provided a good point from which to project down. As explained in Chapter 4, on Fibonacci expansions, with a 1×1 expansion you are merely taking the length of the first run and using that for the expected distance of the second run. This, just like the 15-period MA, can be used on any time frame. For this example, the high of 3725 measured down to the low of 3291 is a total distance of 434 points. When the market begins to roll on October 5, you will project 434 points down from the intermediate high made on October 5 at 3492. You will then subtract 434 from 3492 and expect the market to fall to 3058. Since you are short at 3550, you expect to make nearly 500 points from the move.

Once the Nasdaq hits 3058 you will cover your short position and possibly look to go long on a short-term basis. The market moves past that point slightly and heads as low as 2990. That is okay, because you are still caught a big move and will wait for a retracement to get back in.

Points 2, and 4 of Chart 12.6 involve a more fluid example of how the market moves with the 15-point MA and 1 × 1 Fibonacci expansion. After entering the short position at point 2 on Chart 12.6 at 3200, you immediately use your 1 × 1 Fibonacci projection to calculate where the market is going to go. You do this by measuring the high on October 20 of 3514 down to its short-term low of 2956. The difference is 558 points. This means that you expect the next move down to be for 558 points as illustrated in Chart 12.8, you will immediately be looking for the market to head 558 points lower from 3369, which would give us a price target of 2811, the area from which you would exit your position and take your profits, which would be about 390 points on the trade. The Nasdaq moved as low as 2742 before rallying back up to our third entry point.

The third entry point got you short at 3000 with a price target of around 2510. The market bounced between those moves to allow you to add to your winner. As long as the market didn't break the 15-period MA, you could add to your positions until your price target is reached. The last exit at 2500 had the benefit of being confirmed by two Fibonacci 1 × 1 expansions down. When such collaboration exists, then it pays not only to close out your short but to strongly consider playing a countertrend move to the long side.

This series of trades is a classic example of how the One Shot – One Kill Method can give you a clear edge by providing an objective means for entering and exiting positions in a logical manner. This advantage will allow you to enter trades with good risk-to-reward ratios and exit them at highly probabilistic points, thereby increasing your overall performance.

As One Shot – One Kill traders, we are looking to capitalize on trade setups like these and potentially capture large profits with minimal risk by adding to winning positions and keeping losses small and manageable.

DAY TRADING IN REAL TIME

To illustrate how to do day trading in real time, let's use a real-life example—my own. Coming into November 8, 2001, the market had rallied very powerfully from the lows of September. The market had been quite extended but still offered very profitable trading opportunities from both the short and the long side. I came into the day expecting, based on the previous night's analysis and the close from the previous day, to see a substantial pullback in the index sometime throughout the day.

The morning turned out to be nearly a 20-point gap up and had everyone running around trying to figure out how to get into the market when things were so overbought. The combination of the 15-period MA and a handy Fibonacci 1 × 1 expansion tool helped me to erase those fears and go about my business. Since the Nasdaq was gapped up, traders would need to be careful when looking to buy at the open, as there was a horrible risk-to-reward ratio if they would want to put their stop in a reasonable place. The market moved up strongly in the first half hour but had not pulled back to the two-minute 15-period MA, which is what can be used to ascertain whether to get long or short. At about 7:35 a.m. PT, the Nasdaq pulled back (see Chart 12.10) and touched the 15-period simple MA and rallied off that point.

This was the first long entry signal seen, which set up a favorable risk-to-reward ratio. After entering the position here, my next step was to immediately measure a Fibonacci 1 × 1 expansion move up from the morning low to the recent pivot high, which gave an initial target of 1567. The trade seemed fair enough and worth the risk of 4 points for the potential to gain around 14.

The next thing to do was to wait for the pullback to the 15-period MA and enter half the position when the market hits the 15 MA and the other half when the position takes out the high of the previous bar. The Nasdaq fell through the 15-period MA, which suggested that there might be a trend reversal, but it quickly recovered and headed higher. Once it moved past the 15-period MA, I could go long again. But this time I would need to do so with a little larger stop, because it would not be wise to trade with so many shares, because of the greater risk. From there, once again I needed to project a 1 × 1 Fibonacci move from the 1549 pivot low to the 1569 pivot high, and add 20 points to 1558, to have a target of 1578. The market moved to 1582, but I was not complaining. The second trade made was more risky than the first. Nevertheless, my experience in those spots said to

CHART 12.10

Once again, waiting for the pullbacks, before entering short, offers the biggest bang for the buck.

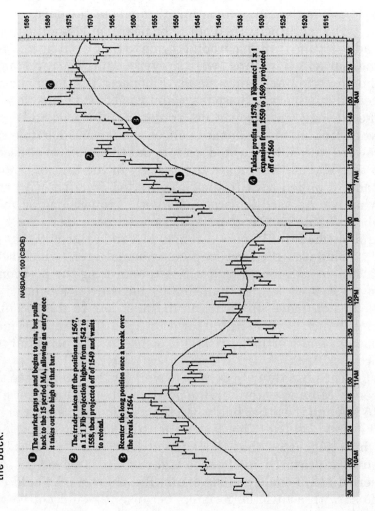

NASDAQ 100 (CBOE)

1. The market gaps up and begins to run, but pulls back to the 15 period MA, allowing an entry once it takes out the high of that bar.

2. The trader takes off the positions at 1567, a 1 x 1 Fib projection higher from 1542 to 1558, then projected off of 1549 and waits to reload.

3. Reenter the long position once a break over the break of 1564.

4. Taking profits at 1578, a Fibonacci 1 x 1 expansion from 1550 to 1569, projected off of 1550

go ahead and take those trades. But if the market fell back below the 15-point MA, I planned to simply exit the position, as in most cases if it falls below that spot twice, then the move has probably lost its steam.

From that point, the market made a 1 × 1 Fibonacci expansion down and hung out in the range for the rest of the morning (see Chart 12.11).

I do not force my will on the market if it is not at a major price target. Therefore, I was going to have to wait for a breakdown to happen, then, hopefully a pullback. If that happened, I would then really get a part of the move using the One Shot – One Kill Money Management Matrix to add and take away contracts. Chart 12.12 shows that at 11:00 a.m. PT, the Nasdaq began to feel heavy and started to break down from consolidation.

The Semiconductor Index, which had been strong all morning, showed that stocks had also broken down from their highs, which served as a sign of ominous things to come. Being that it was afternoon, and the pace of the market tends to be a little bit different in the afternoons than in the mornings, I had my charts set at three-minute time intervals. The Nasdaq broke down and I was not a part of the first move, because, as you know, if this were a major move, it would usually consolidate to the 15-period MA before resuming the move down. So instead of chasing it, I just let it go until that time came.

At 11:51 P.M. PT, right before the Power Hour, the market pulled back to the 15-period MA and then dumped again. I entered the short position and put the stop above the 15-period MA. The first thing I did was measure a 1 × 1 Fibonacci expansion move down to arrive at a price target of 1508. I did this by measuring from the recent pivot high of 1576 down to 1538, which gave me 38 points. I projected that off of the1547 pivot high to get the 1508 price target (see Chart 12.12). I waited for one more move, to the 15-period MA, thinking I might be able to milk a few more points from this move, as the Nasdaq rallied nicely to the 15-period MA one more time and rolled down about 22 points from there. I only netted 10 points from that, as I used a trailing stop after such a long move down. I didn't want a natural countertrend move to wipe out my profits.

CHART 12.11

After the market ripped up during the first 90 minutes, it began to whipsaw traders in and out of positions, until finally succumbing hard to the sellers.

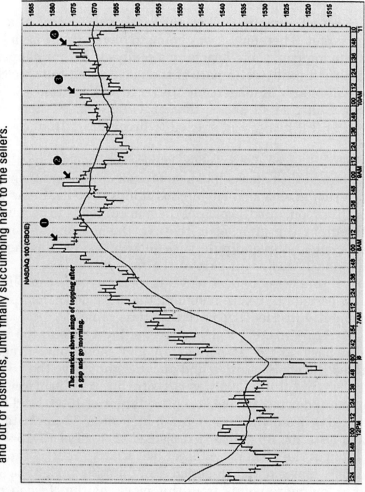

CHART 12.12

After confirming a downward bias in the price action, use the 15-MA as guidance on when to enter.

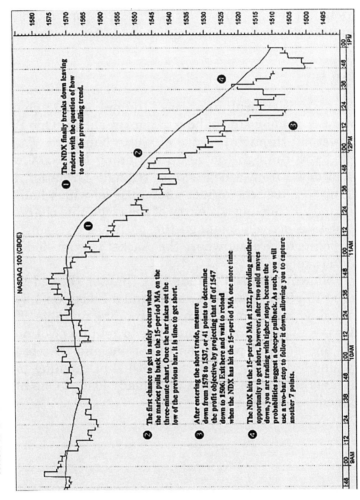

NASDAQ 100 (CBOE)

❶ The NDX finally breaks down leaving traders with the question of how to enter the prevailing trend.

❷ The first chance to get in safely occurs when the market pulls back to the 15-period MA on the three-minute chart. Once the bar takes out the low of the previous bar, it is time to get short.

❸ After entering the short trade, measure down from 1578 to 1537, or 41 points to determine the profit objective, by projecting that off of 1547 down to 1506. Exit there and wait to reload when the NDX has hit the 15-period MA one more time

❹ The NDX hits the 15-period MA at 1522, providing another opportunity to get short, however, after two solid moves down, you are trading with tigher stops, because the probabilities suggest a deeper pullback. As such, you will use a two-bar stop to follow it down, allowing you to capture another 7 points.

These opportunities emerge on a fairly regular basis in the market and provide all traders an opportunity to enter the market and have a predetermined, probabilistic price target. These are the means that the very best traders in the world use get it done. If you wish to emulate them, put the odds of the trade in your favor. Understand that you are not going to catch every move but, if you just are ready when the opportunities arise, you should do very well.

SUMMARY

Chapter 12 is the culmination of the previous 11 chapters and shows you step-by-step of how to implement the One Shot – One Kill Method through the use of Netto Numbers. This chapter walked you through the setup of finding the NDX which had broken down from a descending triangle formation and came back up to retest the former support level which had turned to resistance. Following the entry of the trade this chapter showed you how to actively manage the positions by using Fibonacci price points to forecast where the market was headed and a good spot to take profits.

Following the NDX trade this chapter showed you how to use the 15 period moving average and a Fibonacci 1 by 1 projection to day trade around strongly trending markets. The idea is to use the 15 period moving average to get into positions on pullbacks and a 1 by 1 projection to get out and take profits. This very simple, yet very powerful method of catching moves provides another tool in what is an already loaded One Shot – One Kill trading arsenal.

13

Implementing the One Shot – One Kill Method into Your Trading

It is not as hard as you may think to change from what you are currently doing in your trading regimen to something more complete with a sound basis for success. Weaning yourself from bad habits and holding yourself accountable for your trading decisions and following up after your trading with smart, savvy record keeping and tax preparation will allow you to take what you learn, and the money you make and actually be one of the success stories you dream about becoming. I only hope that you enjoy the trip as much as I have.

CREATING YOUR TRADING GOALS

Determining your trading goals and the thought behind that determination is the foundation on which you should build your livelihood as a trader. Everyone should have his or her own set of trading goals and realize that the time spent trading should be made as enjoyable as possible. After all, the enjoyment of living your life the way you want to is something that you—and every-one—should strive for. Not only does trading offer a lifestyle unlike any other I know, it also affords you the opportunity to set attainable goals as well as time to realize them and enjoy some of your dreams.

Some people are drawn to trading because of its unique-ness. Others start out with lots of money that they came upon without much effort, and as such, they don't understand its true value. Still others believe that trading is not as difficult as it surely is. And some people know that it takes effort and smarts, and they want to be successful, but either they end up not doing the work or they don't follow a proven method. They will all soon perish. If they do not quickly find a sound trading plan, they will not be able to hang around long enough to ever realize their trading goals. The one underlying reason for this failure is lack of self-discipline. There is no one dragging you out of bed in the morning and making you think smart. It's all you. You have to figure out how to wake up in the morning. You have to find your way to the computer screen, and you have to do the work to make it work.

What the One Shot – One Kill Method does is serve as your guide, so you make sure each and every trade you make has been reviewed in specific detail. Doing so lessens your chances of making a mistake *before* you make a trade. Because of this work ethic, when the execution of your trade does take place, it will very likely be profitable, if you follow through with everything taught to you in this book.

To some extent, trading goals are really an extension of your goals for life. Every trader (and every person, for that mat-ter) has things he or she wants to accomplish while on this earth. Trading can be the vehicle to makes those things happen. The important thing to remember about a goal is that it differs from a dream, in that a goal must have a date of achievement attached to it. It is that date that puts time into the equation and, as such, requires some kind of plan of action to take place (which, in turn, requires work on your part). Once you achieve, you have conquered.

As far as your personal goals go, don't limit them. You can accomplish an enormous amount as a successful trader. Really, I cannot tell you the best goals you should pick for yourself. However, as far as goals for becoming a better trader go, the best one, I believe, is to keep actively pursuing an education in trading.

If you can take a relatively short amount of time and money and invest it in learning a method that works well, you will earn the peace of mind and financial freedom that go with it.

PROACTIVE MONEY MANAGEMENT

The money manager is always the commanding officer when using the One Shot – One Kill Method. And, *you* are the money manager. It's just that simple. It is the most precise title and description of your job I can think of, whether you think of yourself as an investor or a trader. That is why it is so important to follow the One Shot – One Kill Money Management Matrix.

Without a doubt, the laughable lack of money management skills many traders have exhibited throughout time marks the most attributable cause of their demise. That fact is exactly why so much of trading revolves around your ability to financially survive over time. (Just because this topic is talked about less than the act of actual trading doesn't make it any less important.) And, the only way to become successful is to become a five-star general when it comes to handling and conserving your capital. If you do not do so, you will relegate yourself to someone who likes trading and following the market but who has two things going against you. First, you will have no more money to "invest" (I smile as I use that term), and second, you will remain someone who has acquired no new and improved skills to make any real, long-lasting comeback a reality. The truth is that you must do your job just as diligently as the professional money managers in the market who bank a profit each week. In fact, if you will just practice the "simple" act of good money management, you will probably be able to achieve success as a trader—or at least prevent yourself from undergoing massive failure.

Many traders understand that good money management is the key to living to trade another day. They have a certain common sense, and they can feel in their bones that bearing too much risk at any time, for whatever reason, is not worth the ultimate risk. The sad outcomes of adopting that tactic could devastate them financially and emotionally, while at the same time putting them indefinitely on the inactive list as traders. Trying for that one big win can always be something to shoot for, but not at the expense of sending you home in a body bag. *Manage your risk.*

To put it another way; trying to find the big-dollar plays and be there as they unfold might be fine and admirable, provided you do your job correctly. True, as a trader you have to do exceedingly hard work, and exercise extraordinary discipline and dedication, to uncover these plays and spot the possibilities. But if your game plan is to always try and hit a home run (as many traders are wont want to try to do), you need to keep in mind how important base hits can be in putting big numbers on the board. We have all heard that "the best offense is a great defense," but rarely in nature can it be exemplified more truly than when it is applied to trading.

The One Shot – One Kill Method does not allow a trader to risk more than 3 percent of his or her total capital on any one trade. By obeying this rule, even if you make many mistakes and many bad trades; you would not be allowing yourself to receive a knockout punch. On the other hand, you might need or want to define your risk factor a little differently than I do. (I don't recommend altering it too much.) If so, always err on the side of safety, by never risking more than 3 percent of your assets on any one trade.

How you define your risk is another issue that needs to be clarified. The way I define risk for my 3 percent rule is by the amount of loss I will incur if I am wrong. For example, if I own 500 shares of WXYZ at \$100 with a \$3 stop, my risk is \$3 × 500 = \$1500. So long as I have capital amounting to more than \$50,000, I am not breaking the One Shot – One Kill trading rule by working with the \$1500 risk.

Let me be clear: By no means does the 3 percent rule guarantee your loss to be only 3 percent. What if, after you get long WXYZ, they get halted and preannounce or come out after the bell with strong warnings? They could gap down to 80 and not look back. Of course, you may not know this information when you retire for the evening, but come sunrise, *surprise!* Say that you find yourself the one in that trade and quickly realize your "guaranteed small loss" is now big enough to change your vacation plans from spending three weeks at the beachfront on Kauai to a long weekend at the local lakefront Holiday Inn. The only thing with which you can reconcile yourself at those times is reflecting on when you have had major gaps go in your favor. (I do hope you have all experienced that more times than you can count). However, except when the situation is out of your control, my advice is to never risk more than 3 percent on any one trade, even if you "know" it's a winner.

What trader hasn't heard a thousand times, the old adage "cut your losses and let your winners run"? If that sounds like a bright idea, you are on the right page. But, oddly enough, doing so successfully is indescribably harder to do than actually knowing that it needs to be done, without a strategic plan in action. When you get to the point where you are really ready to let your profits run in real time, then you have got a successful foundation for your trading. But you must keep losses under control— or else. By doing so you ensure that no one trade does too much damage. And if you keep the losses small, the profits will take care of themselves. But, how do you classify a small loss? How do you define a large-enough profit? There is no one answer. What's right for one person will probably not be right for another. Putting every trader in the same box and determining one cohesive strategy would be the wrong way to go.

The One Shot – One Kill Method offers viable means of entering and exiting trades in a way that should keep you objective and out of troublesome circumstances. But you still must make a decision. Does your personality allow you to embrace this method? If you find it a struggle to limit yourself to such a small amount of controlled risk (3 percent) instead of what you have possibly allowed yourself in the past (10 to 20 percent), success is farther away for you than it has to be.

THE TAXMAN COMETH (AND WE KNOW WHERE HE CAN GOETH)

One of the uglier (but necessary) parts of the One Shot – One Kill Method is dealing with your records for tax purposes. There is an old Wall Street saying: "Even a thief worth his weight in gold can't tap dance on his own forehead." And so be it also with trading and traders. In this business, what you stand to pay in taxes depends on where you sit as a trader, because it is entirely possible that Uncle Sam could deem you an "investor" and not a "trader." It's important for you to decide which one you are, and equally so for you to know what is required to be classified as such. It is not within the realm of this book to prescribe each reader with a tax plan, but it is my intent to point some things out to you, so you can be more aware of your surroundings. Taking full advantage of your situation affects your bottom line as much as a winning or losing a trade. Having the correct preparation in this department can amazingly increase your financial happiness when the time comes—and it will come.

Up to this point, this book is has been devoted to providing skills and techniques to help you become a consistent and profitable trader. These forthcoming pages have been written to help you learn how to keep those profits, utilizing and making you aware of legitimate and proven tax reduction and planning strategies allowed by the Internal Revenue Service (the IRS). Taxes are the single largest expense for a profitable trader, and it is crucial that you learn the following:

1. Where and how to deduct all possible expenses
2. How to elect Section 475, if you trade stocks and options, to hedge against an unprofitable year and to utilize current-year trading losses to offset prior or future years' trading gains
3. When, why, and how to create a legal entity once you start making consistent profits or trade other people's capital

Trading in one form or another has existed for centuries. With the creation of the IRS, special rules were created to define and tax traders and investors on profits. As the need for government revenue has increased over the years, most of the deductions once available to investors have either been specifically eliminated or phased-out based on income limitations. It is essential that, if you qualify, you file your tax return as a trader, not as an investor. Special tax rules for traders are constantly evolving, and a huge need exists (especially in volatile markets) for professional tax advice customized for traders that utilizes all possible tax-planning advantages available.

Tax planning requires year-round diligence, research, and foresight. Trading, education, and trading research are more time consuming than most full-time jobs. But you really should concentrate on trading and realizing profits, because anything that takes you away from that pursuit could be detrimental to your results. Tax planning should be an interactive process with a tax professional that specializes in traders. That person should provide premium client service and should be available year round to answer questions or suggest tax reduction and planning strategies.

IRS Code Sections and Regulations define three categories of market participants—broker-dealers/market makers, investors, and traders—and list different tax rules and requirements for each category. This chapter discusses the advantages and considerations of filing as a trader or as part of a trading entity. Discussion of each category, each specific type of trader or each entity structure, would require an entire book.

Table 13.1, in plain English, summarizes the distinctions between traders and investors.

Qualified traders trading in their own name or in a single-member Limited Liability Company, or LLC, are specifically allowed and directed to deduct all trading expenses and margin interest as fully deductible on Schedule C (as indicated in IRS Publication 550, IRS Form 1040 Instructions).

Investors, on the other hand, are directed to deduct "allowable" investment expenses on Schedule A as a miscellaneous itemized deduction or investment interest. These costs are then subject to various income limitations as well as other restrictions. Incredibly, certain expenses fully deductible to traders, such as education, 100 percent write-off of computers or software, office in home, and even travel to stockholders' meetings, are specifically disallowed to investors (as specified in IRS Publication 550).

Apparently, then, merely by filing as a trader, rather than as an investor, you can save yourself thousands of dollars in taxes, which enhances your capital and cash flow. Other planning techniques can save you even more tax money.

Table 13.1

Traders versus Investors

	Traders	Investors
Definition	Buy and sell securities, commodities, etc,. for their own accounts with the expectation of deriving profits as a result of frequent transactions over a short period of time by taking advantage of market fluctuations	Buy and sell securities, commodities, etc., for their own accounts with the expectation of deriving profits from appreciation, interest, and dividends over a indeterminable period of time
Characteristics	• Numerous trades • Short holding periods • Trade frequently, regularly, and continuously • Have significant assets in the market • Have an office • File a Schedule C • Significant time devoted to trading and research • Insignificant income from interest/dividends	• Few transactions • Long holding periods • Seek asset appreciation • Receive interest and dividends • Do not spend significant time on market research, although they may

---

Tax planning should be individualized and is specific to your unique tax situation. For example, a 25-year-old single scalper will have different needs than a 45-year-old swing trader with three children and another business venture. Because of this uniqueness of each individual trader, a discussion of techniques for each specific situation would obviously be beyond the scope of this section; therefore, I strongly recommend that you consult with a trader tax professional.

EVOLUTION OF THE TAX LIFE OF A TRADER

Filing as a Trader on Schedule C as a Business

If you qualify as a trader, file Form 1040 Schedule C and report to the IRS that you are in the business of trading as a sole proprietor. There is no election, preapproval, or application for the commonly misused term *trader status*.

Once you establish that you are running a business, IRC Code Section 162 states that you can claim the following allowances and deductions:

There shall be allowed as a deduction all the ordinary and necessary expenses paid or incurred during the taxable year in carrying on any trade or business.... Now that you are no longer filing as an investor, all legitimate business expenses become deductible on Schedule C and are no longer reported as investment expenses. These expenses then avoid the trap of being expressly forbidden as itemized deductions or expenses subject to various phase-out limitations based on income or other defined thresholds.

The following are some examples of business-related trading expenses:

- Online and real-time data retrieval services
- Trading publications
- Computer software, trading systems, and hardware
- Margin interest
- Office rent
- Expenses for office in the home
- Trading seminars, education, and consulting
- Business-related meals and entertainment with other traders

These expenses can total thousands, or tens of thousands of dollars, if you incur significant startup or operating expenses such as education or computer hardware and software. If you are fortunate enough to be in the top federal tax bracket of 35 percent for 2003, each dollar of expense will save you 35 cents in taxes. In effect, the IRS is subsidizing your trading business by rebating back to you 35 percent of each expense, just as it promotes home ownership by allowing homeowners to write off mortgage interest and real estate taxes paid. The actual tax savings can be significantly higher once you factor in state tax savings.

Business (trading) expenses that exceed total taxable income may also create a net operating loss, which can be carried forward to offset future income or carried back to offset prior years' income and to obtain a refund of taxes paid in prior years.

Trading gains and losses from the sale of securities continue to be reported on Form 1040 Schedule D as income from the sale of capital assets (as defined in IRC Section 1221). Traders who have not elected Mark-to-Market Accounting Treatment report trades in the exact same manner as investors—as capital gains and losses on Form 1040 Schedule D. They are also prohibited from writing off (offsetting other income) in excess of $3000 in net capital loss in any one tax year.

Trading income from trading your own account is not considered self-employment income. That has both positives and negatives. Self-employment tax is not required to be paid, which is a huge tax savings. The negatives are that trading income cannot be used to fund a retirement plan or deduct self-employment health insurance costs. These deductions are only available by utilizing a legal entity to create self-employment income or salary income.

An unincorporated trader does not need to create an entity if retirement planning or deductible health insurance premiums are not important issues. All expenses deductible at the entity level are deductible to unincorporated traders merely by the filing of a Schedule C Form.

Electing Section 475 Mark-to-Market Accounting Method for Traders in Securities

The provisions of the Taxpayers' Relief Act of 1997 were very beneficial to traders. The IRS finally recognized qualified traders as running a business and formally created new rules applicable to qualified traders—while being careful not to actually provide an exact definition of what qualifies you as a trader. In the ensuing years, the IRS has published additional information, rules, regulations, and procedures concerning traders. And the tax laws applicable to traders continue to evolve. The existence of traders and specific instructions for tax reporting for traders have even made their way into IRS publications such as *Income Tax Instructions for Individuals, Partnerships and Corporations*.

Qualified traders are now able to elect to be taxed in the same manner as broker-dealers/market makers. In effect, their portfolios of securities are now eligible to be treated in much the same manner as the inventory of products held for resale by a retail store. The 1997 tax act required broker-dealers/market makers under Section 475 to mark their positions to market at year end and report any unrealized gain or loss as current year gain or loss. Both realized and unrealized gains were recognized as ordinary income to the brokers-dealers/market makers, and they were subject to self-employment tax.

Traders can now elect to have the same tax rules apply to their trading, although trading income for non-broker-dealers/market makers remains specifically exempt by law from self-employment tax. The election does not change the fact that trading income is exempt from self-employment tax and is not considered earned income. Traders trading stocks, options, single stock futures, and all securities not subject to Section 1256 now can utilize a Section 475 Election, which has huge potential advantages and almost no disadvantages, in most situations. There are many possible planning techniques utilizing Section 475. Space constraints prevent discussing these in depth.

A Section 475 Election (as with all tax decisions) must be discussed with a competent trader tax professional to verify that it is appropriate for your unique tax situation. It should be carefully considered if you have unused capital loss carryovers or if you trade Section 1256 contracts such as regulated futures contracts, foreign currency contracts, nonequity options, or dealer equity options. This election must be made by April 15 of a current year. Failure to make a timely election can cost a taxpayer thousands of dollars. Having an informed decision and planning for this election is a great reason to seek competent tax help from a tax accountant who understands and is knowledgeable about the trading business.

The Section 475 election allows an unprofitable trader to receive immediate payback of prior or current year's taxes paid by allowing a deduction for an unlimited amount of trading losses. This amount is in addition to the previously mentioned 100 percent write-off of trading expenses, which by itself may create a net operating loss.

The Section 475 election allows a profitable trader to ignore wash sales (similar to broker dealers since you are trading "inventory" rather than capital assets) and it reports income and expenses in a more professional and businesslike manner, presumably one that would help validate that you are running a business with legitimate and reasonable expenses. Stock and option traders typically have short-term gains only, and the tax rates for short-term capital gains and ordinary income are identical, resulting in no additional tax arising from the election.

ADVANTAGES OF A SECTION 475 ELECTION

- The $3000 limitation on deductible capital losses does not apply.
- Net operating losses created by ordinary trading losses can be carried forward to offset future income.
- Net operating losses can be carried back two years (five years for losses occurring in 2001 or 2002) to offset prior years' income and to obtain a refund of taxes paid on income in prior years.
- Deferred losses on wash sales are fully deductible against gains, and cumbersome recordkeeping requirements related to wash sales are eliminated.
- Segregating investment profits (potential long-term capital gains) from trading profits is easier and reporting is simplified.

WHO BENEFITS FROM A SECTION 475 ELECTION

- Traders with current year-to-date losses
- New traders without a proven track record
- Traders who have had both very profitable and unprofitable years due to market volatility
- Position traders with significant year end unrealized gains
- Trading entities such as partnerships, LLCs, Family Limited Partnerships, and C and S Corporations
- Almost all traders who use this election as a hedge or insurance policy against a bad year or a difficult market environment

The Section 475 election, due to the unlimited deductibility of ordinary trading losses and the removal of wash sale accounting, is a must for any trader trading stocks or options.

Some traders have recovered hundreds of thousands of dollars by carrying back trading losses in recent years and offsetting gains realized in the late 1990s to receive a refund of tax dollars paid in recent years.

The election will have the effect of transforming capital gains and losses into ordinary income and loss and require you to report trading gains and losses on Form 4797, Ordinary Gains and Losses.

Expenses continue to be reported on Form 1040 Schedule C as indicated above

SPECIAL NOTE: SECTION 1256 CONTRACTS TRADER

A Section 1256 Contract is any of the following:

1. Regulated futures contract
2. Foreign currency contract
3. Nonequity option
4. Dealer equity option

Section 1256 contracts are subject to special tax rules. Section 1256 contracts are marked-to-market by law. *Mark-to-market* means that a contract held at the end of the tax year is treated as if sold at its fair market value on the last business day of the year and you must include this unrealized gain or loss in your taxable income for the year, just like Section 475 accounting. One key difference is that gains and losses are still capital in nature and subject to a maximum write-off of $3000 in any year. This unrealized gain or loss becomes an adjustment to the cost basis and reverses itself in the following year when the contract is actually sold.

Sixty percent of the capital gain or loss from Section 1256 contracts is deemed to be long-term capital gain or loss, and 40 percent is deemed to be short-term capital gain or loss. Gain or loss and the 60/40 split from these contracts are reported on IRS Form 6781.

Long-term gains are now subject to a maximum tax rate of 15 percent.

Because of the volatile nature of these securities, a special loss carryback election is allowed. Net Section 1256 contracts losses can be carried back three years instead of being carried forward to the following year. These losses can only be carried back to a year in which there is a net Section 1256 contracts gain, and only to the extent of such gain, and cannot increase or produce a net operating loss for the year. The loss is carried back to the earliest carryback year first; any unabsorbed loss can then be carried to each of the next two years.

As a result of the very preferential low rates on long-term capital gains for Section 1256 contracts traders and the special carryback election already available, it very rarely makes sense for this type of trader to elect Section 475 accounting. One rare exception might be if there were very significant losses immediately prior to the April 15 deadline for making the election in that calendar year.

Trading in a Single-Member Limited Liability Company

Trading in your individual name and filing a Form 1040 Schedule C is an adequate way to file and, in fact, recommended for most traders. It is also the simplest, least expensive, and least burdensome method, from a recordkeeping standpoint. However, there are certain limitations to operating in this structure.

One of the limitations is that trading income is not considered earned income and therefore not available to fund a retirement plan. To fund a retirement plan or deduct self-employed health insurance premiums, you must convert some of your trading income to earned income. One way to accomplish that is to pay a management fee to the managing member of the LLC. Recent tax legislation has encouraged the creation of very low fee and low maintenance mini-401(k) plans by many mutual funds and brokerage firms, enabling a single-owner company to set up and fund a retirement plan. Prior to this legislation, the cost and hassle of setting up and maintaining a 401(k) plan was too cumbersome for a small, single-owner company.

Profitable traders are often asked to manage money for their relatives or friends. Most of us realize that the best way to break up a happy family or a long-lasting friendship is when finances are involved, as money does strange things to people. It would be extremely unwise to collect a fee, manage someone else's money or brokerage account, or enter into a verbal or written contract without providing yourself and your family some measure of legal and financial protection.

Any legal entity that is properly structured and properly run can provide liability and asset protection. Entity assets, income, and expenses must be strictly segregated from your personal assets, income, and expenses; there can be no commingling of any monies. All state legal requirements must be steadfastly adhered to or this protection can be pierced. The time and expense involved in setting up any entity is wasted without this protection. Many traders do not manage an entity as well as they trade, or they underestimate the time and planning required to properly safeguard their liability and asset protection.

The single-member LLC has some cost and time advantages as compared to other entities. For tax purposes, the IRS disregards single-member LLCs, which has some distinct advantages. Income and expenses are reported in the exact same manner for federal tax purposes as if you were trading in your individual name. Expenses are reported on Form 1040 Schedule C, and trading gains and losses are reported on Schedule D, unless you have elected Section 475 accounting, in which case, gains and losses are reported on Form 4797.

There is no need for a separate tax return for this entity, which saves you tax preparation costs and simplifies bookkeeping and accounting requirements. Maintaining a balance sheet and a separate set of company accounting records is unnecessary.

Trading in a Multimember LLC, Family Limited Partnership, Limited Partnership, or S Corporation

Profitable traders often are asked to trade other people's capital. If they do so, asset and liability protection is essential. To receive these protections, traders must trade in the proper form of entity. In addition, trading is much easier and more efficient when trades are in one pooled brokerage account than when orders are entered for each individual account. A brokerage account set up in an entity's name allows you to combine a client's capital into one easily manageable brokerage account for trading and recordkeeping purposes. Because each of the above entities pays no federal tax, income and expenses are passed through to the individual partner-shareholder on a Schedule K-1 allocated by the entity operating agreement. This form is easily prepared as part of the partnership or corporation tax return. Tax reporting for the individual partner-shareholders is simplified, because they do not have to track and report each trade and expense. Their accountants can just report the relevant tax numbers as shown on the K-1.

Multimember LLCs, family limited partnerships (FLPs), limited partnerships, and S Corporations that are properly managed and set up can all provide asset and liability protection, and they allow the trader to have management flexibility and control. They all share the characteristic of being considered a "flow-through" entity for tax purposes. These entities are governed by state legal and tax requirements that will differ for each state. A competent legal and tax advisor should talk with you about which entity is best for you based on state law and your specific goals for setting up an entity. In New York City, for example, S Corporations are taxed as corporations while trading partnerships with no other business are exempt from the city's Unincorporated Business Tax.

An S Corporation is treated for legal purposes as a C Corporation (see the following section for a description of the latter), but for tax purposes it is treated very much like a partnership. The primary difference is the requirement that reasonable compensation must be paid to a shareholder performing services.

Family limited partnerships, or FLPs, may be set up as part of an estate plan or to shift income to other family members who may be in lower tax brackets. Another advantage to FLPs is that management can be retained by the general partner, either directly or through another legal entity.

Hedge funds are typically set up as limited partnerships, but they can be set up in any legal form. Section 475 elections can be made at the entity level, giving you some flexibility as to whether to report trading gains or losses as ordinary or capital.

In addition, there are special IRS rules concerning entities qualified as a trading business that affect how expenses are reported. These rules can be quite beneficial to partner-shareholders, which allow them ordinary loss treatment of expenses as opposed to having them flow through as itemized deductions.

Unfortunately, many fringe benefits available to C Corporations are either unavailable or are severely limited to partners or shareholders of the above entities.

Income and expenses are reportable on the entity's separate tax return. In the case of a S Corporation, Form 1120S is used; for the other entities, Form 1065 is used. Trading gains and losses are reported to partner-shareholders as capital in nature, unless Section 475 accounting was timely elected at the entity level. If the entity is in the business of trading, expenses are reported as ordinary in nature and can be used to offset partner-shareholders' taxable income from other sources.

Creating a C Corporation as a Management Company

A *C Corporation* is a separate legal entity recognized as a separate and unique legal and taxable entity with its own rights and obligations distinct from the shareholders'. Income and expenses do not flow through to the individual shareholders' tax returns as they do for all other entities. The C Corporation pays its own tax based on net income, and shareholders are typically compensated for their capital contributions by the payment of dividends. Unfortunately, dividends paid to shareholders are taxable to the shareholder while the corporation receives no tax deduction for the payment of dividends. This despite the fact that the corporation has already been taxed on the income that allowed the corporation to pay the dividends.

This commonly known "double taxation" issue has been a problem for many years. The recent 2003 tax law has attempted to mitigate this problem by reducing tax rates on qualifying dividends paid by corporations. Nevertheless, the double taxation issue is still a problem for corporate distributions.

The two most common ways of distributing cash from a corporation are through the payments of dividends or as compensation for services rendered. This is another disadvantage unique to traders. If you pay trading profits out of the corporation as compensation, you are essentially converting income not subject to social security tax into income subject to social security tax, paying an unnecessary 15.3 percent of wages to the Social Security Administration.

For these reasons, and for other lesser-known and arcane IRS rules such as the accumulated earnings tax, I recommend that you never trade in a C Corporation. However, consistently profitable traders may have reasons to consider a C Corporation in their business plans.

A properly managed C Corporation of any size can offer the same fringe benefits that General Motors offers its employees. Health benefits, education expense reimbursement, and dependent care reimbursement are examples of possible fringe benefits of which a trader can take legal advantage. If these benefits are available through other businesses or through your spouse, then of course they have less value to you.

The C Corporation can receive revenue from managing trading activities of another entity such as a FLP, LLC, partnership, or S corporation. The management fee is typically based on trading profits realized. This management fee is deductible to the *flow-through entity* paying it, which reduces taxable income to the individual trader partner-shareholder. Taxable income of the C Corporation is reduced by the payment of compensation to the trader and the direct payment of trading-related expenses.

The above structure is commonly sold by many promoters to new traders, and all traders need to be extremely careful that this is the right structure for them. If you do not have trading profits, then there are very small or zero management fees to be received by the corporation. Yet, you still must incur costs for accounting and tax preparation fees, state filing fees, and minimum state taxes, even you have an operating loss. For this reason, C corporations are only cost effective and feasible for consistently profitable traders with a proven track record.

Income and expenses are reported on Form 1120 and the corporation pays its own income taxes, with nothing flowing to the individual shareholder's tax return, with the exception of any dividend payments or compensation received.

For purchasers of this book, a free consultation with the tax advisors for One Shot – One Kill Trading is available by contacting www.taxesfortraders.com.

The preceding information is presented to provide authoritative and accurate information with respect to the subject matter covered. In publishing this book, neither the author nor publisher is engaged in rendering legal, accounting, or other professional services. If legal, tax, or other advice is required, the services of a competent professional should be sought and advice given based on your unique and specific legal and tax situation.

For taxwise purposes in the United States, there is a distinct difference (some would call it an annoyance) between an *investor* and a *trader* in securities. Most individuals who make trades a few times a week are considered by the IRS to be investors, not traders. It is because of the *investor classification* that those participating in this activity and engaged in its practice are not considered to be carrying on a business. Therefore, they are tightly handcuffed in the amount and types of expenses they can deduct relating to their investments.

A trader, on the other hand, is considered to be carrying on business and may therefore deduct almost all the expenses she or he incurred in the course of trading. Such expenses can include software, seminars, workshops, computer equipment, subscriptions, and related travel. There are also other advantages to being a trader for income tax purposes, which will not be discussed here.

The line between an investor and a trader, for tax purposes, is faint at best. And the IRS continually steps up to the plate and makes it nearly impossible for most people reading this book to definitively decide how they are perceived. You may know how you would *like* to file, but you need to have the records to substantiate your claim. Having these on hand is what you need to guard against getting yourself shot (figuratively speaking, of course) by one of those big, bad tax bullies.

SUMMARY

The market is an ever-changing dynamic, which needs to be studied on a continual basis. The profession of trading is different from no other when it comes to training and honing one's skills. In order to compete with some of the brightest minds on the planet, you must stay faster, stronger, and sharper, with the intent of being one step ahead of the competition at all times. Because most traders are *re*active rather than *pro*active, the process of being proactive in your trading will give you a cognitive edge.

Throughout the course of this book, I have emphasized the importance of creating a coherent trading strategy so as to reduce your susceptibility to the two emotions that plague every trader who has attempted to profit from a market: greed and fear. By applying the One Shot – One Kill Method to your trading, you are effectively taking the emotional component out of your trading. As a One Shot – One Kill trader, you are simply looking to buy weakness in rising markets, sell strength in falling markets, and take profits at predetermined price points. The process of determining whether what you are seeing is weakness in a rising market is done through the use of selected moving averages, Fibonacci measurements, as well as other ancillary indicators within the respected time frame you are trading, whether that be a three-minute chart or a daily chart.

The price targets you use to take profits are largely influenced by the Fibonacci measurements. You create those measurements from the previous moves leading up to that trade, backed by historical support and resistance lines. The goal behind this endeavor is to consistently put yourself in at a good spot as a trader. If you do so, and if the trade doesn't work out and you are subsequently stopped out, the reason probably will be because there was a change in trend. It won't be because the trade was entered at a bad spot on the charts and your stop didn't allow for the position to wiggle. This idea of taking on trades for a premium is the basis of the One Shot – One Kill Method. It is how a number of market makers work their order flow on a daily basis.

This book has touched upon a number of subjects, all significant. They ranged from creature comforts as a trader, to systematically adding to winning positions, to reducing your tax liability. With the knowledge you have acquired from this book and from your experiences, you will be at a trading advantage.

But your efforts will be significantly undermined if you fail to make the proper adjustments to execute on your plan. With traders, one of the biggest reasons the attrition rate is so high is the failure to adhere to the discipline of one's own plan of attack.

For anyone to make it this far in the book is a commendable feat and speaks highly of your commitment to learning about the markets and how to trade them. I thank you for your time and wish you the best of luck in your efforts!

APPENDIX

Chart Formations

The purpose of this first appendix is to provide more examples of charts and highly favorable formations. Please use these charts to gain the necessary familiarity with charts that would earn high bullish and bearish Netto Numbers.

BULLISH FORMATIONS:

CHART A.1

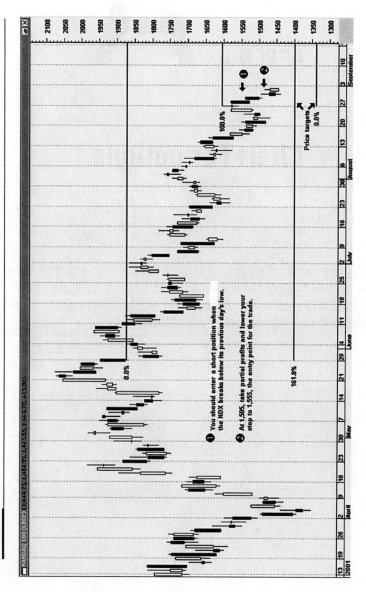

BEARISH FORMATIONS:

CHART A.2

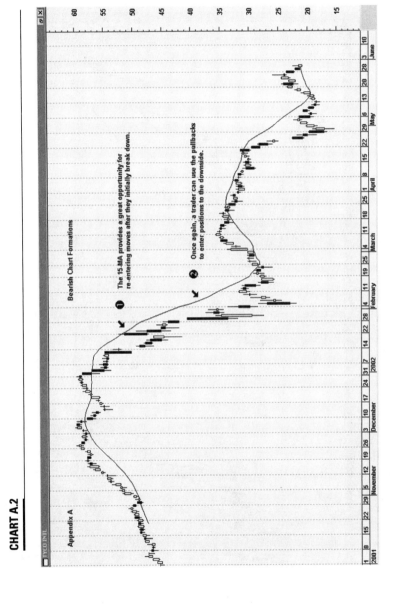

Appendix A

Bearish Chart Formations

❶ The 15-MA provides a great opportunity for re-entering moves after they initially break down.

❷ Once again, a trader can use the pullbacks to enter positions to the downside.

BEARISH FORMATIONS:

CHART A.3

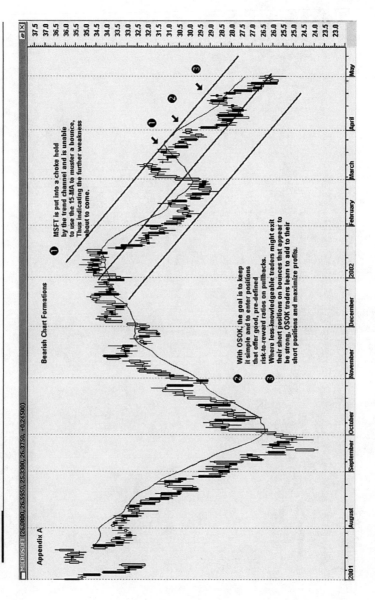

MICROSOFT (26.0080, 26.5950, 25.3300, 26.3750, +0.2(500)

Appendix A

Bearish Chart Formations

① MSFT is put into a choke hold by the trend channel and is unable to use the 15-MA to muster a bounce, Thus indicating the further weakness about to come.

② With OSOK, the goal is to keep it simple and to enter positions that offer good, pre-defined risk-to-reward ratios on pullbacks.

③ Where less-knowledgeable traders might exit their short positions on bounces that appear to be strong, OSOK traders learn to add to their short positions and maximize profits.

BEARISH FORMATIONS:

CHART A.4

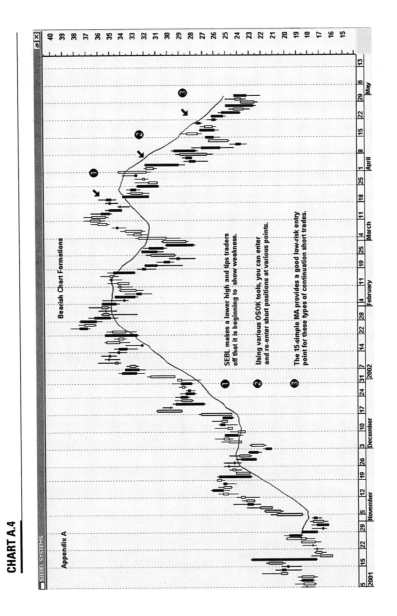

Appendix A

Bearish Chart Formations

1. SEBL makes a lower high and tips traders off that it is beginning to show weakness.

2. Using various OSOK tools, you can enter and re-enter short positions at various points.

3. The 15-simple MA provides a good low-risk entry point for these types of continuation short trades.

APPENDIX

Top 12 Sector Indexes

More than 550 symbols divided into 12 different sectors with some redundancy.

BASIC INDUSTRY

FCX	ATI	N	SEE
EC	PDG	LPX	X
BMS	NUE	WLL	GP
AVY	HPC	BCC	EMN
VMC	ROH	ABX	APD
AL	GLK	TIN	PTV
NEM	PPG	WY	DOW
AA	WOR	BLL	SIAL
ECL	PX	IP	DD

FINANCIALS

PVN	UNM	MTG	AOC
SPC	BEN	JHF	GDW

NTRS	CMA	SV	ABK
CF	LTR	SCH	LEH
AFL	SLM	STT	HIG
TMK	UPC	MBI	XL
PNC	MET	HI	BK
MMC	ALL	ZION	JP
ASO	KEY	MEL	KRB
FITB	USB	ONE	FRE
HBAN	MCO	RF	PGR
BBT	MER	MWD	JPM
FNM	WFC	CCR	CINF
LNC	COF	NCC	FBF
WB	BAC	AIG	C
BSC	SNV	SOTR	CB
STI	WM	AXP	

ENERGY

MDR	EOG	KMG	DVN
APA	BR	MRO	RDC
KMI	NBR	WMB	RIG
BHI	APC	SUN	COC
AHC	UCL	EP	SLB
CVX	ASH	NE	HAL
OXY	P	XOM	

CONSUMER STAPLES

BCR	CHIR	FO	CLX
MCK	CPB	GDT	WWY
FRX	MEDI	ADM	CAG
HNZ	GIS	SLE	SYY
KR	BGEN	STJ	CCE
CVS	SWY	UN	G
WAG	SGP	ZMH	BMET

HSY	AVP	CL	BUD
BMY	LLY	ABT	UST
ABC	BDX	IMNX	CAH
AMGN	PEP	MRK	KO
KG	AGN	BSX	ABS
BAX	PHA	PG	JNJ
GENZ	PBG	SYK	K
KMB	MDT	MO	PFE

UTILITIES

PGL	TE	NI	CIN
AEE	EIX	DTE	GAS
MIR	KSE	REI	PEG
FE	ETR	FPL	CMS
AES	CEG	XEL	PGN
AEP	D	EXC	PGN
DYN	SRE	PCG	TXU
SO	BLS	PNW	AYE
PPL	ED	AT	DUK
VZ	SBC		

CONSUMER SERVICES

AM	DLX	HMA	HLT
RX	AET	HOT	NYT
QTRN	DRI	MAR	HRB
WLP	IPG	MHP	TRB
MDP	DNY	HET	UVN
CI	GCI	CMCSK	THC
TMPW	WEN	IGT	SBUX
OMC	HCA	CCU	MCD
HCR	RHI	KRI	CTAS
CD	UNH	DIS	HUM
DJ	HRC	YUM	CCL

INDUSTRIAL

IR	NAV	ABI	COL
PCAR	PH	GLW	ETN
PKI	APCC	TMO	ITT
JCI	DE	DHR	NOC
CR	PLL	WAT	TXT
WMI	ITW	EMR	LMT
CUM	DCN	ROK	MIL
FLR	CBE	TRW	CAT
HON	BA	TYC	AW
GR	RTN	DOV	GD
UTX	MMM	GE	

TECHNOLOGY

NVDA	VTSS	CTXS	CPWR
AMD	NTAP	NSM	GWW
SANM	JDSU	TER	XRX
PMTC	CNXT	MERQ	BMC
TSG	ALTR	CSC	INTU
LXK	AAPL	FISV	YHOO
ANDW	TEK	ADCT	NXTL
SLR	Q	PBI	KLAC
CA	PCS	LLTC	XLNX
PALM	CIEN	SFA	UIS
PSFT	NT	ADI	MXIM
LU	CEFT	EMC	AMAT
ADSK	CMVT	JBL	LSI
MOLX	ADBE	A	CPQ
EDS	FDC	ADP	MOT
GTW	PMCS	TLAB	CTL
WCOM	SEBL	PAYX	QCOM
HPQ	T	DELL	AOL

AMCC	AV	NCR	EFX
NVLS	EK	FON	SUNW
ORCL	CSCO	INTC	MSFT
SBL	CZN	QLGC	CVG
BRCM	VRTS	MU	AWE
TXN	IBM		

CYCLICAL/TRANSPORTATION

KM	VC	PHM	SWK
BDK	CC	SHW	JNY
VFC	WHR	TUP	DDS
DAL	DG	GPC	FDO
CSX	FD	NSC	AZO
RBK	BC	LIZ	LEG
MAT	MAY	BBBY	BNI
TJX	GPS	BLI	KBH
TOY	TIF	LTD	MAS
FDX	BBY	HDI	S
R	HAS	CTX	JCP
DPH	LUV	COST	LOW
GM	CTB	AMR	GT
RSH	SPLS	UNP	KSS
TGT	HD	SNA	JWN
MYG	ODP	NWL	NKE
F	WMT		

SOFTWARE INDEX, $GSO

ADBE	ADSK	ADSK	AMSY
BEAS	CA	CDN	CHKP
COGN	CPWR	CTXS	DOX
ERTS	IFMX	INTU	JDEC
MSFT	NATI	NETA	NOVL

| ORCL | PSFT | RATL | SEBL |
| SEIC | SNPS | SYMC | VRTS |

SEMICONDUCTOR INDEX, $SOX

ALTR	AMAT	AMD	INTC
KLAC	LLTC	LSCC	LSI
MOT	MU	NSM	NVLS
RMBS	TER	TXN	XLNX
MXIM			

BIOTECH INDEX, $BTK

GENZ	AMGN	GILD
BTGC	BGEN	IMNX
MEDI	CEPH	CHIR
PDLI	CORR	

APPENDIX C

TRI and Other Useful Resources

TREND REVERSAL INDEX CALCULATIONS

Trend Reversal Index–MetaStock formula

$$RSI(13) + Mov(RSI(3),3,S$$

RESOURCES ON THE INTERNET

The One Shot – One Kill Web site, www.oneshotonekilltrading.com, keeps an updated list of useful trading and hedge fund web sites.

INDEX

About the Author

John Netto is a former U.S. Marine and professional hedge fund manager. He has taught his One Shot – One Kill Method of trading to hundreds of professional and non-professional traders, brokers and money managers.

Deemed a stock market prodigy at an early age, Mr. Netto is President and Founder of One Shot – One Kill Trading, LLC and Chief Investment Strategist for Semper Fidelis Capital Management, LLC, a Commodity Trading Advisor (CTA). He is recognized as a technical analysis expert and is the creator of 'Netto Numbers', a quantitative and objective assessment tool for determining the quality and appropriate asset allocation of a trade, before actually entering it.

Mr. Netto has gained the respect of traders for his tireless devotion to providing poignant market insight and forecasts via his nightly newsletter and real-time online educational service, 'SniperScope'. His One Shot – One Kill Method of trading teaches his students the discipline to succeed and is taught online and at workshops throughout the year.

Besides being an avid student of the financial markets, John speaks, reads, and writes Japanese and Chinese. He worked abroad for nearly four years throughout the Far East including the US Embassy in Tokyo, Japan. During his matriculation at the University of Washington, John's curriculum focused on Japanese, Chinese, and Finance.